lonely planet

PARIS

Jean-Bernard Carillet, Eileen Cho, Fabienne Fong Yan,
Catherine Le Nevez, Jacqueline NGO MPII, Danette St. Onge

Contents

PASCALE GUERET/SHUTTERSTOCK ©

Above Pont Neuf and Île de la Cité

HOURS & RESERVATIONS

Restaurants generally open noon to 2pm and 7.30pm to 10.30pm. Most shut at least one day (usually Sunday). Many close for summer holidays in July and August. Reserve *well* ahead for popular and/or high-end places.

BON **APPÉTIT**

Bien manger (eating well) is an inextricable part of Parisian life. While the city doesn't have its own 'local' cuisine, it's the crossroads for regional dishes that encompass the Mediterranean south's olive oil, garlic and tomatoes, the pastoral north's butter and cream, Alpine cheeses, Atlantic coast seafood, Breton crêpes and galettes, Basque *pintxos* (tapas) and more. As a multicultural hub, Paris' dining landscape also incorporates the full spectrum of global flavours.

Left French pastries, tea and coffee **Right** *Formule* menu **Below** Charcuterie board

→ MENUS

For the best-value dining, forgo ordering à la carte (from the menu) for daily *formules* or *prix-fixe* menus (fixed-price, multicourse meals). Some establishments, particularly market-driven neobistros, have no *carte* (menu).

BISTROS, BRASSERIES & CAFES

Bistros are small neighbourhood restaurants serving French standards; neobistros are experimental and contemporary. Classic cafes offer inexpensive meals, becoming bars around 5pm. Brasseries offer all-day dining.

↑ WINE-BAR DINING

Caves à manger typically serve *fromage* (cheese) and charcuterie (*saucisson*, pâté) to accompany *un verre* ('a glass'). *Bars à vins* often create gastronomic small, tapas-style sharing plates.

▶ See our cheese guide on p130

Best Food Experiences

▶ **Slurp sublime oysters in the vestiges of Paris' former wholesale markets around rue Montorgueil.** (p72)

▶ **Fire up the spice at the noodle shops and family-run restaurants of Paris' biggest Chinatown.** (p188)

▶ **Taste the flavours of Africa in Paris' northern neighbourhoods.** (p96)

▶ **Dine overlooking Notre Dame at revered restaurant La Tour d'Argent.** (p142)

WHAT'S ON

LYLO (lylo.fr) Les Yeux, Les Oreilles has the low-down on live music performances.

Sortir à Paris (sortiraparis.com) Food and drink, culture, nights and bars, and beyond.

L'Officiel des Spectacles (offi.fr) Theatre, cinema, concerts, events.

PARISIAN **NIGHTLIFE**

La Ville Lumière (the City of Light) comes into its own after dark. A night out in Paris can be anything from sipping cocktails made from rare French spirits at a specialist bar to watching a film in an atmospheric cinema, catching a cabaret, taking in a concert at a hallowed music hall or jazz club, hitting the clubs, or attending a lavish opera or ballet production.

Left Cocktail and macarons **Right** Jazz singer, Latin Quarter **Below** Cinema seats, Grand Rex

→ JAZZ IN THE CITY

A centre for jazz for over a century, Paris' scene remains strong. Jam sessions, concerts and festivals are posted on parisjazzclub.net, and streamable radio station tsfjazz.com.

LIFE IS A CABARET

Part of the city's mythology, cabarets span intimate works to over-the-top spectacles with dazzling sets, costumes and dance routines, often accompanied by Champagne.

▶ Catch glamorous cabaret shows on the Champs-Elysees (p54) and in Pigalle (p84)

↑ CINEMATIC PARIS

In the 19th century, the world's first paying public film screening took place in Paris, and today its wonderful array of movie houses screen classics and new releases.

▶ Discover some of Paris' best-loved cinemas on p158

Best Nightlife Experiences

▶ **Combine cocktail bar-hopping with cabaret shows on a night out in Pigalle.** (p84)

▶ **Watch a film in a classic cinema in the Latin Quarter.** (p158)

▶ **Discover the cabarets around av des Champs-Élysées.** (p54)

▶ **Listen to jazz at the intimate, authentic club Bab-Ilo.** (p89)

City-run museums (parismusees.paris.fr) are free.

Temporary exhibitions usually cost extra, even at free museums.

Students, seniors and children generally get discounted or free admission (bring ID).

National museums (culture.gouv.fr) are free for all under 18s and EU citizens under 26.

TOP TREASURE **CHESTS**

Parisians have an insatiable appetite for art, and there are scores of museums and galleries in the city, from venerable repositories like the Louvre, showcasing artworks and artefacts from antiquity, and the impressionist-filled Musée d'Orsay, to groundbreaking newcomers like former foundry Atelier des Lumières, projecting digital art onto its walls. Even those with the most niche of interests will find an exhibition or whole institution that hits the spot.

Left Apartments of Napoleon III, Louvre
Right *The Age of Bronze*, Musée Rodin
Below Musée d'Orsay

→ PARIS MUSEUM PASS

The money-saving Paris Museum Pass (parismuseumpass.com; two/four/six days €52/66/78) is valid for entry to over 50 venues in and around the city (excluding their temporary exhibitions).

RESERVATIONS

Be aware that for many museums, such as the Louvre, advance reservations for allocated time slots are mandatory, even for visitors who qualify for free admission.

↑ OPENING & CLOSING TIMES

Most museums shut on Monday or Tuesday. General hours are 10am to 6pm, though all museums' gates close up to an hour before their stated closing times.

▶ Learn more about business hours in Paris on p219

Best Museum Experiences

▶ **Be seduced by love-themed art at the Louvre.** (p62)

▶ **Wander amid world-famous works in the Musée Rodin's sculpture garden.** (p179)

▶ **Learn how life on the planet evolved at the Grande Galerie de l'Évolution.** (p157)

▶ **Appreciate fashion as an art form at the Palais Galliera and Musée Yves Saint Laurent Paris.** (p43)

▶ **Catch contemporary installations and exhibitions at the Palais de Tokyo.** (p43)

ARCHITECTURE MUSEUMS IN PARIS

Cité de l'Architecture et du Patrimoine (citedelarchitecture.fr)

Pavillon de l'Arsenal (pavillon-arsenal.com)

Musée des Plans-Reliefs, Hôtel des Invalides (musee-armee.fr)

ARCHITECTURE **FOR THE AGES**

Paris' architectural layers serve as a living document of its history: Roman ruins like the 2nd-century amphitheatre Arènes de Lutèce, medieval masterpieces like the stained-glass Sainte-Chapelle, art nouveau structures like original metro station entrances, past French presidents' *grands projets* like the 'inside-out' Centre Pompidou, Mitterand's glass pyramid at the Louvre and Chirac's Musée du Quai Branly. Visionary architects continue to make their mark on the skyline.

Left View over bd Haussmann from Printemps **Right** Haussmannian building, rue Tolbiac **Below** Ceiling, Galeries Lafayette

→ QUINTESSENTIAL CITYSCAPES

Boulevards lined by cream-coloured apartment buildings with wrought-iron balconies and grey metal mansard roofs are a defining legacy of Baron Haussmann's 19th-century 'modernisation' of Paris under Napoléon III.

DANIELE SCHNEIDER/GETTY IMAGES ©

OLYMPIC PREPARATIONS

As the clock ticks down to the Paris 2024 Summer Olympic Games and Summer Paralympic Games, renovations, redevelopments and grand-scale infrastructure projects are taking place around the city.

RIGHT: WJAREK/SHUTTERSTOCK © LEFT: BEBOY/SHUTTERSTOCK ©

↑ ART NOUVEAU

Characterised by curves and flowing, asymmetrical forms, and typified by the Eiffel Tower, art nouveau flourished during La Belle Époque in the late 19th and early 20th centuries.

Best Architectural Experiences

- **Toast your ascent of Paris' elegant Eiffel Tower at its top-floor champagne bar.** (p37)
- **Survey the art nouveau splendour of Grands Boulevards department stores Galeries Lafayette and Printemps.** (p53)
- **Peek behind the scenes of Paris' historic opera house, the Palais Garnier.** (p68)
- **Admire some of Paris' oldest buildings in Le Marais.** (p104)
- **Revel in the palatial surrounds of the Château de Versailles.** (p196)

Grands magasins (department stores) are an ideal first stop for up-to-the-minute Parisian fashion.

Galeries Lafayette (Champs-Élysées & Grands Boulevards)

Printemps (Champs-Élysées & Grands Boulevards)

La Samaritaine (Louvre & Les Halles)

Le Bon Marché (St-Germain & Les Invalides)

CREATIVE LAB/SHUTTERSTOCK ©

IN VOGUE

One of the great shopping cities, Paris is famed for its increasingly sustainable fashion, from up-and-coming designers' ateliers (workshops) to small, one-off boutiques, luxury *haute couture* (high fashion) flagships and magnificent department stores. Parisians favour personal style above trends or labels, pairing quality pieces with statement-making accessories such as scarves.

Best Shopping Experiences

- **Personalise your purchases with monogramming services at luxury stores on av des Champs-Élysées.** (p51)
- **Heed fashion editors' advice and scout out their favourite addresses** (p40)
- **Infuse your wardrobe with Left Bank chic on a shopping spree in St-Germain.** (p166)
- **Create a timeless look with vintage flea-market pieces.** (p88)

UNDER THE **RADAR**

Big-hitting sights abound in France's capital – iconic monuments like the Arc de Triomphe, Eiffel Tower and the domed Sacré-Cœur basilica are everywhere you turn. But tucked in between them are the small shops, restaurants, charming streetscapes and creative spaces that make the city great. Discover the hidden secrets of Paris.

ADISA/SHUTTERSTOCK ©

CULTURAL CENTRES →

Some of the most happening places in Paris today are hybrid cultural venues that host diverse programs of music gigs, art exhibits, food festivals, beer tastings and countless other events, often in previously disused industrial spaces.

BILD MEDIA/LE HASARD LUDIQUE ©

Best Hidden Experiences

▸ **See massive murals in the 13e *arrondissement*.** (p184)

▸ **Follow the trails blazed by Montmartre's female historical figures.** (p80)

▸ **Explore southern Paris' charming villages.** (p186)

▸ **Party in the abandoned train station Le Hasard Ludique.** (p92)

▸ **Find workshops, food trucks and pop-up events at Ground Control.** (p125)

← FLÂNERIE

Coined by the Parisian writer Charles Baudelaire, *flânerie* – city strolling without a destination in mind – is the ideal way to make serendipitous discoveries and understand what makes the city tick.

Far left Street style, Paris **Above left** Montmartre **Bottom left** Performer, Le Hasard Ludique

FAVOURITE PARISIAN PARKS

Jardin du Luxembourg (St-Germain & Les Invalides)

Parc Monceau (Montmartre & Northern Paris)

Parc Montsouris (Montparnasse & Southern Paris)

Parc des Buttes Chaumont (Montmartre & Northern Paris)

URBAN **OASES**

Paris' beautiful parks and gardens are its apartment-dwelling residents' communal backyards. Green squares, rooftop gardens and other secluded pockets are complemented by sprawling parks with old-fashioned children's activities such as puppet shows and modern sporting facilities, and – at the eastern and western edges of central Paris – its two rambling forests, Bois de Boulogne and Bois de Vincennes.

Best Park Experiences

- **Stroll the chestnut-shaded paths of Paris' most popular park.** (p171)
- **See the Seine close-up at the tiny Square du Vert-Galant.** (p145)
- **Catch the sun setting over Paris from the Parc de Belleville.** (p112)
- **Traverse an elevated park atop a 19th-century viaduct.** (p124)

THE MARKETS **OF PARIS**

Paris' vibrant *marchés* are a cornerstone of local life. Along with produce-laden street markets in virtually every *quartier* at least once a week (never Mondays) and *rues commerçantes* ('commercial streets' with pavement stalls), there are historic, delicacy-filled covered markets, perfumed flower markets and treasure-packed flea markets.

GOLERO/GETTY IMAGES ©

FLEA MARKETS →

Haggle for clothes, homeware and collectables at *marchés aux puces* (flea markets) like Porte de Vanves (pucesdevanves.com). See sortiraparis.com for ephemeral *brocantes* (second-hand markets) and *vide-greniers* ('empty the attic' sales).

ELENA DIJOUR/SHUTTERSTOCK ©

Best Market Experiences

▶ **Browse farm-fresh produce and gourmet stalls at Marché d'Aligre.** (p132)

▶ **Shop for tasty fruit, veggies and cheeses at the Marché St-Eustache.** (p73)

▶ **Sample epicurean treats inside covered market Marché St-Germain.**

▶ **Unearth antique finds at the vast flea market Marché aux Puces de St-Ouen.** (p88)

← FOOD MARKETS

Browse Paris' *marchés alimentaires* (food markets), including *marchés biologiques* (organic markets) by day or by *arrondissement* at paris.fr/equipements/marches-alimentaires/tous-les-horaires.

Far left Parc Monceau **Above left** Food stall **Bottom left** Brooches, flea market

Demand for accommodation peaks in the warmer months. Book tours, flights and insurance in advance at lonelyplanet.com/bookings.

↓ Bastille Day

France's national day features a morning military parade along av des Champs-Élysées and night-time fireworks at the Champ de Mars.

↖ Fête de la Musique

This national music festival welcomes summer on 21 June with live performances at outdoor stages citywide.

JUNE

Average daytime max: 22°C
Days of rainfall: 8

JULY

Paris in SUMMER

Parisians take summer holidays in July and/or August, when many restaurants and smaller shops shut for several weeks.

↓ Tour de France

The famous cycling event finishes on av des Champs-Élysées on the third or fourth Sunday of July.

▶ letour.com

↘ Cinéma en Plein Air

From mid-July to mid-August, free French and international new-release and classic films screen outdoors at Parc de la Villette.

La Villette, p95

▶ parisinfo.com

Assumption Day (L'Assomption), 15 August, is a public holiday. Many businesses and services are closed on this day.

Average daytime max: 25°C
Days of rainfall: 8

AUGUST

Average daytime max: 27°C
Days of rainfall: 7

← Paris Plages

From around mid-July to late August, 'Paris Beaches' set up along the Parc Rives de Seine and Bassin de la Villette.

The Seine, p146

▶ parisinfo.com

Packing notes

Flat, thick-soled shoes are invaluable, along with a light jumper for cooler evenings.

Check out the full calendar of events

↓ Journées Européennes du Patrimoine

Step inside otherwise off-limits buildings and monuments during European Heritage Days on the third weekend in September.

▶ journeesdupatrimoine.culturecommunication.gouv.fr

← Fête des Vendanges de Montmartre

Montmartre's grape harvest is celebrated with costumes, concerts, food events and a parade over five days in early October.

▶ fetedesvendangesdemontmartre.com

← Nuit Blanche

Sundown on the first Saturday of October until sunrise sees museums stay open (for free), art installations and concerts.

▶ parisinfo.com

SEPTEMBER

Average daytime max: 22°C
Days of rainfall: 6

OCTOBER

Paris in AUTUMN

↓ Salon du Chocolat

Five days of chocolate tastings, workshops, demonstrations and children's activities take place at Paris Expo Porte de Versailles.

▶ salon-du-chocolat.com

→ Festival d'Automne

The long-running Autumn Festival of arts incorporates painting, music, dance and theatre at venues throughout the city.

▶ festival-automne.com

All Saints' Day (La Toussaint), 1 November, and Armistice Day/ Remembrance Day (Le Onze Novembre), 11 November, are public holidays.

Average daytime max: 17°C
Days of rainfall: 8

NOVEMBER

Average daytime max: 11°C
Days of rainfall: 8

In September, *la rentrée* marks residents' return to work and study after the summer break, with cultural life shifting into top gear.

← Beaujolais Nouveau

From midnight on the third Thursday (ie Wednesday night) in November, the first bottles of Beaujolais Nouveau are opened in Paris wine bars.

Packing notes

By late autumn the weather is chilly: bring warm clothing and a jacket.

There are public holidays for Christmas (Noël), 25 December, and New Year's Day (Jour de l'An), 1 January.

↖ Africolor

Starting in mid-November and running to late December, this five-week-long African-music festival is primarily held in outer suburbs.

▶ africolor.com

← New Year's Eve

The Eiffel Tower, 7e, and av des Champs-Élysées, 8e, are the ultimate Parisian locations for welcoming in the New Year.

DECEMBER

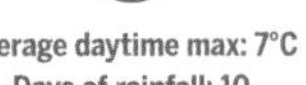

Average daytime max: 7°C
Days of rainfall: 10

JANUARY

Paris in WINTER

← Paris Cocktail Week

In late January, participating cocktail bars and pop-ups create signature cocktails; other events include workshops and masterclasses.

▶ pariscocktailweek.fr

← Epiphany (Three Kings' Day)

On 6 January, patisseries bake frangipane-filled puff-pastry *galettes des rois* (kings' cakes) concealing a *fève* (trinket), accompanied by a cardboard crown.

← Le Festival du Merveilleux

The Pavillons de Bercy – Musée des Arts Forains celebrates the festive season with fairground attractions of yesteryear and shows.

▶ arts-forains.com

Average daytime max: 6°C
Days of rainfall: 9

FEBRUARY

Average daytime max: 8°C
Days of rainfall: 8

← Outdoor Ice Skating

Open-air rinks pop up across Paris in picturesque spots like Galeries Lafayette's panoramic rooftop (venues change annually).

▶ parisinfo.com

Packing notes

A warm jacket, scarf, gloves and boots all help keep winter temperatures at bay.

There are public holidays on May Day (Fête du Travail), 1 May, Victory in Europe Day (Victoire 1945), 8 May, Ascension Thursday (L'Ascension), 40th day after Easter, and Whit Monday (Lundi de Pentecôte), seventh Monday after Easter.

→ Foire du Trône

This huge ride-filled funfair is held on the Pelouse de Reuilly of the Bois de Vincennes in April and May.

▶ foiredutrone.com

→ Marathon International de Paris

Starting on the Champs-Élysées and looping through the city, the Paris Marathon is held on a Sunday in early April.

▶ schneiderelectricparismarathon.com

Easter heralds the arrival of spring. Easter Sunday and Monday (Pâques and Lundi de Pâques), in late March/April, are public holidays.

MARCH

Average daytime max: 12°C
Days of rainfall: 8

APRIL

Paris in SPRING

↓ Banlieues Bleues

For four weeks each spring, the Suburban Blues jazz, blues and R & B festival is held at venues in Paris' outer suburbs.

▶ banlieuesbleues.org

← La Nuit Européenne des Musées

On one Saturday typically in mid-May, key museums across Paris stay open until midnight with free entry for the European Museums Night.

▶ nuitdesmusees.culture.gouv.fr

← Portes Ouvertes des Ateliers d'Artistes de Belleville

Hundreds of artists open their Belleville studio doors over four days in mid-May.

Belleville, p112

▶ ateliers-artistes-belleville.fr

Average daytime max: 16°C
Days of rainfall: 8

MAY

Average daytime max: 19°C
Days of rainfall: 9

← French Open

France's tennis grand slam hits up from late May to early June at Stade Roland Garros at the Bois de Boulogne.

▶ rolandgarros.com

Packing notes

Bring layers for the fickle weather, and an umbrella for the inevitable showers.

MY PERFECT DAY IN **PARIS**

By Eileen Cho
@yo_cho
@eileenwcho

SWEETS, SIGHTS & SHOPPING

Start the day with *viennoiseries* (sweet baked goods) from Ritz Comptoir. Continue to the Musée de l'Orangerie and spend the morning with Monet, Van Gogh, Cézanne and more. Stroll through Jardin de Tuileries to rue de Rivoli and promenade along the colonnades and over the mosaic floors. Walk to the Samaritaine, a fashion emporium that has completed a 16-year facelift. Refuel with Paris' best teatime at Limbar, hidden inside the Cheval Blanc hotel. Take the metro to Abbesses and walk it all off in Montmartre. Spend the evening painting the town red in electric Pigalle.

WHY I LOVE PARIS

I've never felt bored in Paris as there's always something to experience. It's an old city that's constantly reinventing itself; there's a lot to keep up with and even more to learn. Everyone becomes a *flâneur* (stroller) the minute they arrive.

↘ BEST JAZZ CLUBS

Cave du 38 Riv'
Atmospheric stone cellar in Le Marais.

Café Universel
Fabulous Latin Quarter club.

Le Baiser Salé
Afro and fusion near Les Halles.

By Catherine Le Nevez

MARKETS, MUSEUMS & RIVERSIDE STROLLS

Start with coffee and flaky croissants on a cafe terrace, then wander through a neighbourhood street market (Marché Bastille is superb). Browse the *bouquinistes* (secondhand book sellers) lining the Seine and take the steps to the Parc Rives de Seine, former expressways transformed into parks by the water's edge. Marvel at contemporary art at the Bourse de Commerce, taste Paris' best onion soup at Au Pied de Cochon, swing by Scilicet or Baby Doll for cocktails, and close out the night listening to jazz.

JARRY/TRIPELON/GAMMA-RAPHO VIA GETTY IMAGES ©

BEST ASIAN EATS

La Taverne de Zhao
X'ian specialities, including noodles and momo buns.

The Hood
Modern takes on Southeast Asian classics.

Fondue Chongqing
Cook-your-own spicy Chinese hotpot.

Sanukiya
Low-key Japanese spot specialising in udon and tempura.

PEOPLE, GLITZ & GASTRONOMY

Spend the morning hunting for treasures at a *brocante* (flea market) or *vide-grenier* (boot sale), then pack for a picnic in the idyllic Parc des Buttes-Chaumont. In the afternoon, hire a boat for a ride down the Canal de l'Ourcq and follow this with some people-watching on a cafe terrace. After *apéro* (predinner drink) at L'Avant-Comptoir and dinner at La Table de Colette, get glammed up for drinks at Prescription Cocktail Club, then head to a jazz club or cabaret, or to La Coupole for dancing till the wee hours.

By Danette St. Onge
@global gastronomiste

KIEV.VICTOR/SHUTTERSTOCK ©

↖ BEST SECRET GARDENS

Alpine Garden
In Jardin des Plantes.

Musée Bourdelle
A sculptural garden.

Jardin-Musée Albert Kahn
Scenic with a Japanese heritage.

Arboretum
A tree study outside of Paris.

TREATS, GARDENS & NIGHTS OUT

Start with coffee in Rue Mouffetard, then head to the Museum of Natural History. Don't leave without visiting the greenhouses. For lunch, head to Mokonuts, near Bastille. Buy a few cookies from Moko to keep you going while shopping for crafts and fashion in the neighbourhoods of Charonne and Le Marais. Don't forget to take an ice-cream break. Is it *apéritif* time already? Meet your friends at Ground Control, then sit back, relax and enjoy the evening. The night is long...

By Fabienne Fong Yan
@a.fab. journey

Left Performer, Le Baiser Salé **Above** Jardin-Musée Albert Kahn

7 Things to Know About PARIS

INSIDER TIPS TO HIT THE GROUND RUNNING

1 The French Art of the Bonjour

French people take their *bonjours* seriously – they're not just a hello but a sign of respect. Always greet someone with a *bonjour* when you enter a shop, museum, train station, restaurant and any public service space. The safest bet is to use it in every situation.

▶ See Language on p220

2 Transport Tips

Despite popular belief, Paris is an incredibly walkable city. If wheels are more your thing, Mayor Anne Hidalgo has made major changes to get more bikes on the road. There are bike rental options from the city-run Vélib', and scooter start-ups that also offer bikes. Public transport is inexpensive and efficient, and taxis and ride-sharing options are plentiful.

▶ See Getting Around on p210

3 Keep Your Belongings Safe

Statistically speaking, Paris is a very safe city, but pickpocketing is quite common. Like a seasoned Parisian, never have your valuables visible.

▶ See Safe Travel on p214

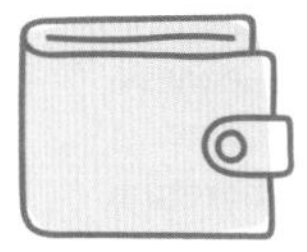

4 Double-Check Opening Times

With COVID-19, business operating hours are changing often. Don't always rely on the hours you find online – call to double-check. In addition, most restaurants close between lunch and dinner unless they are *service continu*.

▶ See Opening Hours on p219

5 Make Reservations

Whether it's for a museum or a restaurant, it is important that you make reservations in advance. Most museums in COVID times will require that you purchase tickets in advance online. Restaurant reservations are often easy to make, online or by phone. Keep in mind that popular dining establishments should be booked months in advance.

6 COVID-19 Considerations

At the time of writing, there were no travel restrictions for fully vaccinated people entering France. During your stay in France, it's recommended that you download and activate the #TousAntiCovid application (gouvernement.fr/info-coronavirus/tousanticovid), available in English or French on Android or iOS.

All international visitors must present proof of vaccination or a negative COVID test within 48 hours to enter public attractions and hospitality venues, including cafes, restaurants, museums, hotels, theatres, sporting events and large shopping areas. The most convenient way to do this is to convert your non-EU vaccination certificate(s) into a French QR code for the *passe sanitaire* (printed or in your #TousAntiCovid app). Non-EU vaccinations can only be converted to a French QR code at a participating pharmacy. Pharmacie Les Filles du Calvaire (2 bd de Filles du Calvaire in the 11e) will do it for €20 with proof of vaccination(s) and photo ID.

▶ See COVID-19 on p214

7 Paris Water Is Accessible

Paris tap water is safe to drink and widely available. If you don't want to pay for bottled water in restaurants, ask for *une carafe d'eau*. Having a reusable bottle is a smart idea as the historic and gorgeous Wallace Fountains offer free tap water all over the city.

Read, Listen, Watch & Follow

READ

A Moveable Feast (Ernest Hemingway; 1964) Hemingway's memoir about his tumultuous life in 1920s Paris.

An Editor's Burial (Wes Anderson; 2021) Collection of essays on expatriate life in Paris.

Mastering the Art of French Eating (Ann Mah; 2013) Journalist's memoir about finding solace through food in France.

Americans in Paris (Adam Gopnik; 2004) Collection of 70 American writers in Paris spanning three centuries.

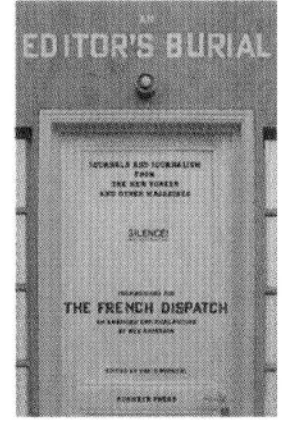

LISTEN

L'Essentiel Des Albums Studio (Serge Gainsbourg; 1961) Collection of Gainsbourg's best works.

Disconova (Margaux de Fouchier; 2022) Parisian Margaux de Fouchier's second album, bringing together her seductive and melancholic vocals with disco covers.

Feeling Dancing Tempo (Jabberwocky; 2021) French electropop trio's latest album highlighting their Italo-disco shift.

Navigating the French (Paris Underground Radio; 2021) American journalist Emily Monaco's podcast takes a deep dive into a new French word each episode.

Héra (Georgio; 2016) Brilliant Parisian rapper who pulls lyrical inspiration from his diverse upbringing in the 18e.

WATCH

Les Misérables (2019) Another side of life in and near the City of Light by Parisian director Ladj Ly.

Ratatouille (2007, top right) Remy the rat dreams of becoming a celebrated Parisian chef.

Amélie (2001, bottom right) A whimsical depiction of life in Montmartre.

Emily in Paris (2020–present) Lighthearted comedy about a young American's Parisian adventures.

Paris, je t'aime (2006) Collection of 18 short films about love in different *arrondissements*.

ALBUM/ALAMY STOCK PHOTO ©

AA FILM ARCHIVE/ ALAMY STOCK PHOTO ©

FOLLOW

@m_magazine Culture and news from daily newspaper *Le Monde*.

Paris Je T'aime (en.parisinfo.com) Official city website.

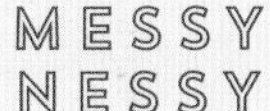

Messy Nessy Chic (messynessychic.com) Parisian blogger sharing Paris' kitschy secrets.

The Local Paris (thelocal.fr) France's news in English.

@mkrs.family Tells the stories of Paris creatives.

Sate your Parisian dreaming with a virtual vacation at lonelyplanet.com/ paris#planning-a-trip

EIFFEL TOWER & WESTERN PARIS

FASHION | ART | ARCHITECTURE

EIFFEL TOWER & WESTERN PARIS

Trip Builder

TAKE YOUR PICK OF MUST-SEES AND HIDDEN GEMS

Western Paris has some of the lushest parks, the highest concentration of museums in the city, and iconic landmarks such as the Eiffel Tower. Home to the sophisticated 16e, the Haussmannian buildings create a charming backdrop. Come for the wide array of museums, picture-perfect views, excellent dining options and posh shopping.

Neighbourhood Notes

Best for Modern museums and classic Paris views.

Transport Metro to Alma-Marceau, Iéna, Trocadéro, Bir-Hakeim or Passy; RER C to Champ de Mars or Pont de l'Alma.

Getting around On foot, bike or bus.

Tip For the best photos of the Eiffel Tower without the crowds, head to rue de la Manutention.

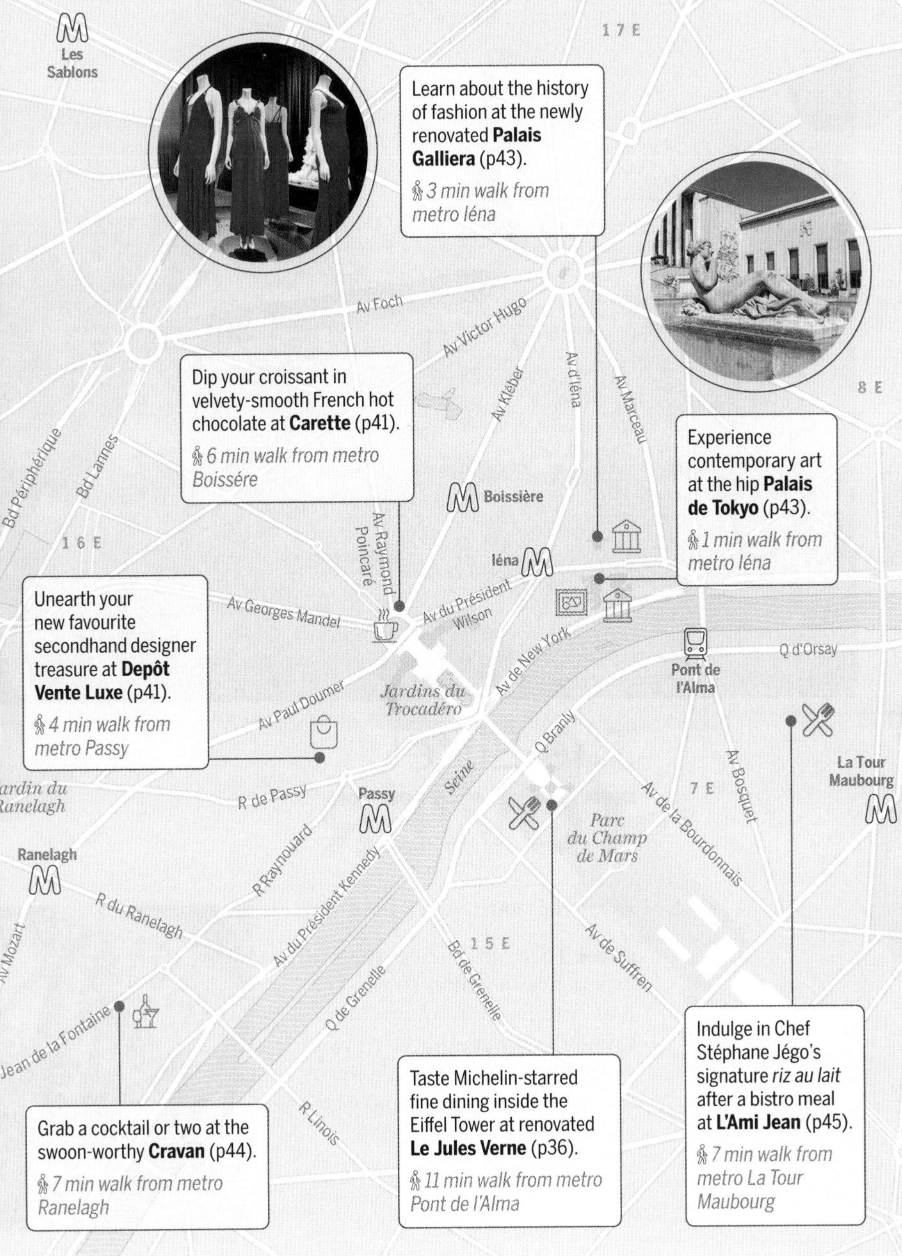
Les Sablons
17 E
Learn about the history of fashion at the newly renovated **Palais Galliera** (p43).
3 min walk from metro Iéna
Av Foch
Av Victor Hugo
Dip your croissant in velvety-smooth French hot chocolate at **Carette** (p41).
6 min walk from metro Boissére
Av Kléber
Av d'Iéna
Av Marceau
8 E
Experience contemporary art at the hip **Palais de Tokyo** (p43).
1 min walk from metro Iéna
Bd Périphérique
Bd Lannes
Boissière
16 E
Av Raymond Poincaré
Iéna
Unearth your new favourite secondhand designer treasure at **Depôt Vente Luxe** (p41).
4 min walk from metro Passy
Av Georges Mandel
Av du Président Wilson
Av de New York
Pont de l'Alma
Q d'Orsay
Av Paul Doumer
Jardins du Trocadéro
Q Branly
Jardin du Ranelagh
R de Passy
Passy
Seine
Av Bosquet
La Tour Maubourg
7 E
Av de la Bourdonnais
Parc du Champ de Mars
Ranelagh
R Raynouard
Av du Président Kennedy
R du Ranelagh
Av Mozart
15 E
Bd de Grenelle
Av de Suffren
Q de Grenelle
R Jean de la Fontaine
Indulge in Chef Stéphane Jégo's signature *riz au lait* after a bistro meal at **L'Ami Jean** (p45).
7 min walk from metro La Tour Maubourg
Taste Michelin-starred fine dining inside the Eiffel Tower at renovated **Le Jules Verne** (p36).
11 min walk from metro Pont de l'Alma
R Linois
Grab a cocktail or two at the swoon-worthy **Cravan** (p44).
7 min walk from metro Ranelagh

01

The Eiffel **TOWER**

ARCHITECTURE | VIEWS | DINING

There are endless ways to experience the Eiffel Tower. The best options are from up close. Climb the tower, dine at its two restaurants – famed Michelin-starred Le Jules Verne and Chef Thierry Marx's 58 Tour Eiffel – clink glasses at the champagne bar, or enjoy the tower from Parc du Champ de Mars below.

CATARINA BELOVA/SHUTTERSTOCK ©

How to

Getting here Metro to Bir-Hakeim or RER C to Champ de Mars – Tour Eiffel.

When to go The Eiffel Tower is open all year, even on public holidays, from 9.30am to 11.45pm (last ascent to the top at 10.30pm).

Tips Entrance tickets to the Eiffel Tower are available two months in advance on the official website toureiffel.paris/en. Book as soon as you know your travel dates as they often sell out. You'll need to reserve and pay in advance to dine at one of the tower's restaurants – they also book up quickly.

ZHUZHU/GETTY IMAGES ©

The Iron Lady

The Eiffel Tower is the most iconic symbol of the City of Light. The tower is made up of four sections: the Esplanade, 1st floor, 2nd floor and the Top. Visitors have multiple different ticket options to choose their own adventure: stairs of 647 steps or lift to the 2nd floor, or the pricier options of stairs and lift or lift only to the top floor (the summit), where views are best. It's imperative that you are on time for your reserved ticket so it is advisable to come 15 to 20 minutes early to explore the Esplanade upon arrival and to navigate the queuing system.

N. VIVIENNE SHEN PHOTOGRAPHY/GETTY IMAGES ©

The 1st Floor

The 1st floor has transparent floors and is worth visiting for the CinEiffel video experience, the largest gift shop in the tower,

Picture Perfect

If you're just after a glimpse up close, go to the **Eiffel Tower Carousel**, also known as Carousel XI, the only clockwise-spinning carousel in the city. Here you can take quick snaps of the tower itself or with the charming carousel.

Top left Paris skyline **Bottom left** Eiffel Tower, detail **Above** Eiffel Tower Carousel

and to see Paris at your feet. There are two dining options: **The Buffet**, a cafeteria with grab-and-go options, and the **58 Tour Eiffel** brasserie led by Chef Thierry Marx (closed for renovations and due to reopen in 2022). At lunch, they offer casual bistro fare but bring in a more upscale menu for dinner. Reservations for 58 Tour Eiffel include access to the 1st floor.

The 2nd Floor

The 2nd floor has the **La Verrière** gift shop, which focuses on reproductions of the tower, as well as two dining options: The Buffet (same as the first floor) and Michelin-starred **Le Jules Verne**. Under the helm of Chef Frédéric Anton, Le Jules Verne is truly a once-in-a-lifetime dining experience. Diners have access to a private lift that will transport them to a chic space by renowned architect and

Ducasse's Eiffel Tower

Chef Alain Ducasse might have passed on the reigns of Le Jules Verne after more than a decade but diners can still get the Ducasse Eiffel Tower experience on his floating restaurant, Ducasse sur Seine. Diners board a luxurious electric boat at Pont d'Iéna for a 90- or 120-minute fine-dining cruise, passing some of Paris' greatest monuments between the Trocadéro gardens and the Eiffel Tower. The menu is French contemporary cooked by a full kitchen team in the lower deck. The three-course lunch is one of the more affordable dining options by the legendary chef!

Far left Alain Ducasse and team, Ducasse sur Seine **Near left** Telescope, Eiffel Tower **Below** Picnickers, Champ de Mars

interior designer Aline Asmar d'Amman, known for her opulent yet contemporary style. The meals are delicious despite the kitchen not being able to cook on open flames, as these aren't allowed in the tower. It is advisable to make reservations here months in advance, by website, phone or email.

The Top

The Top is divided into two smaller floors, one open-air and another indoor. Beyond breathtaking views, you can also delve deeper into the history of the tower with panoramic maps and a reconstruction of Gustave Eiffel's office. The champagne bar serves Champagne and fruit juice to help you celebrate.

The Tower for Free

There are also great ways to experience the tower up close for free. Pack a picnic with your favourite market finds – try the **Marché Président Wilson** – and head to the **Champ de Mars**, a gorgeous green space located at the foot of the Eiffel Tower that once served as a fruit and vegetable garden for Parisians.

DON'T LEAVE
Paris Without...

03

01 Condiments
Confiture, mustard, and even artisanal hot sauce. Great selections at La Petite Épicerie de la Tour and La Grande Épicerie.

02 Officine Universelle Buly Hand Cream
The most luxurious hand cream in the world is Buly 1803's Pommade Concrète. Visit its original Left Bank store.

03 Eiffel Tower Replica Keyring
Tacky but chic. Be like Timothée Chalamet on the red carpet and turn this into a fashion accessory.

04 Le Beurre Bordier
Le Beurre Bordier comes in many flavours, including algae, smoked butter and raspberry.

05 Shakespeare & Company Stamped Book
Visit the legendary bookshop and get the inside of your purchase stamped.

06 Fine Chocolates
Paris has many craft chocolate shops run by the finest cacao artisans. Try Patrick Roger or Le Chocolat Alain Ducasse.

07 Macarons
No trip to Paris is complete without a box of macarons to take home. Pierre Hermé or Ladurée have the best.

08 Opinel Knife
Beautiful knives from the Savoie region that make great gifts.

09 Café de Flore Crockery
Many Parisian bistros sell crockery but the ones at Café de Flore are the most sophisticated.

10 Mariage Frères Tea
The quality blended, loose-leaf teas by France's oldest tea house can be packaged in its iconic tin canisters.

11 Gourmet French Salt
Gourmet salts are affordable in France and beloved by all. Look for Sel de Guérande or Fleur de Sel de Camargue.

12 Postcards
Parisian postcards are works of art. Browse unique postcards by artists in Paris at Epiphania.

13 Poilâne Treats
From Punitions (its famous butter cookies) to *miches* (large rustic loaf bread), Poilâne has delicious fresh treats.

02 FASHION Hotspots

STYLE | CHIC DINING | SHOPPING

A seasoned fashion editor in Paris has all the best-kept secrets on where to shop for enviable, one-of-a-kind pieces and where to dine to exhibit these stylish finds. Lily Templeton, a fashion editor and writer, has lived in the 16e when in Paris and shares her favourite destinations in the neighbourhood that can be visited in a half day.

ADRIENC/GETTY IMAGES ©

How to

Getting here Take the metro to Trocadéro.

When to go The French sales (*soldes*) take place twice a year on dates mandated by the government. Discounts happen in increments, with the biggest bargains to be found towards the end.

Tip Put on a pair of your best comfortable walking shoes for a fun day of shopping and exploring. For excellent style-spotting, visit during Paris Fashion Week, where you will see fashion editors and celebrities. Dates can be found at fhcm.paris/en.

DKSSTYLE/SHUTTERSTOCK ©

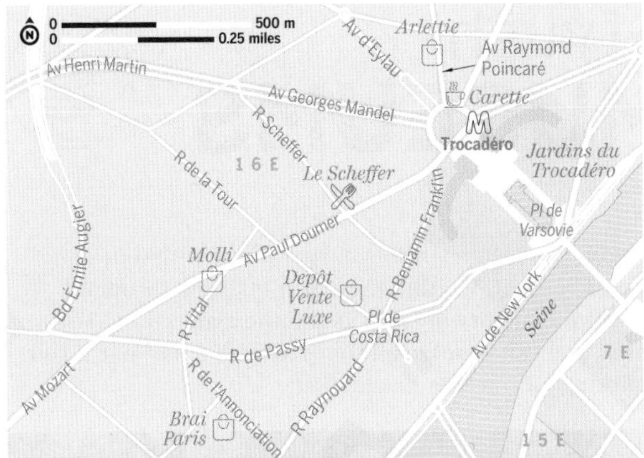

Top left Pl du Trocadéro Bottom left Street style, Paris Fashion Week

People-Watch at Carette, place du Trocadéro This feels like an obvious tourist spot – and don't get me wrong, it is – but for locals, this is people-watching central. We come here off-peak, on-peak, for takeaway coffee or savoury canapé sandwiches, all of it. The patrons are made up of colourful characters, from the Chanel-clad fashion executives to the decorated military personnel in full regalia, and even the odd high-flying public face discreetly meeting their lawyer (or lover) at the back of the house, mingling with oblivious parents taking their little ones for a *goûter* (afternoon snack) and out-of-town visitors.

Finding Secondhand Treasures If you don't mind a bit of a rummage, try your luck at the secondhand stores in this upscale 'hood. The digital presence of **Depôt Vente Luxe** (14 rue de la Tour) is almost non-existent but the boutique itself is a must-see for vintage lovers, as it has a dedicated set of well-to-do Parisiennes who leave their items here.

Lunch at a Kitschy French Bistro If you want an old-fashioned bistro with excellent French cuisine that has not been overrun by tourists, **Le Scheffer** is it. Its iconic red gingham table covers and walls tastefully covered in retro posters transport you to a different time.

Designer Bargains Every fashion insider's guilty pleasure – barely anyone admits they shop at **Arlettie**'s Trocadéro outpost but everyone does. It used to do clearance sales and now handles the sample sales for many luxury brands. The discounts aren't as big as they once were, but still worth a visit!

Parisian Luxury Staples

Molli, the original luxury knitwear brand, before Barrie and Maison Eric Bompard really cemented their place as leading purveyors of cashmere, is now led by cool and capable female entrepreneur Charlotte. One of its historic stores is still there on av Paul Doumer.

I love the PJs and robes best at **Brai Paris**, a loungewear brand founded by two Parisian sisters. The prints are always cute and designed by them in-house. They're big on sustainability and only use organic cotton, non-toxic ink, and they upcycle any excess fabrics. Their products are modestly priced and are size inclusive.

With thanks to Lily Templeton, *a fashion writer and editor, born and raised in Paris.* *@lilytempleton*

03 Stylish MUSEUMS

FASHION | ART | CULTURE

There are many incredible museums in this part of town, with four trendy ones located close to each other. Visiting these will take you through contemporary art, modern art, the history of fashion and the glamour of Yves Saint Laurent. If you're quick, you can squeeze all four into half a day, but if you have time, take it slow, exploring all the area has to offer.

LUC CASTEL/GETTY IMAGES ©

How to

Getting here Take metro line 9 to Iéna.

When to go Avoid this experience on Mondays as Palais Galliera, Musée d'Art Moderne de Paris and Musée Yves Saint Laurent Paris are closed. The Palais de Tokyo is open late until midnight but closed on Tuesdays.

Tip If you need to relax your eyes and legs in between museums, head to The Pavilion, the outdoor space at the back of the Palais de Tokyo. Chill out on the steps in the midst of the monumental art deco jewel, while watching the stylish Parisian skaters perform tricks.

STEPHANE DE SAKUTIN/AFP VIA GETTY IMAGES ©

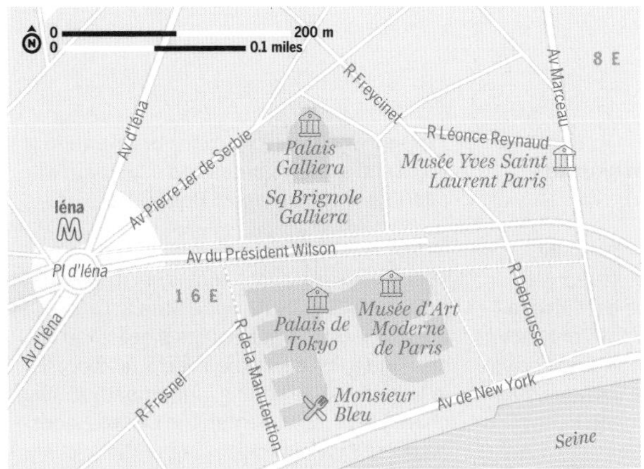

Palais de Tokyo The largest contemporary art space in Europe doesn't have a permanent collection but exhibits edgy and provocative temporary exhibitions. The art might not be for everyone, but the museum also has a large bookshop, two restaurants and the hip nightclub-cum-event-space, YOYO. The bookshop is run by Walther König & Cahiers d'Art, two icons in the art world, and offers a wide selection of books, magazines and trinkets from all over.

Musée d'Art Moderne de Paris (MAM) This museum shares the same building as the Palais de Tokyo, on the eastern wing. Owned by the City of Paris, it offers free entry. One of the most awe-inspiring works of art – a vibrant mural that spans the whole room depicts the history of electricity – is found in the Dufy Room.

Palais Galliera Reopened in 2021 after a renovation, this is one of the few museums in the world dedicated solely to fashion and its history. With the help of funding from Chanel, the museum now has more space to show off its permanent collection of over 200,000 pieces, including garments, accessories, photographs, drawings, illustrations and prints.

Musée Yves Saint Laurent Paris This is located in the atelier where the designer and his team worked for over three decades. The exhibitions display pieces from the museum's vast archive collection, accessories, sketches, photos and films. Highlights include the designer's studio and an original Picasso.

Top left Musée Yves Saint Laurent
Bottom left Temporary exhibition, Palais Galliera

Dining Options

Although the exhibitions at Palais de Tokyo might not be for everyone, the dining options in the building are.

Ritzy **Monsieur Bleu**, where French president Emmanuel Macron and other notable locals have been spotted a few times, has one the best *terrasses* in the city and a grand art deco interior. The menu is simple and straightforward – the filet mignon is a must for omnivores.

Bambini is the Paris Society hospitality group's 'grown-up trattoria' project, serving up cocktails and Italian comfort food, plus pasta and pizzas.

Over at the east wing, you'll find celebrity chef Julien Sebbag's newest restaurant, **Forest**, where vegetables are in focus.

Listings

BEST OF THE REST

Other Noteworthy Museums

Musée Marmottan Monet

This museum is housed in a former hunting lodge and has the largest collection of Monet paintings in the world as a result of a generous donation from the artist's only heir. The museum also exhibits its comprehensive impressionist collection, which includes masterpieces from Pissarro, Manet and Renoir.

Musée de la Contrefaçon

This small and wonderfully odd museum, dedicated to counterfeit goods, exhibits more than 350 seized items from customs or court settlements beside their authentic originals.

Fondation Louis Vuitton

Housed in a stunning Frank Gehry creation, this art museum is a bit off the beaten path near the Bois de Boulogne but is absolutely worth the visit for the exhibitions and the views.

Musée Guimet

One of the world's largest collections of Asian art can be found here in the 16e. The collection spans over 5000 years on the Asian continent and also highlights contemporary Asian artists.

Musée du quai Branly – Jacques Chirac

This museum and research centre, dedicated to showcasing and studying indigenous art and cultures found around the world, was completed by President Jacques Chirac. Close to the Eiffel Tower, this is a great place to seek out greenery thanks to its plant wall and the surrounding hectare of trees and plants.

Maison de Balzac

The charming home of Honoré de Balzac now serves as a free museum dedicated to the Parisian writer and his works. Upon entering, you'll find a lovely garden and a tearoom with offerings from the famed Rose Bakery.

Musée Baccarat

This crystal glass museum is set in a mansion decorated by Philippe Starck. On display are major Baccarat heritage pieces. You'll also find a Baccarat shop and a restaurant in an impressive setting, underneath shining chandeliers, aptly named the Cristal Room.

Gourmet Dining

Café Lignac — €€

Beloved local spot Café Constant was recently passed on to chef Cyril Lignac. Café Lignac continues to pay homage to Parisan bistro offerings and, like other Lignac establishments, is consistently delicious.

Cravan — €€

Located on a quiet street, Cravan is a captivating cocktail bar in a tasteful cafe setting with mirror-filled walls. Its small plates are perfect for *apéro* (predinner drink) but it also serves snacks and coffee during the day. Come early to secure a table.

Peacock, Parc de Bagatelle

L'Ami Jean €€€

Located near the Eiffel Tower, this loud but inviting bistro serves up generous portions of bistro classics, like *ris de veau* (sweetbread) and fish of the day, with a Basque touch. You cannot leave without trying chef Stéphane Jégo's signature rice pudding.

Shang Palace €€€

This Michelin-starred Chinese restaurant on the ground floor of the Shangri-La hotel offers a Cantonese fine-dining menu. The dining room is adorned with magnificent jade accents. The dim sum is the best in Paris!

Unwind

Hotel Molitor

The historic art deco Piscine Molitor swimming pool was revived, with its luxury hotel addition causing quite a scandal in the city. The stunning pool, now a historic monument, still remains the star and can be accessed by hotel guests, club members or those who splurge on a one-hour spa.

Parc de Bagatelle

This botanic garden, one of four maintained by the city, lies in the centre of Bois de Boulogne, and came to be because of a bet between Marie Antoinette and King Louis XVI's brother. Here you'll find peacocks roaming freely and 1200 species of roses, manicured to perfection.

Le Chalet des Îles €€

This cosy and calm restaurant is located on an island on Lac Inférieur, the smaller of two lakes in the Bois de Boulogne. A free water shuttle that consistently runs throughout the day will help you cross over to the island and back. The food and drinks here are pricey but great.

Love Juice Bar €

This healthy spot serves up the best smoothie bowls and gluten-free avocado toast in the city. A great spot to catch your breath and fuel up in between adventures.

LUDOVIC MARIN/AFP VIA GETTY IMAGES ©

Marché Président Wilson

Market, Vintage & Views

Marché Président Wilson

The largest open-air market in Paris pops up every Wednesday and Saturday. Here you'll find myriad stalls with the best of French *terroir*. It's a great place to shop but also the quintessential location to watch how locals interact with each other and food. Best to go before lunch.

Passy Brocante

This treasure trove of antiques is tucked away in a cul-de-sac off the posh rue de Passy. The prices are a bit higher than a pop-up *brocante* (flea market) in the city, which is reflective of the shop's location, but you're guaranteed to find something that sparks your wonder.

Trocadéro

Located across from the Eiffel Tower, this spot is made up of a collection of museums, sculptures and a public garden that surrounds the famous Warsaw fountains. This busy area is a great place to take in the views, but be extra careful with your belongings.

CHAMPS-ÉLYSÉES & GRANDS BOULEVARDS

FASHION | CULTURE | NIGHTLIFE

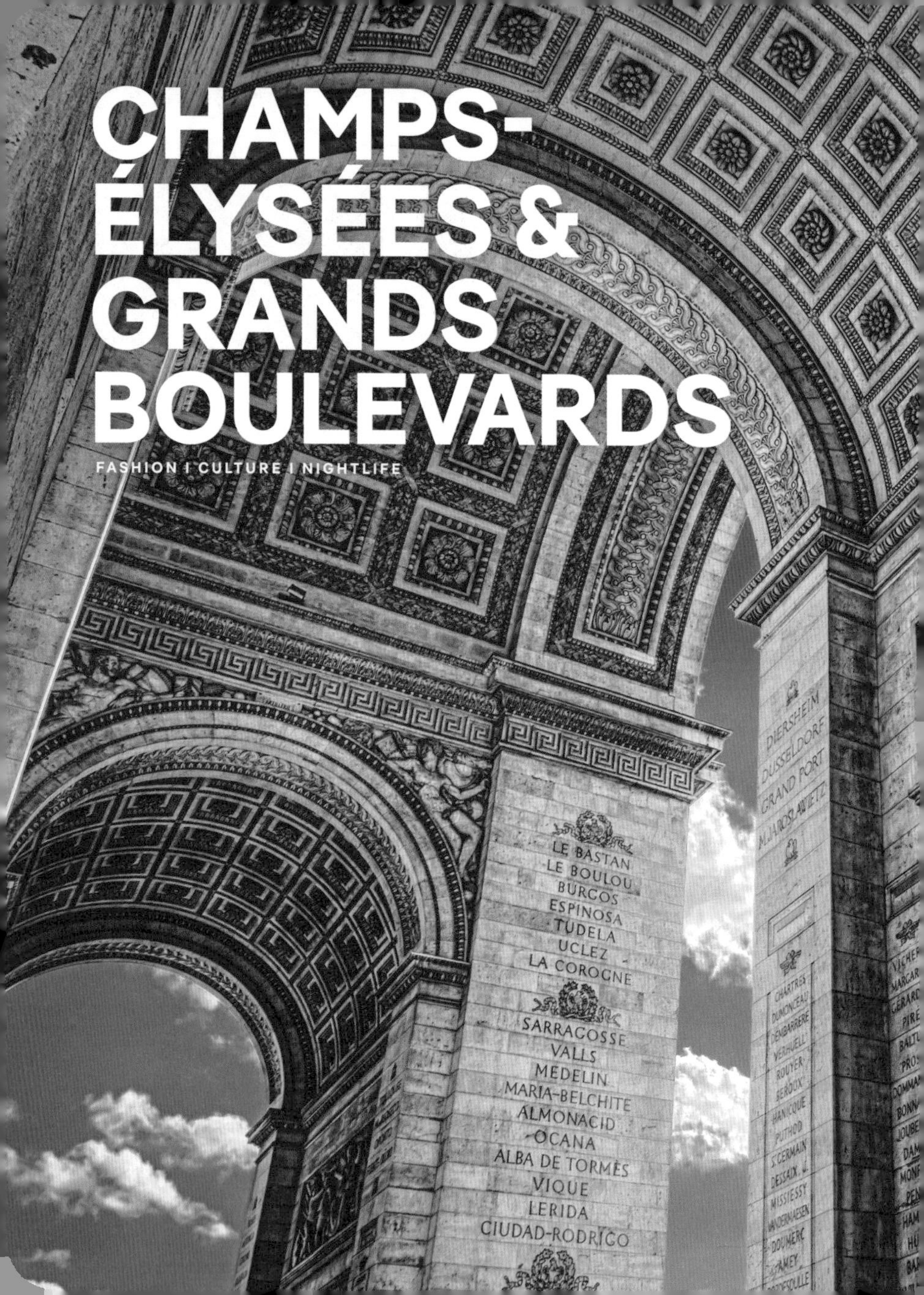

LUXEMBOURG
BRESLAW
BERG-OP-ZOOM
AUSTERLITZ
IENA
FRIEDLAND
ULM
WAGRAM
EYLAU
NEIGRE
ROTTEMBOURG
DESVAUX
MICHEL
FOULER
DALESME
PERCY
PETIET
VILLEMANSY
BURCY
LOCHET
BROUSSIER
GRATIEN
CHAMPMORIN
QUENTIN
DAVID
OLIVIER
MALHER
LEVAL
SAHUC
MONTRICHARD
BOYER
MARCOGNET
LAROCHE
GUILLEMINOT
FAUCONNET
DORSNER
DUHESME
GIRARD
LETORT
FRIANT
MONTCHOISY
MERMET
POINSOT
DARNAUD
PETIT
TESTE
PAJOL
CAMBRONNE
DAUMESNIL
COUVION
BASTOUL
SCHNEIDER
J^e BONAPARTE
AMBERT
LAUBADERE
TAPONIER
LAMARCHE
COLAUD
HATRY
DUFOUR
LIGNEVILLE
BONNARD
DEJEAN
SOUHAM
KILMAINE
VANDAMME
LEMAIRE
HARVILLE
SPARRE
PONCET
DELAAGE
BARBOU
BONNEAU
DESENFANTS
MORLOT
LEMOINE
MEUNIER
MARCEAU
DEBELLE
HARDY
LORGE
LAHOUSSAYE
GILLOT
PAILLARD
WATRIN
CRUNDLER
GROUCHY
VILLARET J^e
DILLON
CHARBONIER
MIRANDA
VALENCE
TILLY
FERRAND
CHAZOT
LANDREMONT
LANOUE
PULLY
DABOVILLE
CARNOT
DUVAL
LEVENEUR
DE S^T MARS
DE SAMBRE ET MEUSE·DE RHIN ET MOSELLE·DE HOLLANDE

CHAMPS-ÉLYSÉES & GRANDS BOULEVARDS
Trip Builder

TAKE YOUR PICK OF MUST-SEES AND HIDDEN GEMS

The chic Champs-Élysées offers luxury flagships and art exhibits at the Grand and Petit Palais, plus glitzy nightlife and the monumental Arc de Triomphe. The lively Grands Boulevards, a shopping and entertainment hub since the Belle Époque, are home to elegant department stores, grand opera houses and theatres and atmospheric covered passageways.

Neighbourhood Notes

Best for High-end shops, fine dining and nights out.

Transport Metro line 1 stops along the Champs-Élysées, while the Grands Boulevards are served by lines 8 and 9.

Getting around Explore on foot or find Vélib' stations throughout both areas.

Tip For panoramic views without queues and admission charges, head up to the Galeries Lafayette Haussmann rooftop terrace.

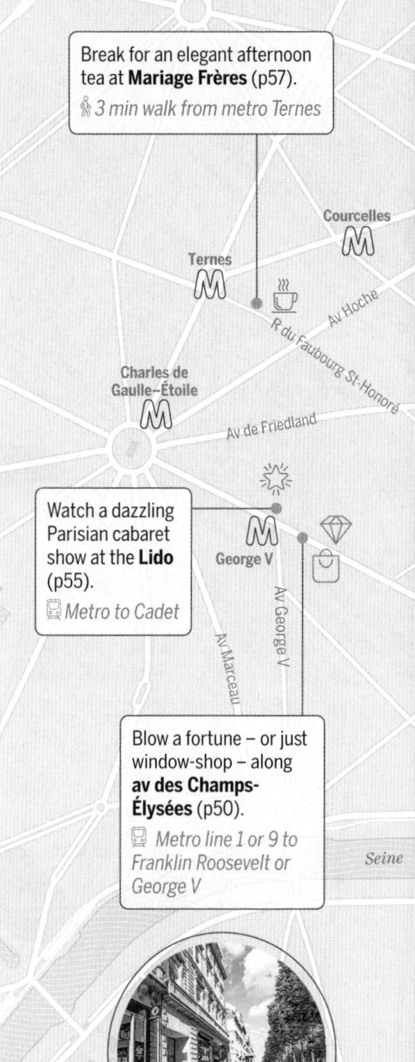

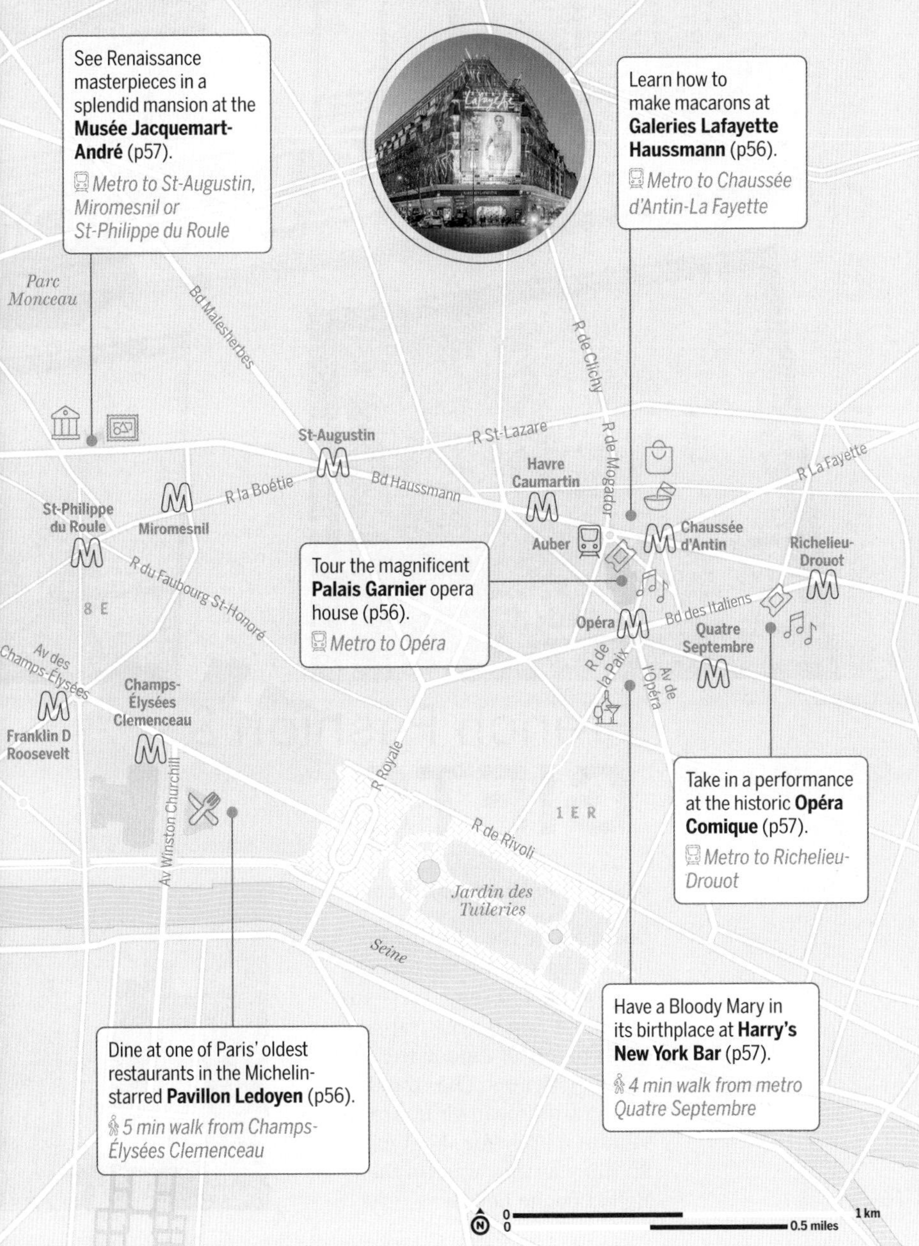
See Renaissance masterpieces in a splendid mansion at the **Musée Jacquemart-André** (p57).
Metro to St-Augustin, Miromesnil or St-Philippe du Roule
Learn how to make macarons at **Galeries Lafayette Haussmann** (p56).
Metro to Chaussée d'Antin-La Fayette
Tour the magnificent **Palais Garnier** opera house (p56).
Metro to Opéra
Take in a performance at the historic **Opéra Comique** (p57).
Metro to Richelieu-Drouot
Have a Bloody Mary in its birthplace at **Harry's New York Bar** (p57).
4 min walk from metro Quatre Septembre
Dine at one of Paris' oldest restaurants in the Michelin-starred **Pavillon Ledoyen** (p56).
5 min walk from Champs-Élysées Clemenceau
Parc Monceau
Bd Malesherbes
R de Clichy
R St-Lazare
R de Mogador
St-Augustin
Havre Caumartin
R La Fayette
Bd Haussmann
R la Boétie
St-Philippe du Roule
Miromesnil
Auber
Chaussée d'Antin
Richelieu-Drouot
R du Faubourg St-Honoré
8 E
Opéra
Bd des Italiens
Quatre Septembre
Av des Champs-Élysées
R de la Paix
Av de l'Opéra
Franklin D Roosevelt
Champs-Élysées Clemenceau
R Royale
Av Winston Churchill
1 E R
R de Rivoli
Jardin des Tuileries
Seine
0
1 km
0
0.5 miles

04 French Fashion & GIFTS

LUXURY | FASHION | FLÂNERIE

While the Champs-Élysées doesn't have quite the cachet it once did and some Parisians dismiss it as a tourist trap, it holds plenty of unique treasures and experiences. The Grands Boulevards, meanwhile, are as vibrant a place for shopping and strolling as they were in their Belle Époque heyday.

AURORE KERVOERN/GETTY IMAGES ©

How to

Getting here Metro line 1 or 9 to Franklin Roosevelt or George V.

When to go Grands Boulevards is most dazzling in winter, with elaborate holiday lights and window displays drawing crowds.

Tip When it's raining, the glass-roofed galleries of Grands Boulevards are perfect for shopping while staying dry.

Pedestrians The Champs-Élysées is pedestrian-only the first Sunday of each month; a great way to experience a leisurely stroll down its 2km length without the usual traffic chaos.

1000PHOTOGRAPHY/SHUTTERSTOCK ©

Indulge in Bespoke Luxury

Though a progressive influx of mass-market chains and fast-food outlets has significantly altered the character of the famous Champs-Élysées, high-end flagship stores, like Cartier, Lanvin and Hermès, can still be found here, with many offering special services and tailor-made gifts that can't be found elsewhere.

The **Guerlain** boutique, for example, offers customised lipsticks, engraved perfume bottles and – if you have a spare €45,000 – their master perfumer can formulate an exclusive scent just for you.

At **Longchamp**, you can design your own version of the signature Pliage folding bag, selecting the colours of the material, trim and hardware and adding a printed message or initials and an embossed monogram.

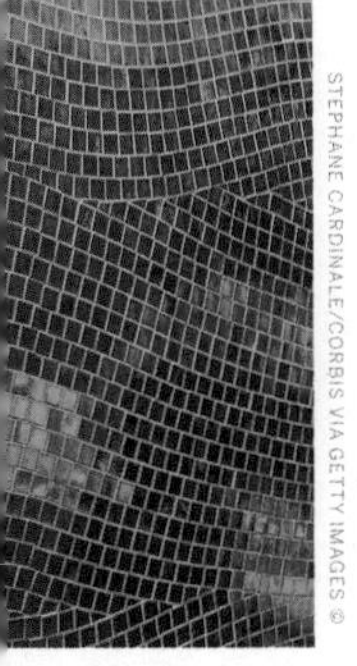

STEPHANE CARDINALE/CORBIS VIA GETTY IMAGES ©

A Macaron Fix

If the Ladurée or Pierre Hermé queues on the Champs-Élysées are too daunting, you can find macarons from Pierre Hermé at **Publicis Drugstore**. Galeries Lafayette's basement food hall, **Le Foodcourt**, has macarons from noted chocolatier Pierre Marcolini.

Top left Louis Vuitton, Champs-Elysées **Bottom left** Maison Guerlain **Above** Macarons

The **Dior Champs-Élysées** store features a personalisation station where customers can have a name or initials embroidered onto certain products, and at the grand, four-storey **Louis Vuitton** flagship store, you can watch artisans at work in the in-house ateliers. A monogramming service is offered and there is a fragrance fountain where clients can refill empty Louis Vuitton perfume bottles.

One-Stop Concept Shops

The multistorey **Galeries Lafayette Champs-Élysées** concept store, opened in 2019, is a huge draw for fashion-forward locals and visitors alike. If you're short on time, the hip new branch of the venerable department store chain is great for finding, all in one place, pieces from classic and cutting-edge French designers, including Isabel Marant and Jacquemus, as well as high-end beauty and homeware products like Diptyque candles.

Make-Up & Hair Supplies

Some of the best hair and make-up suppliers are in this area.

For hair accessories, quality brushes, grooming combs, beautiful hairpins for wedding dos, hats and more: **Maison Caillau** on rue du Faubourg St-Honoré.

On the same street, **Plein Fard** has lots of hard-to-find pro cosmetics brands. This shop's big secret is that the general public can avail of a professional discount when buying certain brands.

At the boutique of the French brand **Make Up For Ever** on rue la Boétie, you can get personalised advice and find special-effects, waterproof and body-painting products.

By Mily Serebrenik, *a professional session make-up artist and hair-stylist in Paris. @milyserebrenik*

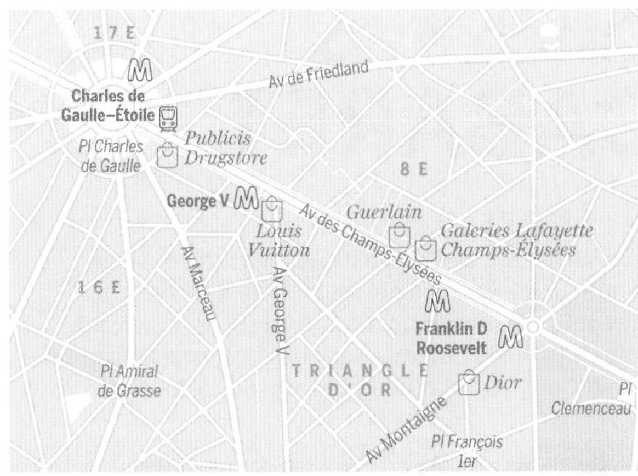

Near the Arc de Triomphe, **Publicis Drugstore** was Paris' first concept store, inaugurated in 1958. It features a cinema, two restaurants and a 24/7 pharmacy, plus a trendy shop selling books, gifts, international press, gourmet food, cigars and wine.

Shop Like It's 1912 in Grands Boulevards

Leafy bd Haussmann is as firmly connected with the Parisian pastimes of *flânerie* (leisurely strolling) and *lèche-vitrines* (window shopping; literally 'window licking') as it was in its Belle Époque heyday. It's home to the **Printemps** and **Galeries Lafayette Haussmann** department stores, both featuring art nouveau glass domes. Both Printemps and Galeries Lafayette have departments focusing on secondhand and vintage fashion in addition to up-and-coming design labels.

Explore the World's First Shopping Malls

For a taste of 19th-century shopping, wander through the vestiges of Paris' network of glass-roofed shopping arcades, each with its own character. The **Passage des Panoramas**, one of the oldest, dates from 1800 and houses shops selling collectable stamps, antique books and prints. The graceful **Galerie Vivienne**, built in 1823, has elaborate mosaic floors and a glass cupola, plus a tea salon and independent boutiques. There's also **Passage Jouffroy** and the elegant **Galerie Colbert**.

Left Lipsticks, Galeries Lafayette
Below Galerie Vivienne

05 Catch a CABARET

GLAMOUR | ENTERTAINMENT | NIGHTLIFE

Paris is the birthplace of cabaret, and while its earliest form – which still exists at places like Montmartre's Lapin Agile (p95) – was simply singers accompanied by piano or accordion entertaining tavern guests as they drank, over the centuries it's evolved into many different varieties. At its most over-the-top, cabarets like the Lido and Crazy Horse offer glittering spectacles.

SORBIS/SHUTTERSTOCK ©

How to

Getting here Metro line 1 to George V (Lido, Crazy Horse) or line 9 to Alma-Marceau (Crazy Horse).

When to go Lido shows start at 9pm or 11pm. They occasionally offer afternoon matinee performances at a lower price. Book in advance.

What to wear A smart outfit; flip-flops, shorts, trainers and sportswear are not allowed.

Alternative cabaret Le Cabaret Burlesque, Le Cirque Électrique, Cabaret Le Secret, Cabaret de Poussière and events at La Coupole for more intimate, edgier shows.

LAURENT VITEUR/WIREIMAGE ©

Far left Lido **Bottom left** Dancers, Crazy Horse **Near left** Performer, Lido

Paris Meets Vegas: Le Lido

The historic **Lido** first opened on the Champs-Élysées in 1928 as a Venice-inspired restaurant and nightclub with a vast indoor marble swimming pool. It later transformed, in the 1930s, into a cabaret. In the postwar years the Lido was one of the pioneers of the 'dinner show' format that continues today. The large-scale showgirl numbers are accompanied by a live orchestra and punctuated by variety acts such as acrobats or mimes. The latest show, created by Franco Dragone, former artistic director of Cirque du Soleil, is a lavish extravaganza that blends elements of Vegas shows and circus acts with French touches like the can-can. Although the dancers are sometimes topless, the show is mostly known for its spectacular costumes, which are heavy on the crystals, feathers and sequins.

Racy and Minimalist: Crazy Horse

In contrast, **Crazy Horse** is more modern, risqué and stripped-down, with no can-can, no dinners and no elaborate costumes. The dancers, in fact, are mostly dressed in wigs and projected light effects – and not much else. Founded in the 1950s as a 'cowboy saloon', it started out with traditional burlesque striptease shows before evolving into its current form. The space is intimate, with cinema-style seating rather than individual tables. In recent years, guest stars like Dita Von Teese and Conchita Wurst have visited for limited-run shows.

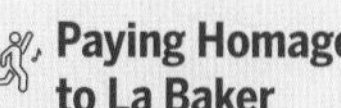

Paying Homage to La Baker

Josephine Baker, my idol and guardian angel, inspired my career in show business and led me to Paris.

When I had the honour of becoming the first African American MC at **Crazy Horse**, I was thrilled to realise that I was performing sandwiched right between two historic spots linked to her. On av de Montaigne, the **Théâtre des Champs-Elysées** was where she gave her first performance in Paris in 1925, and what's now **Hôtel Château Frontenac**, on rue François 1er, was where she opened her second cabaret, the Chez Joséphine Baker Club des Champs-Elysées, in the 1930s.

By Brian Scott Bagley, *a cabaret performer who leads Gay Paris Noir and Josephine Baker tours. @brianscottbagley*

Listings

BEST OF THE REST

Activities & Tours

Palais Garnier

See the ceiling painted by Chagall and the setting that inspired *The Phantom of the Opera* at this opulent 1860 opera house. Self-guided and guided tours are available in English.

Galeries Lafayette Haussmann

The department store offers a fashion show every Friday afternoon (booking required), plus macaron-making classes and guided visits. Classes and tours are in French and English.

Views

Arc de Triomphe

The roof of Napoléon's monument to himself affords breathtaking views of the surrounding boulevards. Below it, the Tomb of the Unknown Soldier's eternal flame is rekindled each evening at 6.30pm.

L'Oiseau Blanc €€€

This Michelin-starred, aviation-themed restaurant atop the Peninsula hotel offers seasonal tasting menus as well as indoor/outdoor seating and striking views of the Eiffel Tower.

Galeries Lafayette Haussmann

The rooftop terrace on this stunning Belle Époque department store affords panoramic views over Paris without queues or admission charges and features pop-up restaurants and bars throughout the year.

Unique Boutiques

Librairie Artcurial

The bookshop of the Artcurial auction house, located in an elegant 19th-century mansion, carries a wide selection of books on contemporary art, photography, design and architecture, including English-language tomes.

Laulhère

A venerable maker of traditional berets since 1840, offering classic and contemporary styles in wool, cashmere and leather in its main boutique, located in a courtyard on rue du Faubourg St-Honoré.

Memorable Meals & Quick Bites

Le Drugstore €€

Chic brasserie at Publicis Drugstore, with international dishes, a takeaway counter and a sidewalk terrace that's perfect for people-watching. Open until 2am daily; rare in Paris.

Bouillon Chartier €

A distinguished institution, founded in 1896, in a lovely and airy art nouveau space. The traditionally dressed waiters serve classic, retro-priced brasserie fare at shared tables.

Alléno Paris au Pavillon Ledoyen €€€

One of Paris' oldest and most elegant restaurants, once a favourite of artists and writers

Palais Garnier

like Degas, Monet and Flaubert. Now run by Michelin-starred chef Yannick Alléno.

Le Foodcourt at Galeries Lafayette Champs-Élysées €

Basement food hall and shop with a natural-wine bar and counter service. Perfect for gourmet gifts like Alain Ducasse chocolates, Crème de Salidou salted caramel or flavoured Edmond Fallot mustards.

Pastries, Sweets & Teatime

L'Éclair de Génie

Forget macarons. Chef Christophe Adam's sleek shops (in rue Montmartre and Lafayette Gourmet food hall) sell the most beautiful and luscious handcrafted éclairs, in creative, seasonal flavours like 'basil mint' and 'lemon yuzu'.

À la Mère de Famille

The oldest sweet shop in Paris, dating from 1761, is a tiny jewel packed with handcrafted chocolates, regional French candies, cakes and more.

Mariage Frères Étoile €€

An elegant tearoom with an old-world ambience and antique decor serving pastries, jelly and savoury dishes made with the brand's gourmet teas, plus refined brunches.

Operas, Films & Art

Opéra Comique

See an opera in the intimate and ornate neobaroque theatre where Bizet's *Carmen* premiered in 1875. From classic operas to contemporary, experimental works. All performances have English subtitles.

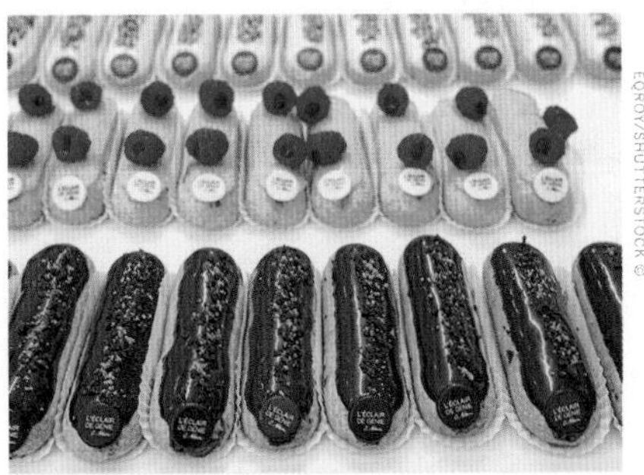

EQROY/SHUTTERSTOCK ©

Pastries, L'Éclair de Génie

Grand Rex

Vast and stunning 1930s art deco cinema. Today it still screens films but is also a concert venue and nightclub. Self-guided tours in English are available.

Musée Jacquemart-André

A museum housing an extensive art collection – with a focus on Italian Renaissance masterpieces – in a lavish mansion on bd Haussmann, the former home of a wealthy 19th-century couple.

Distinguished Drinks & Chic Nightlife

Harry's New York Bar

A cosy, wood-panelled hang-out founded in 1911. Legend has it that the Bloody Mary was invented here and Gershwin composed *An American in Paris* in the piano bar.

Silencio

Eclectic and dimly lit club owned by David Lynch, with a program of concerts, DJs, films and exhibitions. It's members-only until midnight, then open to the public.

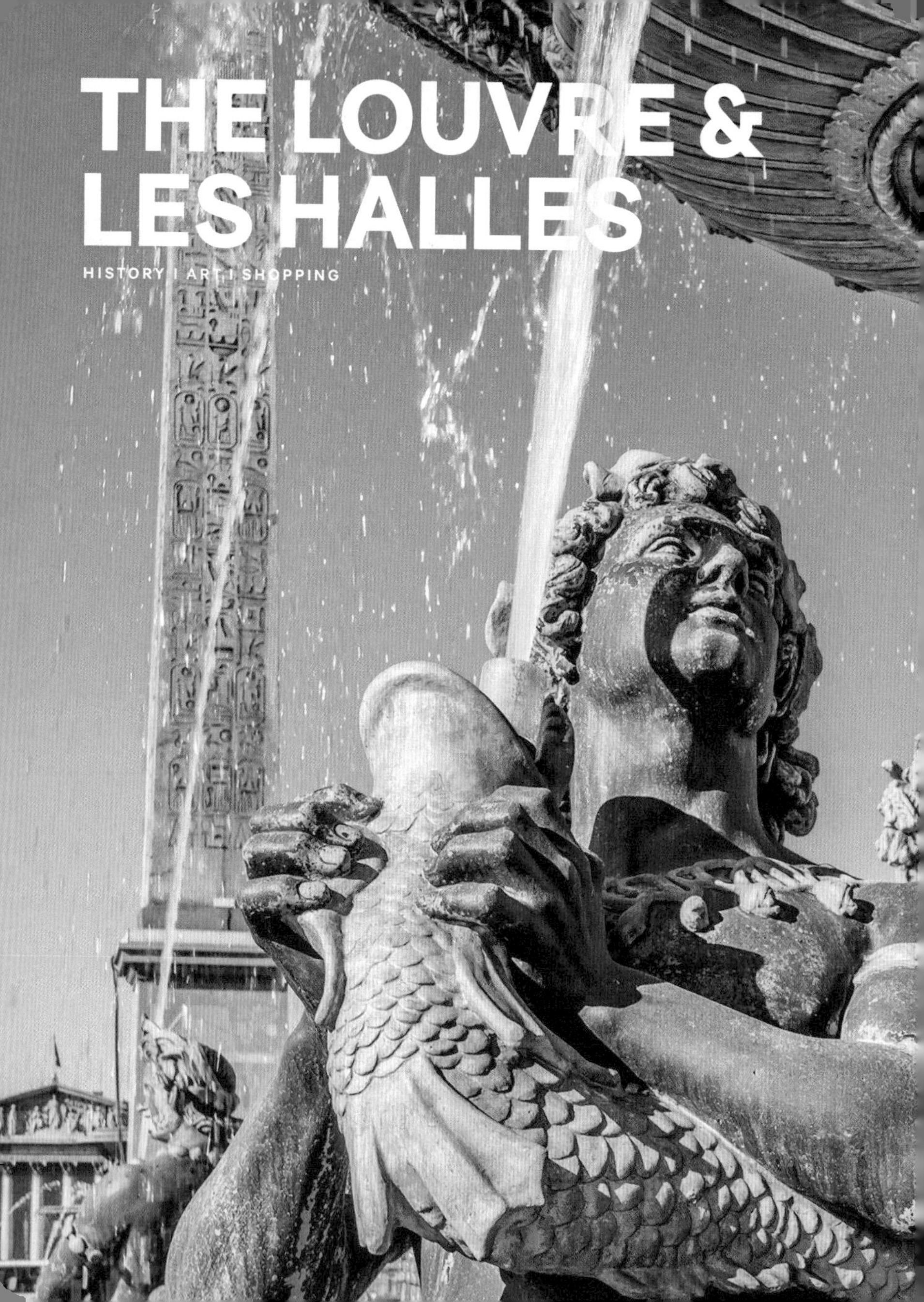
THE LOUVRE &
LES HALLES
HISTORY | ART | SHOPPING

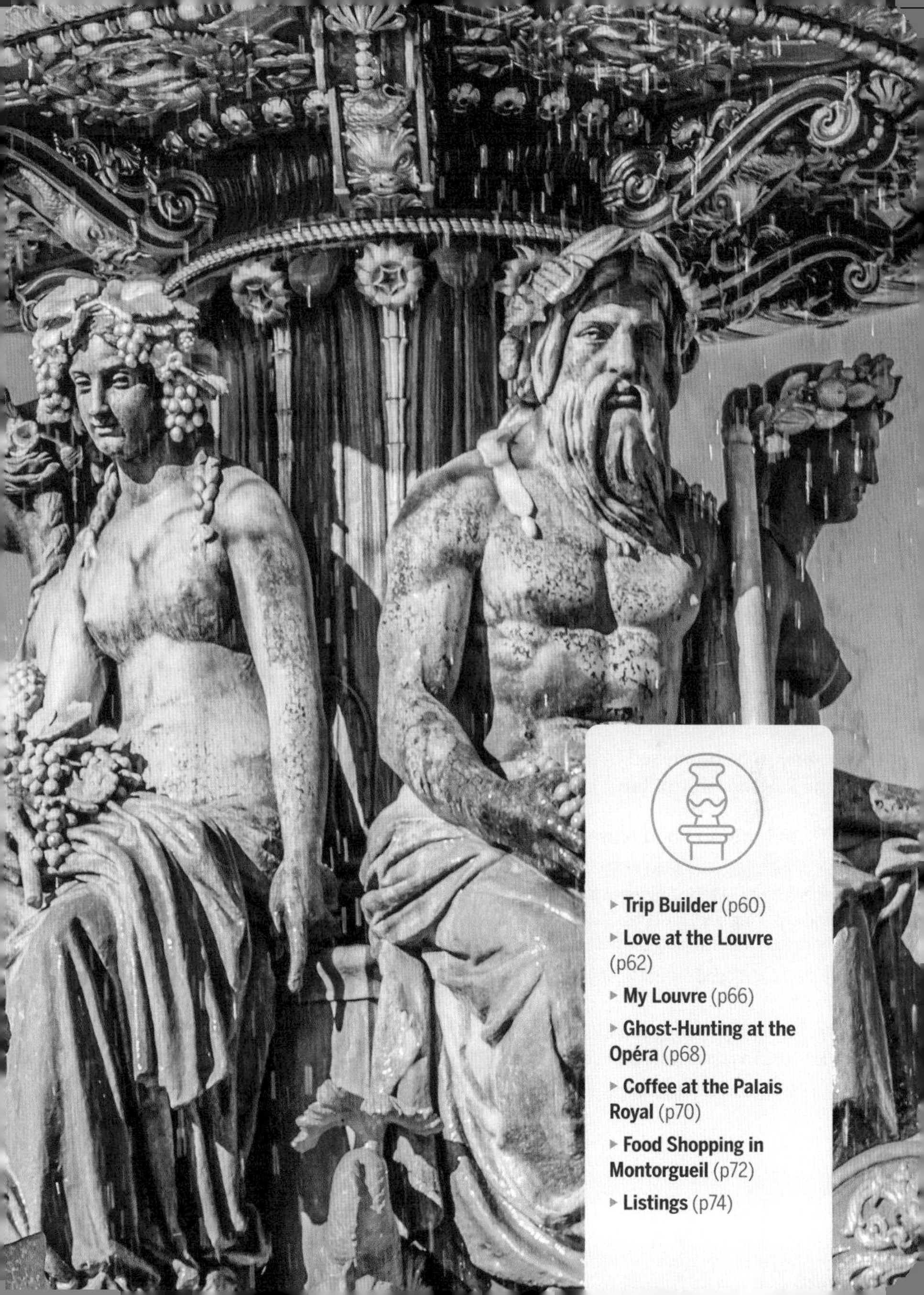

THE LOUVRE & LES HALLES
Trip Builder

TAKE YOUR PICK OF MUST-SEES AND HIDDEN GEMS

Old meets new in this historic centre, home of the world's largest art museum, former royal palaces and the city's oldest commercial streets. Royals, politicians, entrepreneurs and artists have left their mark on the neighbourhood and its architecture. Come to be immersed in history and the Parisian way of life.

Neighbourhood Notes

Best for Marvelling at art and architecture. Drinking coffee at a terrace and exploring quiet galleries. Shopping for fresh food and sampling the best pastries.

Transport Around central Châtelet–Les Halles.

Getting around Explore on foot so you don't miss any architectural detail or shop.

Tip Mind your personal belongings.

Take your time strolling from the Louvre to place de la Concorde through the **Jardin des Tuileries**.

5 min from metro Palais Royal–Musée du Louvre

Take a coffee break on the terrace of **Café Marly**, facing the Louvre's Great Pyramid (p66).

5 min from metro Palais Royal–Musée du Louvre

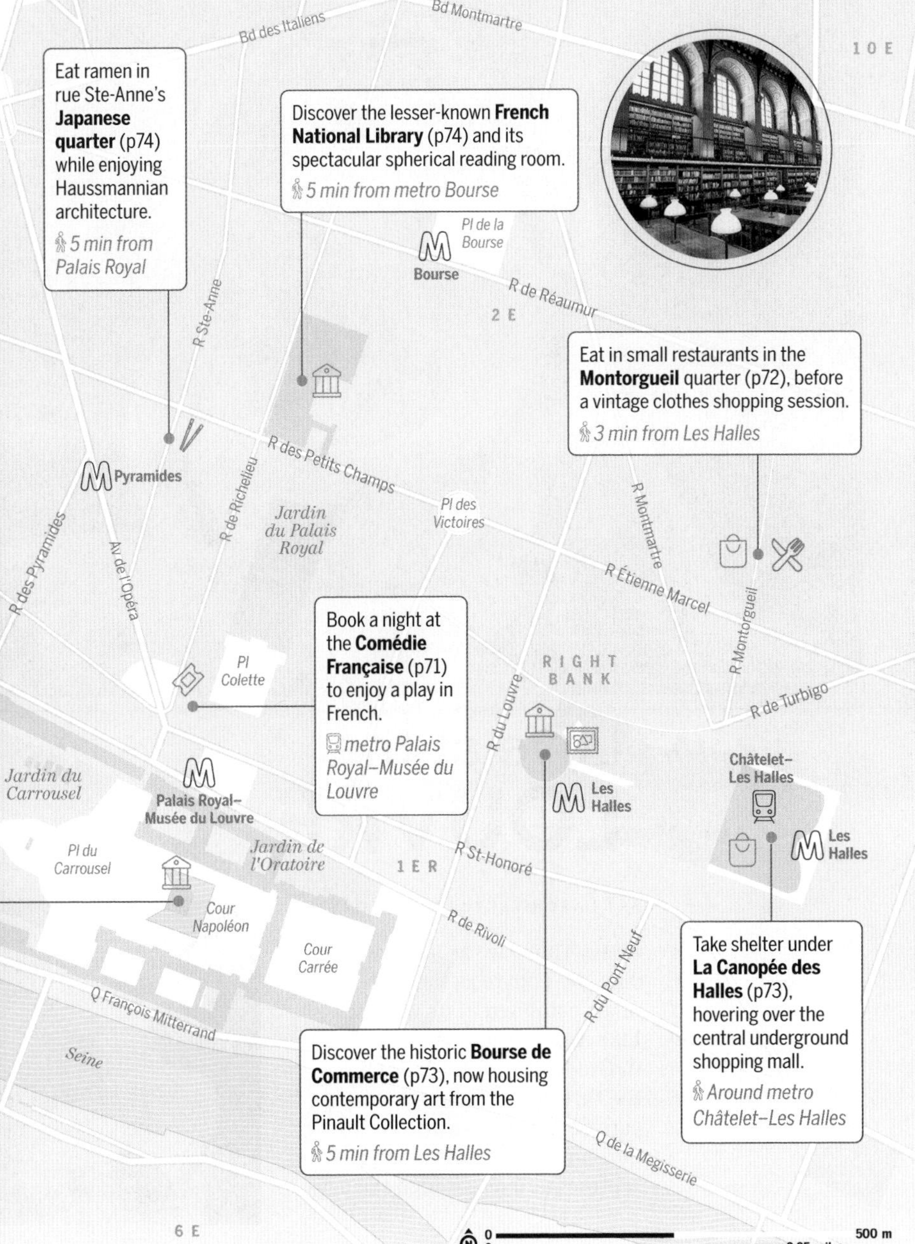

Bd des Italiens
Bd Montmartre
10E
Eat ramen in rue Ste-Anne's **Japanese quarter** (p74) while enjoying Haussmannian architecture.
5 min from Palais Royal
Discover the lesser-known **French National Library** (p74) and its spectacular spherical reading room.
5 min from metro Bourse
Pl de la Bourse
Bourse
R de Réaumur
2E
R Ste-Anne
Eat in small restaurants in the **Montorgueil** quarter (p72), before a vintage clothes shopping session.
3 min from Les Halles
Pyramides
R des Petits Champs
R de Richelieu
Jardin du Palais Royal
Pl des Victoires
R Montmartre
R des Pyramides
Av de l'Opéra
R Étienne Marcel
Book a night at the **Comédie Française** (p71) to enjoy a play in French.
metro Palais Royal–Musée du Louvre
Pl Colette
RIGHT BANK
R Montorgueil
R du Louvre
R de Turbigo
Châtelet–Les Halles
Jardin du Carrousel
Palais Royal–Musée du Louvre
Les Halles
Les Halles
Pl du Carrousel
Jardin de l'Oratoire
1ER
R St-Honoré
Cour Napoléon
Cour Carrée
R de Rivoli
R du Pont Neuf
Q François Mitterrand
Seine
Take shelter under **La Canopée des Halles** (p73), hovering over the central underground shopping mall.
Around metro Châtelet–Les Halles
Discover the historic **Bourse de Commerce** (p73), now housing contemporary art from the Pinault Collection.
5 min from Les Halles
Q de la Megisserie
6E
0
0
500 m
0.25 miles

06 Love at the LOUVRE

ART I ARCHITECTURE I HISTORY

There are as many ways to visit the Louvre as there are works of art exhibited in its galleries. Like Ariadne guided Theseus in Greek mythology, let's follow the thread of 'love' down the corridors of the world's largest art museum, and discover some of its representations through the ages.

DEAGOSTINI/GETTY IMAGES ©

How to

Getting here Take the metro to Palais Royal–Musée du Louvre.

Online booking Buy tickets on ticket louvre.fr.

How much A full-price ticket is €17 but the museum is free of charge for anyone under 18 and for residents of the European Economic Area (EEA) up to the age of 26. For other visitors, entry on the first Sunday of each month is always free.

Tip Start with the paintings section, preferably in the morning, as it's the most popular and tends to fill up by 11am.

DEAGOSTINI/GETTY IMAGES ©

Mythical Figures of Love

Who else to begin our love journey with than the ***Venus de Milo***? Dating to c 150 BCE, she was identified as a 'Venus', the Roman counterpart of Greek goddess Aphrodite and an antique representation of love and female beauty, because of her nudity and curves. Excavated and made famous in the 19th century, she remains one of the world's most notable Venuses, along with Botticelli's painting *The Birth of Venus*.

Now walk to room 403 in the Denon wing. ***Psyche Revived by Cupid's Kiss*** is much admired for the delicateness in the choice of the scene, composition and textures. Its sculptor Antonio Canova represented the climax of Psyche and Cupid's story in this ode to love. The lovers are reunited after overcoming all obstacles, including travelling to hell and

PAOLO GALLO/SHUTTERSTOCK ©

Louvre Explore

The museum has rich online resources to help you prepare for or extend your visit, and admire its masterpieces on screen. Browse the 'Explore' tab of its website to dive into major courtyards, rooms and galleries. Visit louvre.fr/en/explore.

Top left *Psyche Revived by Cupid's Kiss* **Bottom left** *Venus de Milo* **Above** *Raherka et Merseankh* (p64)

back. Impressed, Zeus allows their union and that's how Psyche, born mortal, enters the divine pantheon as the goddess of the soul.

Marital, Courtly and Sacred Love

Skip the *Seated Scribe* in the Department of Egyptian Antiquities and focus on ***Raherka et Merseankh*** in room 635: a warm gesture by the woman expresses her feelings towards her husband. The modelled couple is believed to have lived under the 4th or 5th Dynasty, between 2600 and 2400 BCE.

Let's travel a few millennia ahead, to room 504 in the Richelieu wing. Have a look at ***L'Offrande du Coeur*** (The Offering of the Heart), a 12th-century tapestry representing courtly love. This refers to courtship between two unmarried people in medieval times. It mainly consisted of poetry and chivalrous gestures. It is worth noting that, eventually, the outcome of such wooing was always supposed to be based on mutual consent.

Indoor Garden

Enter the Louvre and discover the Cour Marly and Cour Puget: two immense courtyards with tiered architecture, hosting two centuries of French sculpture. Are we inside or outside? Both courtyards used to be open before architects IM Pei and Michel Macary started the renovation of the museum in 1983. But how can you exhibit sculptures intended for outside, without them suffering any damage? The idea of a glass-covered space was born, bathing the marble masterpieces in natural light. Walk among the statues and olive trees, enjoy the vistas and sunbathe in the morning light.

FINE ART IMAGES/HERITAGE IMAGES/GETTY IMAGES ©

Far left Nicolas Coustou's *La Seine et La Marne*, Cour Marly **Near left** *L'Offrande du Coeur* **Below** Bernardino Luini's *Madonna and Sleeping Child with Three Angels*

Going through European religious art and Renaissance masterpieces, you will come across many painted representations of the Madonna and Child, central figures in Christian imagery. This image of sacred love created a lasting impression of maternity, which influenced people's perception of femininity through the centuries.

A Controversy

Walk to room 929 in the Sully wing and look for a painting which hangs in complete contrast to the religious artworks: ***Le Verrou*** (The Bolt), by Jean-Honoré Fragonard. It is famous for its erotic tension, expressed by the lascivious movement of the characters, the undone bed and a reference to original sin in the discreet apple. However, the interpretation of the scene is controversial: she seems to be pushing his face away, and his decided posture makes him look like he could be forcing himself on her. In the context of the emerging ideas of freedom in 18th-century France, it is unclear whether the woman in this piece is consenting or being forced.

FAR LEFT: ISOGOOD_PATRIC/SHUTTERSTOCK ©
LEFT: FINE ART IMAGES/HERITAGE IMAGES/GETTY IMAGES ©

■ **By Fabienne Fong Yan**
French-Chinese born and raised on Réunion Island, Fabienne has travelled between Europe and Asia for the past 15 years. She now works in Paris as a digital content strategist.

My Louvre

A DIFFERENT WAY TO EXPERIENCE PARIS' BEST-LOVED MUSEUM

So many visitors walk into the Louvre everyday, lining up in front of the pyramid, sometimes for hours. As a Parisian, I visit the museum only on special occasions. But enjoying the Louvre from outside? That, I indulge in regularly!

SANTIAGO CASTILLO CHOMEL/SHUTTERSTOCK ©

From left Musician under the Pavillon de l'Horloge; Façade detail, Louvre; Cour Carrée

A central landmark in Paris, the Louvre happens to often cross the path of my daily commute. There is one special itinerary I love because I secretly enjoy looking for the numerous signs left by the successive kings, queens and architects who have contributed to the grandeur of the palace over the centuries. Many have left their marks on façades, medallions, locks and gates, sometimes on the ground.

Coming from the left bank of the Seine, I usually enter the Louvre from the Pont des Arts, directly into the **Cour Carrée**. This perfectly symmetrical square is often overlooked by visitors. Its tranquillity is my playful haven. I enjoy rotating while looking around at the surrounding façades: it makes me dizzy like a child to look at the infinite succession of windows!

Under the **Pavillon de l'Horloge** (Clock Pavilion), the acoustics are amazing. That's why classical musicians like to play under the arches. I've always thought it created a soothing transition before the surprise majestic view offered by the **Great Pyramid**, which appears suddenly before your eyes when you walk into the main courtyard. It's even better on a bright sunny day when the sun reflects upon each and every glass triangle.

I like to carefully look around at the façades and galleries, ornate with hundreds of sculpted busts and faces. Whole chapters of the French monarchy's history are ready to be discovered by those who know what to look for. For instance, almost all the kings who lived here left a monogram somewhere on the walls. The one I like best is an H with two interlaced Ds: they stand for Henri II and

GAUTIER WILLAUME/SHUTTERSTOCK ©

G. DAGLI ORTI/DE AGOSTINI PICTURE LIBRARY VIA GETTY IMAGES ©

Diane de Poitiers, his favourite mistress. How could a mistress have her initials engraved on the royal palace? Because the king made the Ds also look like two Cs...the initials of his actual wife, Catherine de' Medicis. Sly king!

Secrets of the Louvre are also hidden in plain sight, for example, the upturned base of the **inverted pyramid** (a smaller version of the Great Pyramid) is invisible from outside, even though it's right in the middle of the roundabout separating the Great Pyramid from the opposite Jardin des Tuileries. Another secret lies at the foot of the small **Arc de Triomphe du Carrousel**: while many take pictures of the standing monument, keen observers might notice the lines traced on the floor, originating from the arch. Those lines serve as a giant sundial!

> Whole chapters of the French monarchy's history are ready to be discovered by those who know what to look for.

Finally, a less concealed but very satisfying stop, before leaving what feels like a quiet capsule at the heart of Paris, is when I head back to the **Richelieu gate**. Under its dark threshold, large windowpanes allow me to see inside the museum. From there, I look at the visitors who seem so small, wandering the **Cour Marly**, a vast room hosting masterpieces of French sculpture. It's as if I could take a glimpse of inspiration from the museum before diving into Paris' intense traffic again. That feels like a small gift from the Louvre.

The Hidden Cross of Paris

'Aérer, unifier et embellir Paris': open up Paris, unify the city and make it more beautiful. That's the order Baron Haussmann received from Emperor Napoléon III in 1853 before beginning the city's great transformation. He created the grande croisée de Paris, a big cross in the city centre at place du Châtelet, which was built to improve links from north to south and east to west. Work on the cross was initially started by Napoléon I, but it was completed by Napoléon III in 1859, and the intersection is still a major hub today. Three arches dot the east–west boulevards: the small arch of the Louvre, the Arc de Triomphe and La Grande Arche de La Défense.

07 Ghost-Hunting at THE OPÉRA

MYSTERY I ARCHITECTURE I LITERATURE

The Palais Garnier, also known as the Opéra, is one of the most opulent buildings of the 19th century. Accessible only to the richest, it was easy for those who had never been there to concoct fantasies. The discovery of a skeleton sparked Gaston Leroux' imagination. In 1909, his novel *The Phantom of the Opera* revealed the ghost whose mystery has remained in the building until today.

MARY416/SHUTTERSTOCK ©

How to

Getting here Take the metro to Opéra or Pyramides, or the train to Auber.

Tours Self-guided tours allow easy access to the public areas of the building and exhibitions. Guided tours can be more educational. Visits to the auditorium may be restricted or impossible for technical or artistic reasons.

Tickets For tours: operadeparis.fr/en/visits/palais-garnier; for plays: operadeparis.fr/en/programme-and-tickets.

GARY YIM/SHUTTERSTOCK ©

RICHIE CHAN/SHUTTERSTOCK ©

The Making of a Ghost

Before electricity made its way to the city, fires were common in theatres. The most deadly happened at Le Peletier theatre in 1963, when ballerina Emma Livry's outfit caught fire on stage. Her statue can now be seen in the magnificent **Glacier salon** at the Palais Garnier. Legend has it that a musician who was also on stage that night was in love with Emma and burnt half his face in the same fire. Mourning his loss, he sought refuge below the newly commissioned Palais Garnier.

A few years later, a skeleton (now identified as that of a revolutionary) was discovered in the foundations, giving birth to the myth of a ghost living in the labyrinthine basement of the Palais Garnier. Erik the ghost rented Box 5, where he could easily plot mischief, such as dropping a chandelier onto the audience. This was inspired by a real event when the opera's great chandelier fell and killed a woman in 1896.

A Mysterious Underground Lake

The novel shows Erik living in a secret lake below the Palais Garnier. And there is actually a water tank below the building. While digging the foundation, the architect Charles Garnier ran into surprisingly high groundwater levels. They tried to pump the water out but that didn't work. In the end, Garnier decided to control the water instead and he created a double-layered basement, filled with water, to protect the structure from moisture. Today, this water tank, closed to the public, is used by Paris firefighters.

Far left Grand Foyer, Palais Garnier **Bottom left** Theatre seats, Palais Garnier **Near left** Exterior, Palais Garnier

Voices from the Past

The ghost of the Opéra may be fictional, but voices from the past can still be heard. In 1907, time capsules were sealed and 'buried' in the caves of the Palais Garnier. They contained gramophone records of the most famous singers of the time, left by Alfred Clark, who ran the Gramophone Company's offices in Paris. The time capsules were apparently not to be opened for a century. In 2008, the time capsules were extracted, listened to and digitised. They are now kept in the archives of the **French National Library**.

08 COFFEE at the Palais Royal

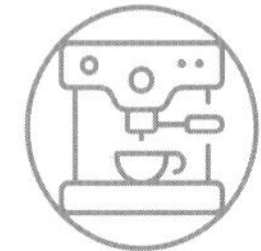

ART I HISTORY I HAVEN

Tucked between the Louvre and the Palais Garnier, the Jardin du Palais Royal can't be seen from the main avenues and is considered a local haven. Enter from hidden passages, under the 18th-century galleries, and breathe in the tranquillity of this peaceful park – fronted by a former royal palace – which is also a major landmark for contemporary art.

MISTERVLAD/SHUTTERSTOCK ©

How to

Getting here Take the metro to Palais Royal–Musée du Louvre or Pyramides.

When to go It's a popular lunch spot for locals who work in the neighbourhood so avoid lunchtime if you want to easily find somewhere to sit.

Takeaway Several cafes have seating under the galleries, but Parisians are used to bringing their own coffee or lunch to the park – there are plenty of takeaway food and drinking options nearby.

STEPHANE DE SAKUTIN/AFP VIA GETTY IMAGES ©

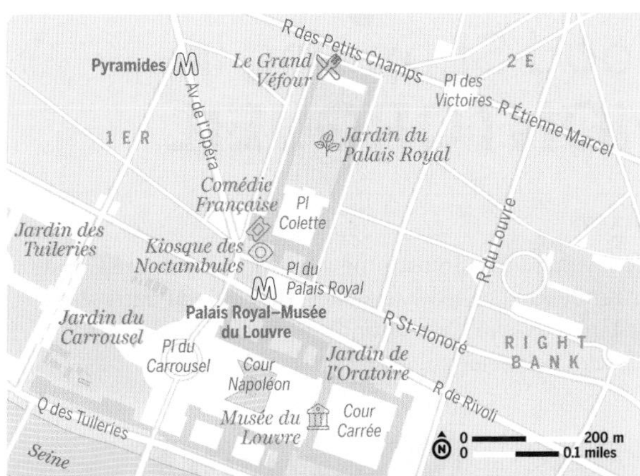

Top left Jardin du Palais Royal
Bottom left Dress rehearsal, Comédie Française

From Royal Palace to Cradle of the Arts

At the end of the 18th century, Duke Philippe d'Orléans transformed the Palais Royal into a popular square with commercial galleries and residences. Soon, it became a location for cabarets, brothels, and gambling houses as the police were not allowed there. This festive period ended in the 1830s, leaving the galleries as we know them today. **Le Grand Véfour**, the only original institution under the arcades, is a historical cafe, where Napoléon Bonaparte met Joséphine, and Victor Hugo used to come for lunch.

A Historical Cultural Residence

Over time, authors and artists took up residence in the Palais Royal, among them Jean-Honoré Fragonard, Stefan Zweig and Colette. The proximity of many giants of the art world – **Comédie Française**, the Louvre and the French National library – made it an inspirational place to be, as well as being conveniently central. Later in 1959, the building also welcomed the headquarters of the French Ministry of Culture.

A Playground for Modern Art

You will see Daniel Buren's zebra-striped **columns**, Pol Bury's **Fontaine des Spheres** (spherical fountain) and, a bit further south on place Colette, Jean-Michel Othoniel's colourful **Kiosque des Noctambules** (Kiosk of the Night Owls). To do it like the Parisians do, buy takeaway coffee and take a seat on one of the gardens' green chairs. Notice the poetry on some: 'Les Confidents' celebrates the moments spent daydreaming in Paris' public gardens, coffee in hand.

Instagram the Invisible

Daniel Buren's 260 black-and-white-striped columns, regularly climbed on by tourists and passers-by, are perfect for Instagram pictures. They were controversial when first erected in 1985 because of the clash between historical heritage and modern art, but are now very much part of the site. The installation is actually named *Les Deux Plateaux* (The Two Levels) in reference to the artist's geometrical work: two invisible plateaus can be visualised through the alignment of some of the columns' tops. Walk around to find the right angle to be able to see them!

09 Food Shopping in MONTORGUEIL

FOOD TOUR I SHOPPING I HISTORY

Paris' largest market was here for almost nine centuries. Fascinated by its teeming life, French writer Émile Zola called Les Halles 'the Belly of Paris'. It is now a trendy pedestrianised area extending to Montorgueil, with many shops still selling fresh food produce. The perfect place to shop and eat.

BRUNO DE HOGUES/GAMMA RAPHO VIA GETTY IMAGES ©

How to

Getting here Take the metro to Sentier, Châtelet or Les Halles.

When to go For a chilled market experience, come between 9am and noon. In the afternoon, the place becomes crowded with shoppers, terrace-lovers and passers-by.

Tip Explore the area on foot starting from the top of rue Montorgueil, or from Les Halles' central hub.

OWEN FRANKEN/GETTY IMAGES ©

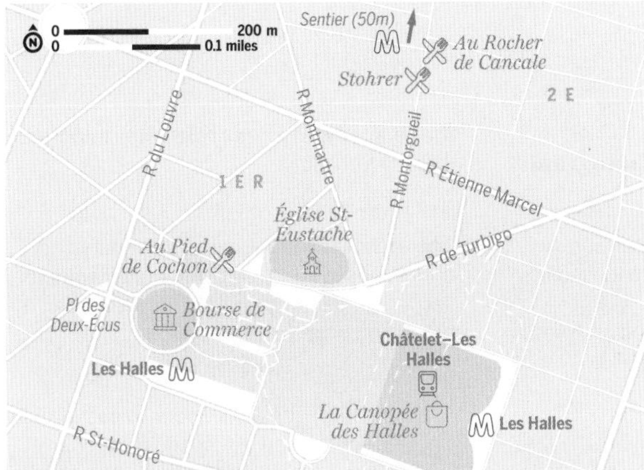

Historical Food Places

When walking along rue Montorgueil towards Les Halles, pay attention to all the vintage shop signs. Always a busy commercial spot, the area became popular for fresh seafood in the 17th century. **Au Rocher de Cancale** (No 78) continues the tradition by serving oysters à la carte. **Stohrer** (No 51), the oldest bakery in Paris, is another historic institution. Try their famous *Puits d'Amour* (wells of love) for a taste of traditional French pastry. If you're curious about French buttered snails, look for the giant golden snail hanging above No 38. The place still serves three dozen snails for the dear price of €80.

The St-Eustache Market

Where rue Montorgueil meets Les Halles, a food market takes place every Thursday and Sunday morning. Beyond it, look for **rue du Jour**, which leads behind the atmospheric St-Eustache church, up to **Au Pied de Cochon**, one of the rare restaurants still open around the clock in Paris! Then, continue either to the **Forum des Halles** shopping mall, under its impressive modern **Canopée des Halles** roof, or to the newly renovated **Bourse de Commerce**, both symbols of the area's bustling commercial past.

Top left Rue Montorgueil **Bottom left** Pastries, Stohrer

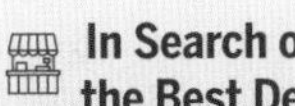

In Search of the Best Deli

What amazes me is the ever-changing atmosphere: at 9am, all you see are early-bird vendors, barely anyone else. One hour later, it's already completely different. It's a great place to relax at a cafe terrace and a definite must for food shopping! There are five bakeries and two cheese shops in this street alone. Some of my favourite things to do include discovering new cheese from all regions of France at La Fermette, tasting Durum's pitta bread, and looking through the windows of every cake shop in search of my cake of the day!

Tasnime Mounavaraly *is a curious foodie and Parisian pastry lover.* *@curioseaty*

Listings

BEST OF THE REST

Literature, Arts & Photography

French National Library – Site Richelieu

The historical site of the National Library. Guided tours give you access to the iconic Henri Labrouste reading room. A larger museum with art collections and archives is expected to be completed by 2023.

Musée des Arts Décoratifs (MAD)

Located in two wings of the Louvre, the MAD aims to keep the French art of living and design alive through permanent collections and exhibitions on contemporary design themes.

Gaîté Lyrique

A cultural institution and performance venue showcasing post-internet culture art: digital art, 3D and video games. It regularly hosts playful workshops and interactive events.

59 Rivoli

Formerly an artist squat, this is now a contemporary art gallery hosting parties, concerts and exhibitions. The building features a huge face sculpted into the façade, contrasting with the classical architecture of rue de Rivoli.

Japanese Quarter

Kodawari Tsukiji Ramen €€

The authentic experience of a traditional Japanese fish market, decor included, except that it's in the heart of Paris. Beware of the hustle and bustle while you enjoy your ramen.

Pâtisserie Tomo €€

Small tearoom tucked behind the Palais Royal. Famous for its *dorayaki* (Japanese pancake) and homemade red bean paste. Sit in the counter with a cup of green tea imported directly from Japan.

Junkudo

One of the largest Japanese stationery and bookshops in Paris. Shop for limited editions, secondhand manga, traditional Japanese paper and origami tutorial books.

Box in Paris

A *kawaii* (cute) gift shop hidden in passage de Choiseul, one of the oldest and most charming Parisian covered alleys. It's worth going just for the surprising cultural differences.

Lively Bars & Cosy Tearooms

La Cantine des Pieds Nickelés €

There's no friendlier and more convivial place than this local canteen. It's been around for ages and serves fresh homemade food along with a good selection of wines.

Sunset/Sunside Jazz Club

One of the most appreciated jazz clubs in the centre of Paris. With a rich and diverse programme, there's a concert – or more – almost every night.

59 Rivoli

Yam'tcha Boutique €€

A quiet sophisticated tearoom that's an offshoot of the Michelin-starred restaurant Yam'tcha. Through the open kitchen, see the traditional baskets in which the bao buns are steamed.

French Tables

Le Verre Luisant €

A friendly restaurant with an open terrace near Châtelet, which specialises in free-range chicken and traditional French food. Open all afternoon and excellent value for money.

La Fresque €

A typical French restaurant with agreeable staff. The mural inside reminds us of what life used to be like when the area was still the largest market in town, known as 'the Belly of Paris'. Good value for money.

Mûre €

A restaurant serving only seasonal dishes, with vegetables coming from their own farm 30km from Paris. Avoid lunch hour (1pm to 2pm) and don't leave without trying the honey madeleines.

Bakeries & Pastry Shops

Bo&Mie €

A creative twist on the most iconic French breakfast and dessert items, with subtle flavours and textures. Try the strawberry cruffin (a mix between croissant and muffin) and the hazelnut and praline flan.

Cloud Cakes €

A small vegan cafe with a large selection of pretty, tasty cakes. Serves good coffee and vegan croissants. The tiny terrace is enjoyable in the afternoon sun.

LEGNA69/GETTY IMAGES ©

Samaritaine

Fou de Pâtisserie €€

The editors of *Fou de Pâtisserie* magazine brought sweet tooth to the next level at their shops, where a selection of pastries made by the greatest chefs is offered, and regularly renewed.

Crafts & DIY

Mokuba

A haberdashery where you will find all sorts of ribbons, conveniently located near Montorgueil and drawing on the textile tradition of the Sentier area.

Rickshaw

A vintage shop where you can find all types of Indian-style furnishings and antiques: knobs and hooks, unusual home accessories and iron-cast letters of the alphabet. Worth paying a visit just for its unique atmosphere!

Luxury Shopping

Samaritaine

Closed for several decades, the oldest department store in Paris is now open to the public again! Once the beating heart of popular shopping, it is now an architectural jewel and home to multiple luxury shops.

MONTMARTRE & NORTHERN PARIS

HISTORY | CULTURE | NIGHTLIFE

Experience Montmartre & Northern Paris online

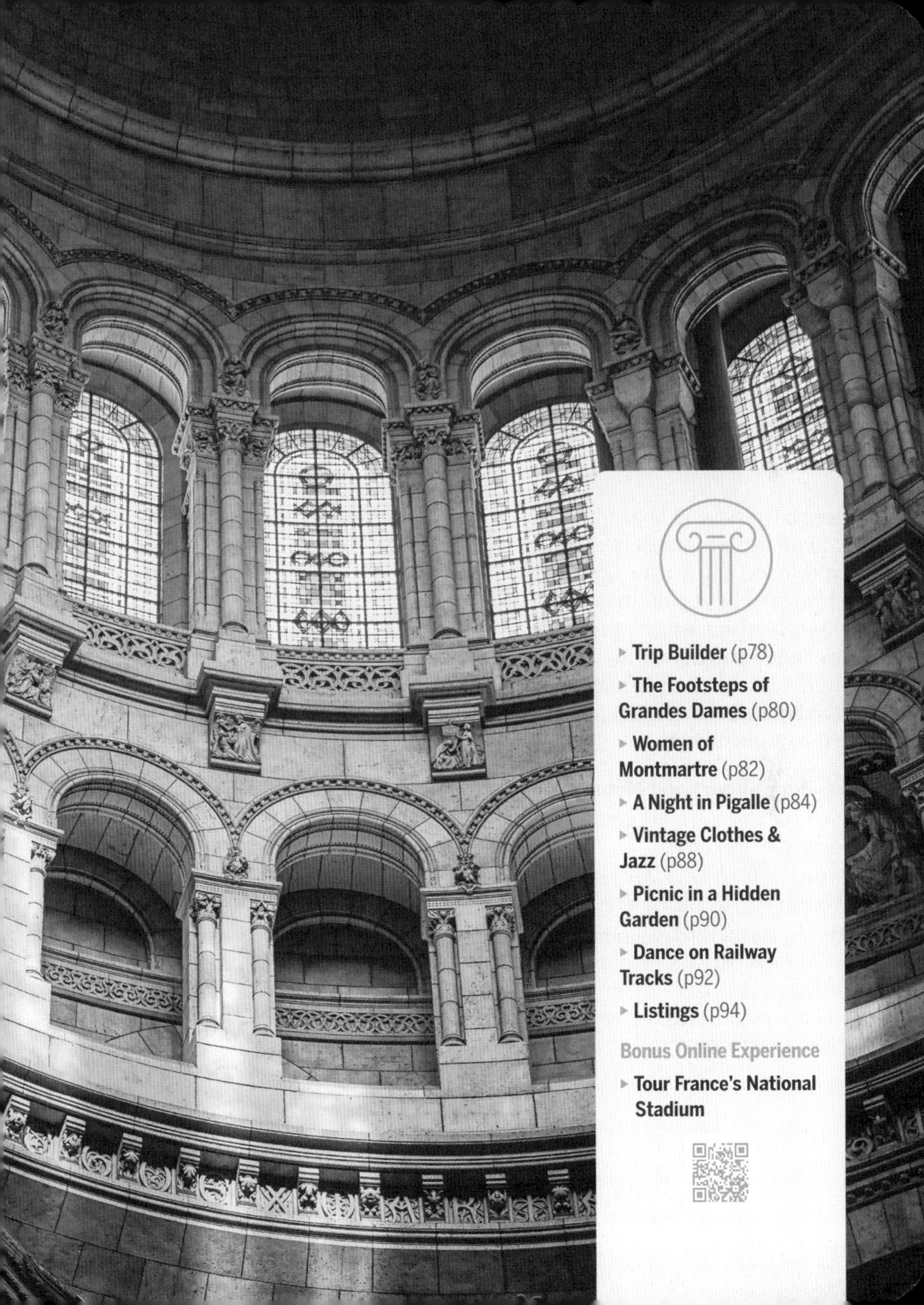

▸ Trip Builder (p78)
▸ The Footsteps of Grandes Dames (p80)
▸ Women of Montmartre (p82)
▸ A Night in Pigalle (p84)
▸ Vintage Clothes & Jazz (p88)
▸ Picnic in a Hidden Garden (p90)
▸ Dance on Railway Tracks (p92)
▸ Listings (p94)
Bonus Online Experience
▸ Tour France's National Stadium

MONTMARTRE & NORTHERN PARIS Trip Builder

TAKE YOUR PICK OF MUST-SEES AND HIDDEN GEMS

Quirky and bohemian Montmartre manages to retain its village feel and artistic sensibilities in spite of its popularity with visitors. Elsewhere in northern Paris, you can find relatively off-the-tourist-track areas that offer tranquil parks, hip cultural centres, live music and vibrant nightlife.

Neighbourhood Notes

Best for Charming streets, traditional cabaret and hip nightlife.

Transport Metro lines 2, 4 and 12 for Montmartre, lines 2 and 12 for Pigalle.

Getting around Hilly Montmartre, with steep slopes and stairs, is best explored on foot.

Tip The area around Barbès and Gare du Nord can be dodgy.

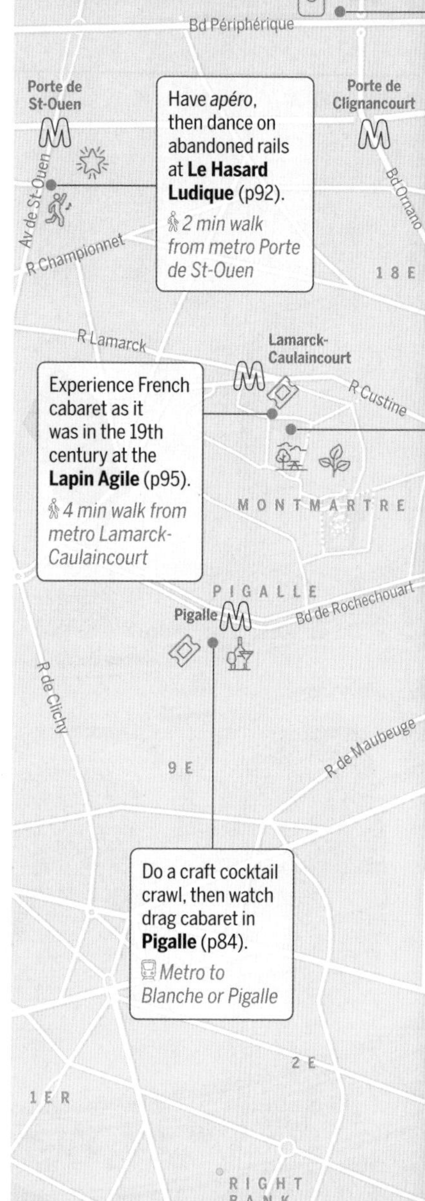

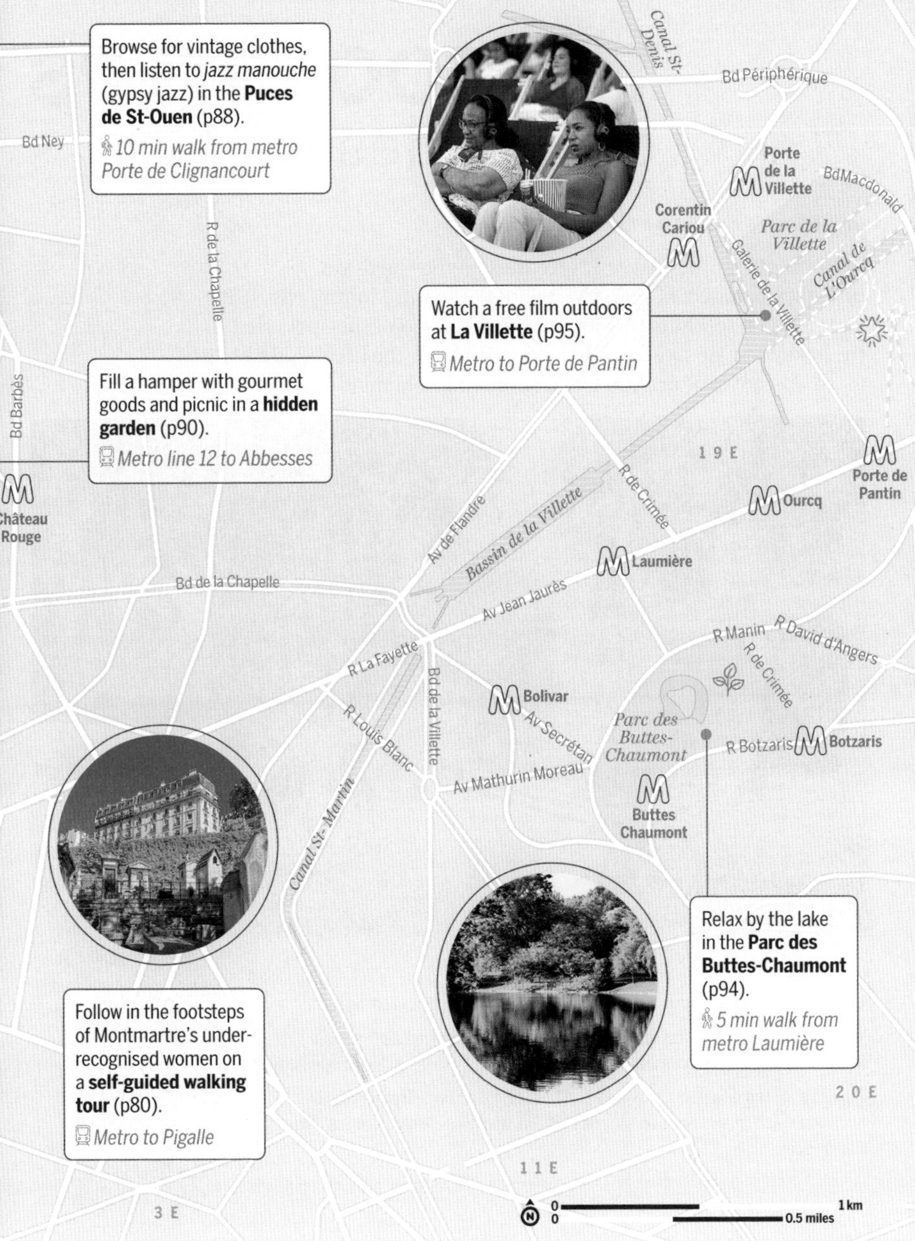

Browse for vintage clothes, then listen to *jazz manouche* (gypsy jazz) in the **Puces de St-Ouen** (p88).
10 min walk from metro Porte de Clignancourt
Watch a free film outdoors at **La Villette** (p95).
Metro to Porte de Pantin
Fill a hamper with gourmet goods and picnic in a **hidden garden** (p90).
Metro line 12 to Abbesses
Follow in the footsteps of Montmartre's under-recognised women on a **self-guided walking tour** (p80).
Metro to Pigalle
Relax by the lake in the **Parc des Buttes-Chaumont** (p94).
5 min walk from metro Laumière
Canal St-Denis
Bd Périphérique
Bd Ney
R de la Chapelle
Porte de la Villette
Corentin Cariou
BdMacdonald
Parc de la Villette
Galerie de la Villette
Canal de L'Ourcq
Bd Barbès
Château Rouge
19 E
Porte de Pantin
Ourcq
R de Crimée
Av de Flandre
Bassin de la Villette
Laumière
Bd de la Chapelle
Av Jean Jaurès
R Manin
R David d'Angers
R La Fayette
R de Crimée
Bd de la Villette
Bolivar
R Louis Blanc
Av Secrétan
Parc des Buttes-Chaumont
R Botzaris
Botzaris
Av Mathurin Moreau
Buttes Chaumont
Canal St-Martin
20 E
11 E
3 E
0 1 km
0 0.5 miles

10 THE FOOTSTEPS of Grandes Dames

HISTORY I WOMEN I ARTS

Many of the places where these remarkable yet underappreciated women lived and worked in Montmartre still exist. Take a self-guided walking tour to some of the spots tied to these key female figures, journeying through the area's long history as an epicentre of artistic innovation and bohemian life.

LOC LAGARDE / 500PX/GETTY IMAGES ©

How to

Getting here and around Metro line 2 to Blanche, then head off on foot.

When to go Weekdays are less busy and spring or autumn has the most favourable weather for climbing the neighbourhood's steep hills and stairways.

Tip Stop for tea or a glass of wine at La Maison Rose, once frequented by Suzanne Valadon and her son Maurice Utrillo, as well as Albert Camus and Pablo Picasso.

Bonus Stops on the Route

Suzanne Valadon also lived for a time at **2-4 rue Cortot**, next door to **6 rue Cortot**, studio of the eccentric composer Erik Satie, with whom she had a brief yet intense love affair in 1893.

In 2021, the park at **14 rue Burq** was renamed **Jardin Louise-Weber-dite-La-Goulue** in honour of the can-can queen.

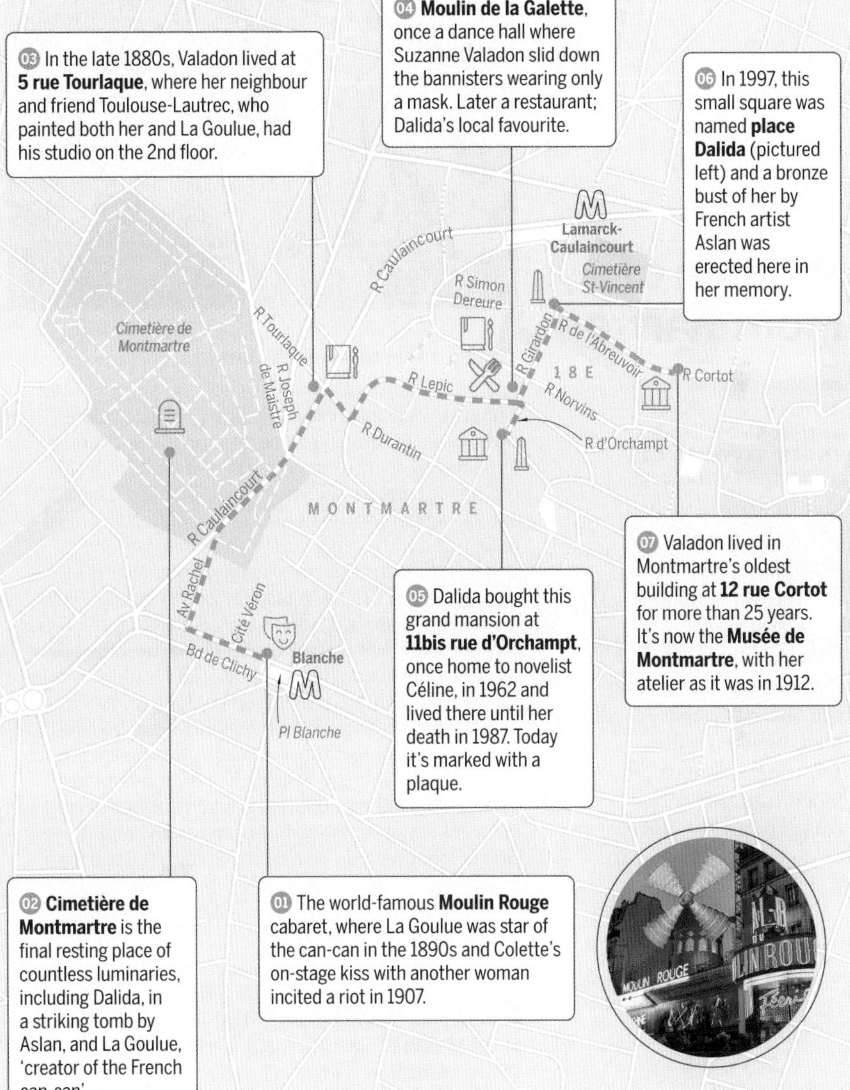

01 The world-famous **Moulin Rouge** cabaret, where La Goulue was star of the can-can in the 1890s and Colette's on-stage kiss with another woman incited a riot in 1907.

02 **Cimetière de Montmartre** is the final resting place of countless luminaries, including Dalida, in a striking tomb by Aslan, and La Goulue, 'creator of the French can-can'.

03 In the late 1880s, Valadon lived at **5 rue Tourlaque**, where her neighbour and friend Toulouse-Lautrec, who painted both her and La Goulue, had his studio on the 2nd floor.

04 **Moulin de la Galette**, once a dance hall where Suzanne Valadon slid down the bannisters wearing only a mask. Later a restaurant; Dalida's local favourite.

05 Dalida bought this grand mansion at **11bis rue d'Orchampt**, once home to novelist Céline, in 1962 and lived there until her death in 1987. Today it's marked with a plaque.

06 In 1997, this small square was named **place Dalida** (pictured left) and a bronze bust of her by French artist Aslan was erected here in her memory.

07 Valadon lived in Montmartre's oldest building at **12 rue Cortot** for more than 25 years. It's now the **Musée de Montmartre**, with her atelier as it was in 1912.

ALXEYPNFEROV/GETTY IMAGES ©

0 — 500 m
0 — 0.25 miles

Women of Montmartre

GET TO KNOW THESE UNDER-RECOGNISED MONTMARTROISES

Montmartre is well-known as the old stomping grounds of countless famous men, among them Picasso, Van Gogh, Debussy and Truffaut. But there are also many women whose achievements have faded into the background.

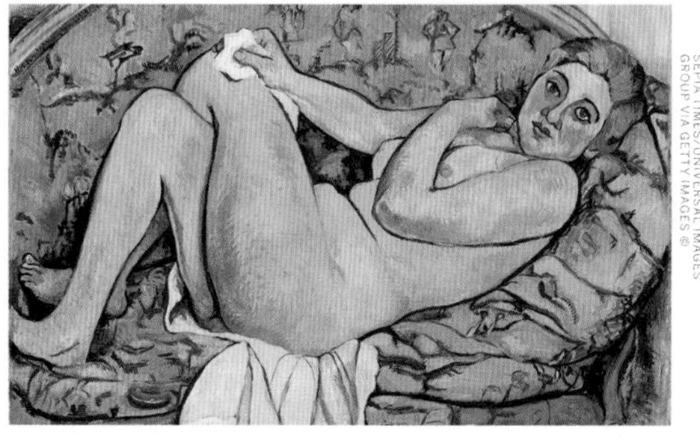

The Painter: Suzanne Valadon

Raised in Montmartre by her mother, an impoverished laundress, Suzanne Valadon started out as a trapeze artist, but a fall put an end to circus work. She turned to modelling for the many artists who lived on the hill, posing for painters such as Renoir, Toulouse-Lautrec and Modigliani. She features in some of Renoir's most recognised works, such as *Dance at Bougival* and *Dance in the City*. But she was far more than just a beautiful artist's muse. A talented and unconventional artist in her own right, she was encouraged by her friend and advocate, Edgar Degas. In 1894, she became one of the first women admitted to the Société Nationale des Beaux-Arts, a stunning achievement for a woman from a working-class background, with no formal training. Her frank and unromanticised nudes were years ahead of their time. Although Valadon achieved substantial success and international recognition during her lifetime, in the following years she has been mostly forgotten outside of Montmartre – and excluded from the history of French art.

The Dancer: La Goulue

Like Suzanne Valadon, Louise Weber grew up poor, the daughter of a laundrywoman. And like Valadon, she modelled for Renoir before finding her own renown. One of the Moulin Rouge's early stars in the 1890s, the boisterous redhead was immortalised in many paintings and posters by Toulouse-Lautrec. She earned her nickname, *La Goulue* (The Glutton), through her healthy appetite and cheeky habit of emptying customers' wine glasses as

From left *Reclining Nude*, Suzanne Valadon; Dalida; Colette

STILLS/GAMMA-RAPHO VIA GETTY IMAGES ©

DEAGOSTINI/GETTY IMAGES ©

she danced past their tables. Credited with developing and popularising the high-energy can-can from an earlier dance called the *chahut*, her fame and fortune were such that she was also known as 'The Queen of Montmartre'. After leaving the Moulin Rouge in 1895 for an unsuccessful turn as a lion tamer, she fell into oblivion and spent her last days in poverty. In 2021, Montmartre's Jardin Burq park was re-named in her honour.

Credited with developing the high-energy can-can, La Goulue's fame and fortune were such that she was also known as 'The Queen of Montmartre'.

The Singer: Dalida

The glamorous *chanteuse* known as Dalida was born Iolanda Gigliotti to Italian parents in Cairo in 1933. In the 1950s, she moved to Paris and quickly became a sensation, first as a pop star and later as a disco diva. She sang in 10 languages, toured the world numerous times and was one of the first singers to be awarded a diamond disc for selling more than 10 million albums. A superstar in France, Europe and the Middle East, she received a lukewarm reception – and remains relatively unknown – in the anglophone world. In 1962, Dalida bought a mansion in Montmartre in rue d'Orchampt and lived there for more than 20 years. Although she was spectacularly successful in her career, her private life was repeatedly marked by tragedy and, sadly, in 1987 she took her own life.

The Writer: Colette

Though Colette is widely recognised as one of France's greatest writers, her early struggles are less known. Her husband Willy published her wildly popular debut novels in his name; when she left him in 1906, he kept all royalties and she turned to performing in music halls to survive. Her 1907 act at the Moulin Rouge with Missy de Morny caused such a scandal that the police threatened to shut down the cabaret. After Willy's death in the 1930s, Colette went to court to have his name removed from the Claudine books and her authorship restored.

11

A Night IN PIGALLE

COCKTAILS I CABARET I NIGHTLIFE

Gritty-yet-trendy Pigalle is one of the best places in town for an expertly crafted drink, and with so many bars, venues and clubs within walking distance of each other, it's easy to spend an entire night out here, transitioning from evening drinks to a raucous cabaret show to all-night dancing.

HELENE PAMBRUN/PARIS MATCH VIA GETTY IMAGES ©

How to

Getting here and around Metro line 2 to Blanche; lines 2 or 12 to Pigalle; from either station, everything is within a 10-minute walk.

When to go Many of these bars are tiny, with limited seating, and get packed on weekends. For a greater chance of snagging a spot, try going either early evening or late at night.

Tip English-language songs are performed at Chez Michou, but Madame Arthur is strictly French-only.

JON BILOUS/GETTY IMAGES ©

A Craft Cocktail Crawl

Bizet allegedly once lived in the opulent 19th-century mansion that's now **Le Carmen**, a plush, ultra-hip bar. Perfect for early-evening cocktails, it specialises in a dizzying array of house-infused gins. Later it morphs into a trendy, all-night club, but it's tough to get past the highly selective bouncers unless you look the part (as in, part of Paris Fashion Week).

In a one-time Belle Époque brothel turned luxury boutique hotel – **Maison Souquet** – this elegant yet relaxed lounge bar features red velvet settees and shelves of leather-bound books. The bartenders mix up artisan cocktails named after famous courtesans.

Steeped in retro charm, **Lulu White Drinking Club** is a cosy little New Orleans–style bar

JOËL SAGET/AFP VIA GETTY IMAGES ©

18th-Century Cabaret Central

Though today only two remain, in the 1780s, nearly half of rue des Martyrs' buildings were cabarets or *guinguettes* (open-air dance halls). Why? Montmartre was outside Paris and not subject to its taxes – so wine was much cheaper there.

Top and bottom left Chez Michou (p86)
Above Rue des Martyrs

offering excellent speciality cocktails, absinthe with all the antique accoutrements and a regular roster of live jazz and blues bands.

Despite its awful name, **Dirty Dick** is one of Pigalle's best cocktail spots. In a compact, dimly lit space, it's a true tiki bar with tropical decor, Hawaiian shirts and modern interpretations of exotic cocktail classics, like the flaming Zombie.

See a Drag Cabaret

In an intimate 1930s space in rue des Martyrs, **Chez Michou** cabaret was launched in 1956 by local celebrity Michou. Known as 'The Blue Prince of Montmartre' for his habit of always dressing in blue head-to-toe, Michou departed on his last 'voyage', as he called it, in 2020, but the show goes on. The shows feature *transformiste* performers who lip-sync as Cher, Lady Gaga, Bette Midler,

More Cocktails & Cabaret

With just the right combination of vintage grit and retro glamour, **Sister Midnight** is the perfect place to celebrate Pigalle's racy past. A regular rotation of drag queens parade through on a near-weekly basis in stilettos to put on crazy-fun cabaret shows. Even on non-cabaret nights, this spot is worth a visit for some of Paris' best cocktails. Try the 'Suicide' for a spicy surprise! The drinks are so good you'll forget your dinner plans. Luckily they have an excellent ploughman's plate with English cheeses, pickled eggs and veg from Emperor Norton, snack suppliers to many bars and cafes around town.

Recommended by Forest Collins, *Paris cocktail expert and France Academy Chair for The World's 50 Best Bars. @52martinis*

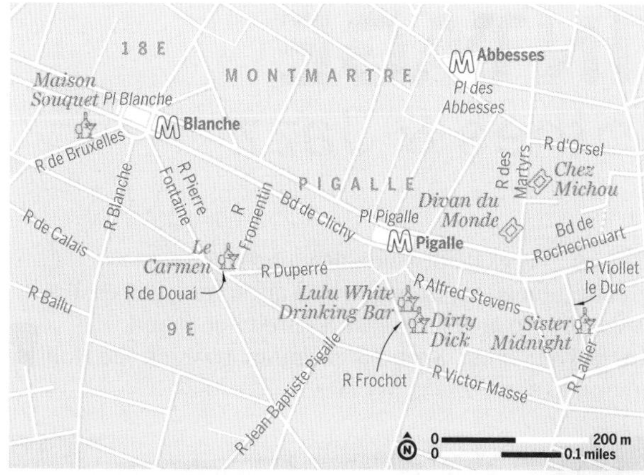

Celine Dion as well as French pop stars. A formula that might feel familiar today, but this venue was one of the first of its kind in Paris. Dinner is served before the show by the performers themselves.

Just across the street at the historic **Divan du Monde** (formerly the Divan Japonais cabaret painted by Toulouse-Lautrec), **Madame Arthur** is a younger and more modern show. Featuring a rotating cast of talented performers, each week the troupe tackles a new musical theme or artist, such as Abba, Queen, Disney or Beyoncé, performing Frenchified versions of the songs. Unlike most drag cabarets, here the performers actually sing, accompanied by live piano or accordion music in the traditional French fashion. The bar makes great cocktails and, once the cabaret show ends at midnight, the venue turns into an all-night dance club, with DJs primarily spinning vintage French hits.

Left Cocktail, Sister Midnight **Below** Le Carmen (p85)

12 VINTAGE Clothes & Jazz

SHOPPING I FASHION I JAZZ

The sprawling Marché aux Puces de St-Ouen flea market – a chaotic labyrinth of stands selling either dodgy tat or overpriced antiques – can easily overwhelm. But if you know where to go, rare treasures are to be found, especially if vintage clothing is your thing. Spend a morning browsing the stalls, then have lunch while listening to some live gypsy jazz.

GABRIELI2/SHUTTERSTOCK ©

How to

Getting here Metro line 4 to Porte de Clignancourt.

When to go The weekend is the best time to visit, since many shops and stands in the market are only open on Saturdays and Sundays.

Tip Stay alert and keep an eye on your valuables – the market is a prime area for pickpockets. The vendors around and beneath the overpass are not part of the official market.

PHOTO 12/ALAMY STOCK PHOTO ©

Browse the Shops and Stalls

Hit the market early for the best finds; most places open between 10am and 10.30am. On the 1st floor of the **Marché Dauphine**, **Falbalas** is one of the market's biggest and best-stocked vintage clothing shops, carrying anything from antique 18th-century outfits to funky '70s duds, plus every period accessory you could imagine. The owners, Erwan and Françoise, also sell their own line of vintage and antique reproduction shoes. **Chez Sarah**, in the **Marché Le Passage**, sells vintage apparel from 1900 through to the 1990s as well as a wide selection of vintage haberdashery. **Les Merveilles de Babellou** has two shops in the **Marché Paul Bert**, at stands 13 and 77. Both specialise in vintage French *haute couture*, from Chanel, Dior and Yves Saint-Laurent to Paco Rabanne. Also in the Marché Paul Bert at stands 112 and 114, **de Laurentis** focuses on vintage avant-garde fashion from designers like Martin Margiela and Comme des Garçons.

Get into the Swing

Once you've combed the racks, head to **La Chope des Puces** for some *jazz manouche* (also known as gypsy jazz, gypsy swing or hot club jazz) and hearty, traditional French fare. The legendary Django Reinhardt, the originator of the style, played here, along with other greats. The low-key, convivial bistro features live performances every Saturday and Sunday afternoon from 12.30pm to 7pm. On the upper floors of the building, there's also a musical instrument store, a luthier workshop, a *jazz manouche* school and a recording studio.

Top left Marché aux Puces de Saint-Ouen **Bottom left** La Chope des Puces

More Live Music in Northern Paris

I feel privileged to be a jazz singer walking the same streets as Brassens, Piaf and Aznavour.

In the evenings I head to **Bab-Ilo**, tucked away on rue du Baigneur. The best of the Paris jazz scene flock to this intimate spot, one of the last genuine jazz clubs in the capital, welcoming musicians from emerging artists to Grammy winners.

For more eclectic concerts, I love the **360 Paris Music Factory** in the heart of La Goutte d'Or, the area's African quarter. The place is always humming with creative activity and a superb world-music programme. There's a bar and restaurant for cocktails and dining, and Sunday brunches have the added joy of a live, local jazz band.

Liv Monaghan *is a singer, songwriter and vintage clothing seller living in Montmartre. @livmonaghan music*

13 Picnic in a Hidden GARDEN

FOOD I GARDENS I LOCAL LIFE

Though it's known for its restaurants, from simple bistros to temples of fine dining, one of the most quintessential Parisian food experiences is a DIY *pique-nique*. When the weather's nice, crowds throng the parks with bottles of rosé and assorted nibbles. For a more intimate setting, head to Montmartre to find top-quality picnic supplies and secluded squares.

ZOLTAN CSIPKE/ALAMY STOCK PHOTO ©

How to

Getting here Metro line 12 to Abbesses.

When to go Many small shops close on Sundays or Mondays and from about 1pm to 4pm on other days.

Order a baguette like a local Ask for *une tradition* (sometimes *à l'ancienne* or *de campagne*), for a tastier baguette than an *ordinaire* or *classique*. *Une tradition* must be handmade on-site rather than factory-produced. For a crisp baguette, order it *bien cuite* (well done), or *pas trop cuite* (not too cooked) for a soft one. You can also order a *demi baguette* (half a baguette).

ROMAN MILAVIN/GETTY IMAGES ©

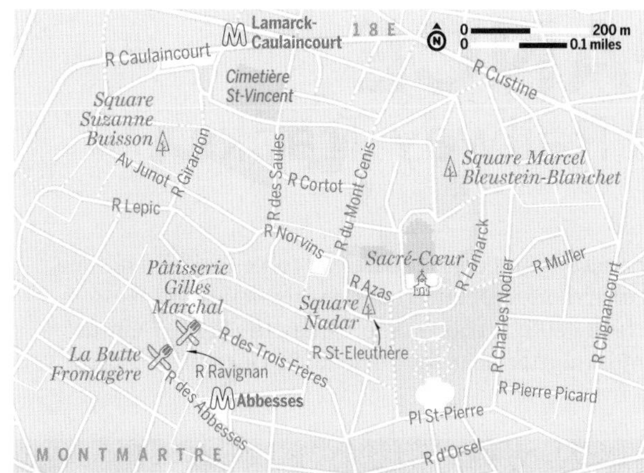

Top left Square Marcel Bleustein-Blanchet **Bottom left** Picnic with *demi baguette*

Shop for Provisions

Montmartre is not the neighbourhood that first comes to mind when a Parisian thinks of picnics, but the abundance of excellent food and wine shops makes it perfect for quickly getting everything you need along a single street: **rue des Abbesses**. Start with artisan cheeses from **La Butte Fromagère**, which also carries some of the world's best butters, like Bordier and Beillevaire. Next, pick up a baguette or two from **Le Grenier à Pain**, two-time winner of Best Baguette in Paris. Across the street, **La Cave des Abbesses** has a great selection of wines, including natural and organic, as well as gourmet snacks. For excellent charcuterie, continue to **Jacky Gaudin**, selling pâtés, *terrines*, *rillettes* and roast chicken, along with foie gras and mustard. Next door, **L'Écaille de la Mascotte** has everything seafood, from smoked salmon, taramasalata and gourmet tinned sardines to caviar and fresh oysters. For dessert, pick up some pastries from **Pâtisserie Gilles Marchal**.

Pick a Peaceful Park

The parts of Montmartre where tourists congregate are anything but peaceful, but there are plenty of tranquil picnic spots nearby. Leafy **Square Marcel Bleustein-Blanchet**, just behind Sacré-Cœur, has romantic, wisteria-covered arbours, stone benches and a grassy lawn. **Square Nadar**, below Sacré-Cœur, has large trees shading rows of benches, where you can enjoy a panoramic view over the city as you picnic. The charming **Square Suzanne Buisson** has a terraced garden and shaded benches.

Behind the Name: St-Denis & Montmartre

In addition to landscaped terraces, **Square Suzanne Buisson** park is home to a fountain with a somewhat morbid statue of a decapitated St-Denis, patron saint of Paris and France, holding his own head. Though it might seem incongruous, it's in fact deeply tied to the place. St-Denis was executed here by the Romans in the 3rd century, giving the hill its name: Montmartre comes from Mont des Martyrs ('Mount of the Martyrs'). He allegedly picked up his head after it was chopped off and carried it several kilometres to the site of the present-day Basilica of St-Denis.

14 DANCE on Railway Tracks

LOCAL LIFE I FOOD I CULTURE

If you're hungry for a taste of modern Paris, head to Le Hasard Ludique, a vibrant, multi-function cultural space, concert venue, nightclub and bar-restaurant set in a former 19th-century train station along the Petite Ceinture. Located just northeast of Montmartre near the Porte de St-Ouen, it's a side of the city well off the tourist track.

EETU AHANEN/LE HASARD LUDIQUE ©

How to

Getting here Metro line 13 to Porte de St-Ouen (two-minute walk) or Guy Môquet (four-minute walk). The closest Vélib' station is on rue Jacques Kellner.

When to go Best in summer, when the bar moves outdoors and there are activities and events on the rails.

Tip Most of Le Hasard Ludique's programming is French-only. For health and safety, only certain portions of the Petite Ceinture are open to the public.

EDWARD BERTHELOT/GETTY IMAGES ©

JULIETTE JEM/LE HASARD LUDIQUE ©

Daytime Offerings

By day, Le Hasard Ludique offers creative workshops, fitness and wellness classes and family-friendly programs, as well as a variety of regular events ranging from art fairs, pop-up shops and by-the-kilo secondhand clothing sales to *pétanque* matches and markets featuring organic fruit and veg from local producers.

Bites and Tipples

The casual on-site eatery, **La Cantine de Léon**, offers coffee, tea, juices and lunch deals in the afternoons. In the evenings, creative fusion tapas, with plenty of veggie and vegan options, are perfect for *apéro* or a low-key dinner. Sunday brunch includes unlimited coffee and tea.

There's seating and tables both indoors and outdoors – on the Victorian railway platform, covered in colourful graffiti, and even along the abandoned tracks themselves, now reclaimed by greenery.

The bar sells draught and bottled beer, with a focus on local craft brews, plus organic and natural wines and cocktails ranging from classic to creative.

After Dark

Things get livelier in the evenings, with tango balls, drag bingo and a diverse schedule ranging from funk, rap and soul to electro-pop, indie, folk and Latin music. There are frequent club nights and DJ sets as well as quirky 'danceoké' nights when attendees copy the moves in their favourite music videos.

Far and near left Le Hasard Ludique
Bottom left Petite Ceinture

What's the 'Petite Ceinture'?

The Petite Ceinture ('Little Ring') is a former railway line surrounding Paris, built in 1852 to connect the city's main train stations. Mostly disused since 1934, it's gradually been taken over by local plants and wildlife and become a sort of open-air, street-art gallery. Unknown even to many Parisians, it's great for peaceful strolls, but access is legally permitted only at certain points and only to some portions of the tracks. In the 18e *arrondissement*, the access points are located at **Le Hasard Ludique** and the **REcyclerie**, both installed in former Petite Ceinture stations.

Listings

BEST OF THE REST

Can't-Miss Sights

Sacré-Cœur

This towering white turn-of-the-century basilica atop Montmartre hill draws visitors from around the globe. It's worth a climb to the top of the dome for the sweeping views.

Green Spaces

Parc des Buttes-Chaumont

A romantic, hilly park with an artificial lake, several bars and restaurants and plenty of gently sloping lawn areas for lounging and picnicking.

Cimetière de Montmartre

This sprawling, leafy cemetery is the final resting place of many famous French and international figures, including Edgar Degas, François Truffaut and Jeanne Moreau. Maps are provided at the entrance.

Unique Boutiques

Antoine et Lili

Colourful boutique of a long-running French brand carrying vibrant, boho-chic women's clothing and accessories, plus home decor.

Flash Vintage

Compact, funky vintage clothing boutique that's worth a dig-through for some well-priced finds, with a focus on '70s and '80s apparel and accessories for men and women.

Memorable Meals

Bouillon Pigalle €

Sprawling, bustling restaurant serving traditional French classics and wines at jaw-droppingly reasonable prices. The menu changes often but is always simple and hearty.

Le Pavillon du Lac €€

Relaxed, airy restaurant in Buttes-Chaumont park serving refined, modern Mediterranean cuisine. In spring and summer, there's also terrace seating and an outdoor bar.

La Mascotte €€/€€€

Elegant 1900s brasserie, a favourite with locals, known particularly for its seafood, including oysters, *bigorneaux* (periwinkles), *bulots* (whelks) and *amandes* (cockles).

Brewpubs & Chic Cocktails

Le Très Particulier

Hidden behind a tall gate on a quiet residential street, the ultra-stylish cocktail bar of this luxury boutique hotel has Twin Peaks vibes, craft cocktails, weekend DJs and idyllic garden seating.

Pavillon Puebla

Stylish hang-out in the Buttes-Chaumont park. In summer, the spacious terrace nestled among the trees features *apéro* cocktails and

Bouillon Pigalle

Mediterranean bites. In winter, an *après-ski* vibe and mulled wine.

Paname Brewing Company

Local craft brewery on the Canal de l'Ourcq offering house draught beers and hearty pub fare. When the weather's nice, snag a table on the floating terrace out front.

Craft Coffee Shops

Café Lomi

Craft coffee shop and roastery in a rustic, industrial space. Besides coffee drinks and cakes, they offer light breakfast and lunch.

Le Pavillon des Canaux

Charming canal-side coffee shop on several floors of an old house furnished with antique decor. Enjoy coffee or tea in the bedroom or curled up on colourful cushions in the bath.

Chocolate & Cheese

Kozak

This tiny store is one of the best places in Paris to find artisan bean-to-bar chocolates from around the world. In the summer, it morphs into an ice-cream shop.

Fromagerie Chez Virginie

With two locations, in rue Damrémont and rue Caulaincourt, this lovely, established cheese shop is one of only a few in Paris that age cheeses in their own cellars.

Museums, Exhibitions & Cultural Centres

Halle St-Pierre

Unusual museum in a former 19th-century market hall. It puts on *art brut* (outsider art) exhibitions and has a tranquil tearoom/cafe as well as an interesting bookshop.

Grande Halle de la Villette

Grande Halle de la Villette

Vast arts and culture complex presenting concerts, dance performances and contemporary art exhibitions and installations. Located in the sprawling Parc de la Villette, which hosts free, open-air film screenings in the summer.

Nightclubs & Cabarets

Bus Palladium

Legendary Pigalle nightclub and rock concert venue where Mick Jagger and Salvador Dalí were regulars. These days, events include concerts, DJs and rock karaoke nights backed by a live band.

Chez Ma Cousine

Convivial wood-lined restaurant and cabaret in the heart of Montmartre village offering dinner and a show, with classic French fare and traditional *chanson* to match.

Le Lapin Agile

Storied cabaret where Picasso used to hang out, preserving the art form as it was in the 19th century – traditional French songs accompanied by piano and accordion.

Scan to find more things to do in Montmartre & Northern Paris online

15 La Goutte D'OR

STROLLING | FASHION | AFRICAN CULTURE

Though Parisians can be guarded at first, they soon warm up. However, in the 18e *arrondissement*, you're likely to be immediately received with open arms. This popular neighbourhood, known as La Goutte d'Or or Château Rouge, has a strong African presence with a warm welcome that's integral to African culture.

LESLY HAMILTON/GAMMA-RAPHO VIA GETTY IMAGES ©

How to

Getting here Metro to Barbès-Rochechouart or Château Rouge. If you come by car, be prepared for traffic and very little parking.

When to go Visiting in the afternoon is best as most shops don't open before noon.

Tip Grab a coffee and sit with locals in Léon Square.

Information The Little Africa Paris Village concept store (6bis rue des Gardes) has maps and tour information.

KEESHASKITCHEN.COM/SHUTTERSTOCK ©

Far left Market, rue Dejean **Bottom left** Thieboudienne **Near left** Shopfront, La Goutte d'Or

Fabrics, Fashion & Inspiration

Whether you decide to explore La Goutte d'Or on your own or via one of the many walking tours available, one of the first things you'll learn is that *le Sac Barbès* originated here. This iconic bag was first used by local people travelling back to their home country, to carry gifts for their families. Over the years, the bag has been popularised by luxury brands, including Louis Vuitton and Balenciaga, who were inspired to create their own €1500 versions. La Goutte d'Or has also been a source of inspiration for the fashion world's fascination with African fabrics. Rue de Léon and rue de Doudeville are full of shops offering hundreds of patterns, ready-to-wear clothing and custom-made services. Today a new generation of designers of African descent are setting themselves up in this creative hub, selling fashion, jewellery, textiles and furniture.

Traditional Food

After wandering La Goutte d'Or for hours looking for that special outfit to turn heads, you may start to feel hungry. Good news: the neighbourhood offers a great choice of restaurants with authentic and generous portions of food inspired by Africa, or more specifically by Northern Africa (Morocco, Tunisia and Algeria), West Africa (Senegal and Mali) and Central Africa (Nigeria and Cameroon). And if you're inspired to give cooking traditional meals, like Thieboudienne, Mafé, couscous, jollof rice and ndolé, a whirl, head to rue Dejean and Marché Barbès to pick up ingredients.

Looking Back in Time

La Goutte d'Or (The Drop of Gold) takes its name from the golden colour of the wine that was produced here up until the 18th century. The neighbourhood was only incorporated into the city of Paris in 1860. Before then, it wasn't subject to its taxes, so attracted a working-class population who had to find different ways to survive, such as selling things on the streets. This led to the creation of the well-known, sprawling **Marché aux Puces de St-Ouen** (p88), the biggest antiques and secondhand market in the world, just 20 minutes away by metro – get off at Porte de Clignancourt.

■ **Jacqueline NGO MPII**
Born in Cameroon and raised in France, Jacqueline NGO MPII is the founder and CEO of Little Africa, a multimedia and cultural agency.

DANIELE SCHNEIDER/GETTY IMAGES ©

Noire Paris

AN INTRODUCTION TO THE CITY'S AFRICAN CULTURE

Every country that has a history of colonisation and slavery will have a history intertwined with immigration, and cities influenced by the people who left their countries, but carried their precious culture with them. Paris is one of those cities.

From left Place Félix Eboué; Josephine Baker; Musée Nationale de l'Histoire de l'Immigration

Paris projects such a strong, and often clichéd image around the world – of romance, rudeness and women draped in Chanel – that it has been difficult for travellers to imagine there is a significant Black population living in the city. From the souvenir shops in Montmartre to the tourist office by Palais Garnier, visitors are presented with a one-dimensional history. When travellers arrive at Charles de Gaulle airport and take the train to the city centre, they're probably not even aware that the train crosses the Seine-St-Denis, a state-region that contains the largest African population in France.

When talking about Black Paris, you should know there are different segments because there are many different communities of African descent. The community the world knows most about is the African American community in Paris from the 1920s to the 1960s. Everyone's heard about Josephine Baker, James Baldwin or Richard Wright and how they found a haven in Paris; a place where their colour wasn't a barrier. This part of Black Paris is well documented in books, documentaries and by tour companies. Many people, however, don't know about the large communities from the former French colonies in Africa (primarily Senegal, Ivory Coast, Cameroon and Mali), and the Caribbean people (primarily from Guadaloupe, Martinique and French Guiana) who have made Paris their home for generations. From the Latin Quarter (p148) – well-known for the Sorbonne University, an institution that welcomed prominent Black figures such as Paulette Nardal, Léopold Sédar Senghor and Aimé Césaire – to the neighbourhoods of La Goutte d'Or (meaning 'drop of gold') and Château d'Eau, which are

BINDER/ULLSTEIN BILD VIA GETTY IMAGES ©

EQROY/SHUTTERSTOCK ©

the beating hearts of the African presence in Paris, there is a lot to see and explore.

One of the easiest ways to recognise the Black French presence is to pay attention to street and metro names: place Félix Eboué (metro Daumesnil), named after the first person of African descent to become governor of a *département* in France and to be buried at the Pantheon; rue Dahomey (11e); rue Congo (12e); rue Soudan (15e); rue Timbuktu (18e); and rue Chevalier de St-George (8e).

> Josephine Baker, James Baldwin and Richard Wright found a haven in Paris; a place where their colour wasn't a barrier.

Then there are museums like the Quai Branly, a garden of classical African art that made history by returning stolen artefacts to their countries of origin. Above all, you should definitely visit Musée Nationale de l'Histoire de l'Immigration. Built for the last international colonial exhibition of France in 1931, the building is massive with an allegorical façade that displays the economic contributions of the former French colonies. Inside, visitors can learn stories about all types of immigrants' contributions ranging from food and art to music.

While debates around immigration increase in Europe, some people still deny what plaques, bridges, buildings, streets, cuisines and faces boldly show: Paris is multicultural and influenced by African culture. Those missing this part of the story (which needs to be told) are missing a vibrant part of Paris, like gold miners missing a lode of gold.

Further Reading

To keep exploring Black Paris, I recommend reading *La France Noire* and *Le Paris Noir*, both by historian Pascal Blanchard. Blanchard specialises in colonialism, and in these two books he covers Black history in France over the last three centuries, including how Paris became the meeting point for Black communities from the US, Caribbean and Africa. He also talks about how the contributions of Black communities have shaped the country's political, artistic, cultural and economic landscape.

LE MARAIS, MÉNILMONTANT & BELLEVILLE

HISTORY | SOCIETY | POP CULTURE

ILLE DEMONJAY

LE MARAIS, MÉNIL-MONTANT & BELLEVILLE
Trip Builder

TAKE YOUR PICK OF MUST-SEES AND HIDDEN GEMS

Le Marais and Belleville both offer very different experiences. Le Marais, now heavily gentrified, was home to dukes and princesses, while Belleville has kept its working-class legacy and still resonates with popular songs. Yet both neighbourhoods are part of Paris, and seeing them helps visitors to understand the city today.

Neighbourhood Notes

Best for Shopping in Le Marais, Chinese food in Belleville.

Transport Take the metro. For Le Marais: Hôtel de Ville or St-Paul; for Belleville: Belleville or Jourdain; for Ménilmontant: Gambetta.

Getting around Because of the narrow streets, it's preferable to walk rather than drive.

Tip Plan to spend several hours in the vast Père Lachaise cemetery.

Admire the 16th-century **Hôtel de Ville** (p107) destroyed during the Paris Commune and rebuilt.
Metro Hôtel de Ville.

Take a moment to gather at the **Shoah Memorial** (p111), tucked in a hidden alleyway.
2 min from metro Pont Marie

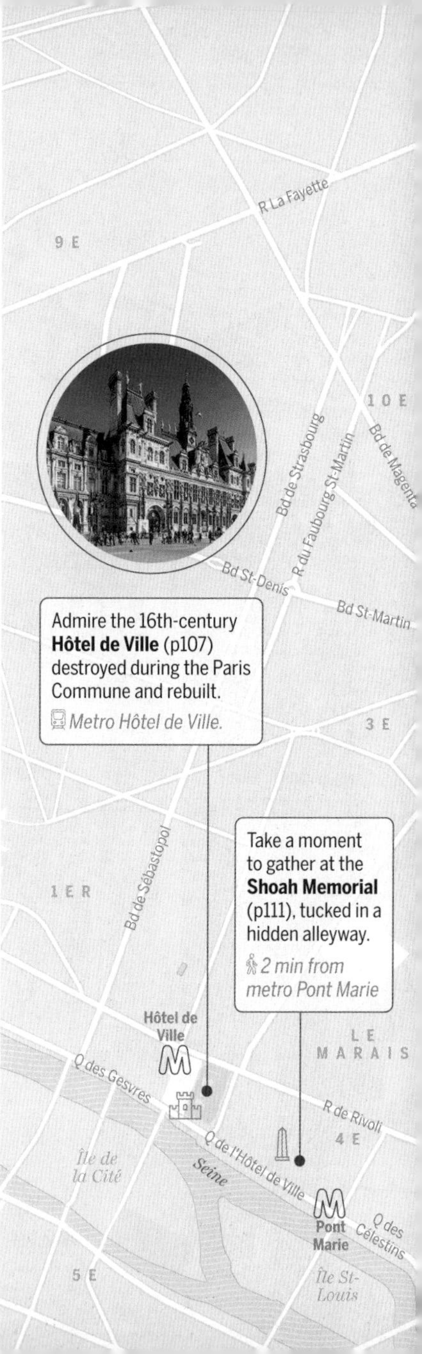

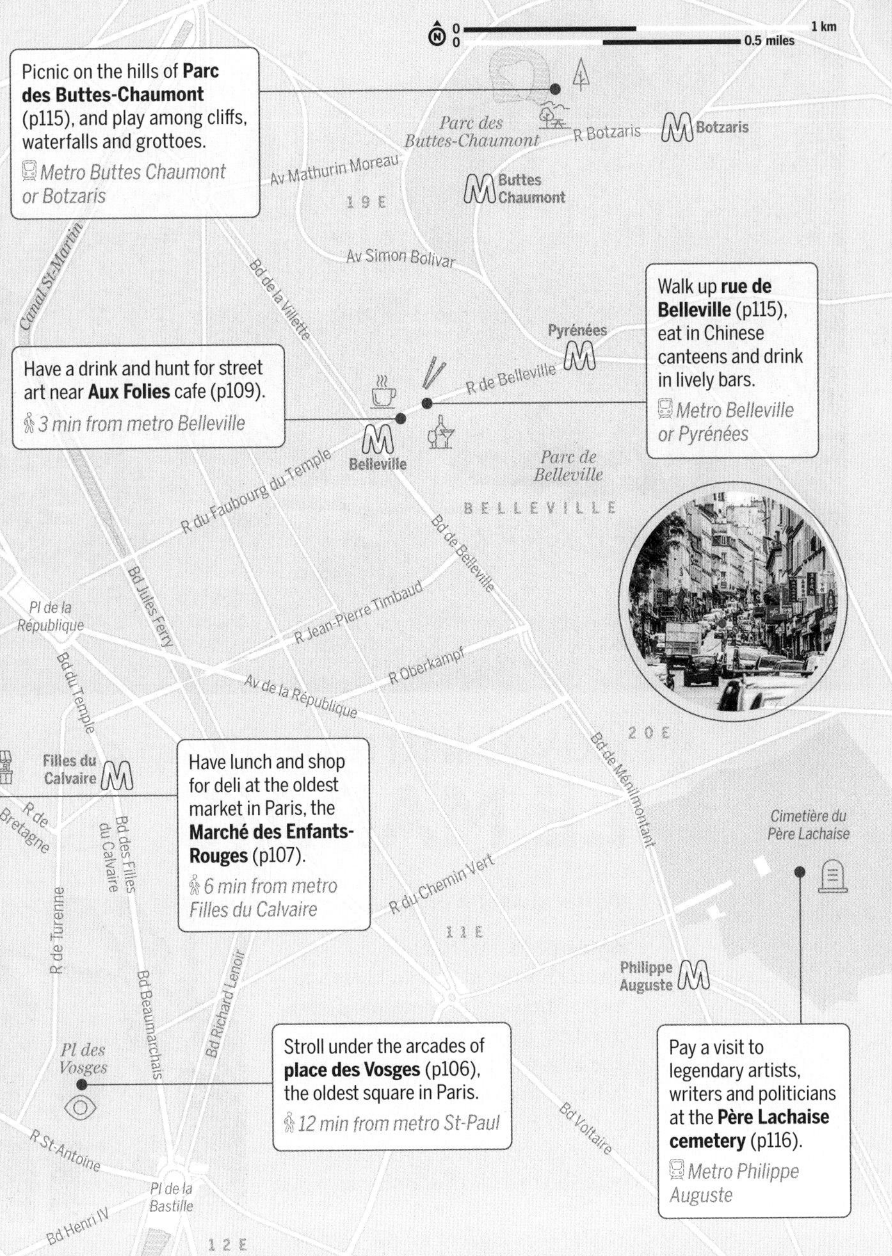
0
0
1 km
0.5 miles
Picnic on the hills of **Parc des Buttes-Chaumont** (p115), and play among cliffs, waterfalls and grottoes.
Metro Buttes Chaumont or Botzaris
Parc des Buttes-Chaumont
R Botzaris
Botzaris
Av Mathurin Moreau
Buttes Chaumont
19E
Av Simon Bolivar
Canal St-Martin
Bd de la Villette
Walk up **rue de Belleville** (p115), eat in Chinese canteens and drink in lively bars.
Metro Belleville or Pyrénées
Pyrénées
R de Belleville
Have a drink and hunt for street art near **Aux Folies** cafe (p109).
3 min from metro Belleville
Belleville
Parc de Belleville
BELLEVILLE
R du Faubourg du Temple
Bd de Belleville
Bd Jules Ferry
Pl de la République
R Jean-Pierre Timbaud
Bd du Temple
R Oberkampf
Av de la République
20E
Bd de Ménilmontant
Filles du Calvaire
Have lunch and shop for deli at the oldest market in Paris, the **Marché des Enfants-Rouges** (p107).
6 min from metro Filles du Calvaire
R de Bretagne
Bd des Filles du Calvaire
Cimetière du Père Lachaise
R du Chemin Vert
R de Turenne
11E
Philippe Auguste
Bd Beaumarchais
Bd Richard Lenoir
Pl des Vosges
Stroll under the arcades of **place des Vosges** (p106), the oldest square in Paris.
12 min from metro St-Paul
Pay a visit to legendary artists, writers and politicians at the **Père Lachaise cemetery** (p116).
Metro Philippe Auguste
Bd Voltaire
R St-Antoine
Pl de la Bastille
Bd Henri IV
12E

16 Royal Intrigue in LE MARAIS

HISTORY | ARCHITECTURE | SOCIETY

Le Marais has known several historical and architectural incarnations and is now one of the trendiest neighbourhoods in Paris. The area was home to influential ladies (and royal mistresses) as early as the 17th century and their *hôtels particuliers* (private mansions) were once the theatre of scandalous plots around the royal court.

STARCEVIC/GETTY IMAGES ©

How to

Getting here Take the metro to St-Paul, Pont Marie or Bastille.

Pedestrian zone Every Sunday, 10am to 6pm (7.30pm in summer).

Narrow streets Traffic isn't great, especially on weekends when the area can get very crowded.

Bookings If you're visiting museums or historical buildings, call to book in advance if possible.

Top left Pl des Vosges (p106)
Bottom left Village St-Paul
Below Philippe-Auguste's wall

PHILAUGUSTAVO/GETTY IMAGES ©

The Affair of the Poisons

In 1666, a scandalous murder affair rocked the court of Louis XIV. It started with Madame de Brinvilliers at her husband's mansion in Le Marais, **Hôtel d'Aubray**. In order to live a luxurious life with her penniless lover, she poisoned her own father and brothers. She was later found out, tortured and beheaded. However, her trial revealed a more intricate network of poisoners, with ramifications throughout the nobility. La Reynie, chief of the royal police, led a thorough investigation, which resulted in the execution of 36 people almost 15 years later.

PACK-SHOT/SHUTTERSTOCK ©

Le Marais and Its Secret Passages

Explore the dozen antique shops around the concealed **Village St-Paul** near Madame de Brinvilliers' mansion. Don't miss **Passage**

At the Heart of Parisian History

Le Marais is one of the only neighbourhoods in Paris where you can still travel through a thousand years of history if you know where to look. Head back to the 12th century at the ruins of Philippe-Auguste's wall in rue des Archives.

■ **By Bohémond Josseran de Kerros**, *a historian, tour guide and former stonemason, who was born and raised in Paris.* @Interkultur_fr

St-Paul, which makes its way inside the church through a side door. Then cross over to **Hôtel de Sully**. At the back of its gardens, look for the passageway to the arcades of **place des Vosges**.

Built under the reign of Henri IV in 1605, place des Vosges is one of Le Marais' most emblematic landmarks, and Paris' oldest square. In the 17th century, the greatest minds flocked to luxury apartments at place des Vosges to exchange ideas. Key Enlightenment ideas were discussed and there was a wealth of intrigue at these literary salons held by noble women of the time.

A Society of Powerful Women

A bit further north, not too far from the hidden Arnaud Beltrame square, Françoise d'Aubigné, known as Madame de Maintenon, used to host her own circle. Louis XIV's mistress, Madame de Montespan, was her best friend and a regular. Ironically, a decade later,

Queen of the Literary Circles

At **No 36 rue des Tournelles**, just behind place des Vosges, Ninon de Lenclos hosted her own literary circle every day. Her '5-to-9' became extremely popular. She rapidly became the symbol of the educated, aristocratic libertines of the 17th and 18th centuries. She was independent, ravishing and won hearts. Ninon led her life freely and opened her *salon* to the greatest politicians, artists and writers of the time, including La Fontaine, Perrault, Lully, Madame de Sévigné, Racine and even Philippe d'Orléans, who became regent of France.

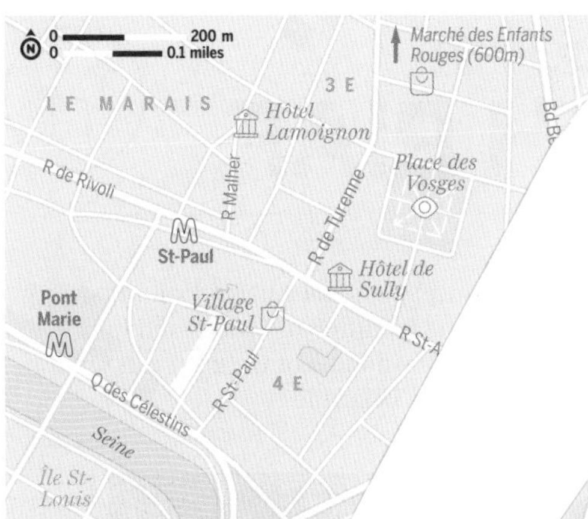

it was Madame de Maintenon wh… king's mistress – even marrying him i…

Another grand *salonnière* was Madame de Scudéry, who held her extremely popular meetings on **rue de Beauce**, a very narrow street tucked behind the oldest market in Paris, the **Marché des Enfants Rouges**. On the way there, you'll pass **Hôtel Lamoignon**, another renowned salon attended by highly recognised Madame de Sévigné, among others. Make your way to the tiny place de Thorigny via rue Payenne, and you'll reach the market. At the back, an alley leads to another hidden garden, commemorating Madeleine de Scudéry.

La Voisin

Denounced by fellow poisoners during the Affair of the Poisons, Catherine Montvoisin, known as 'La Voisin', was a powerful occultist, abortionist and potion-maker. She didn't live in Le Marais but served many high-ranked courtiers, including Madame de Montespan, the king's mistress. She was arrested in 1680 and accused, not only of poisoning, but also of witchcraft – a high crime in the religious patriarchal society of the time. Catherine Montvoisin was burnt alive on the former place de Grève, where the **Hôtel de Ville** stands today.

Left Ninon de Lenclos **Below** Hôtel de Sully

Rediscover ÉDITH PIAF

WALKING TOUR I MUSIC I POP CULTURE

Walk in the footsteps of Édith Piaf, France's national singer. Born in poverty in Ménilmontant, she led an incredibly romantic, eventful and successful life. Discover a glimpse of the old Paris she knew in the middle of the 20th century, and the tribute Parisians continue to pay to her in Belleville.

How to

Getting here Take the metro to Gambetta (line 3). Finish at metro Belleville (lines 2, 11).

Hilly areas Be ready to climb Ménilmontant's hills; wear comfortable shoes.

Which direction Works both ways. Start from either La Môme's grave, or with a coffee at Aux Folies.

Père Lachaise The closest entrance to Édith Piaf's grave is Porte de La Réunion, south of metro Gambetta.

A Rural Glimpse

On the Belleville-Ménilmontant trail, you will often see signs that these villages used to be on farmland. Look for almost hidden staircases and courtyards, and behind vines and bushes. Explore the small village-like allotments. Take pictures discreetly to respect residents.

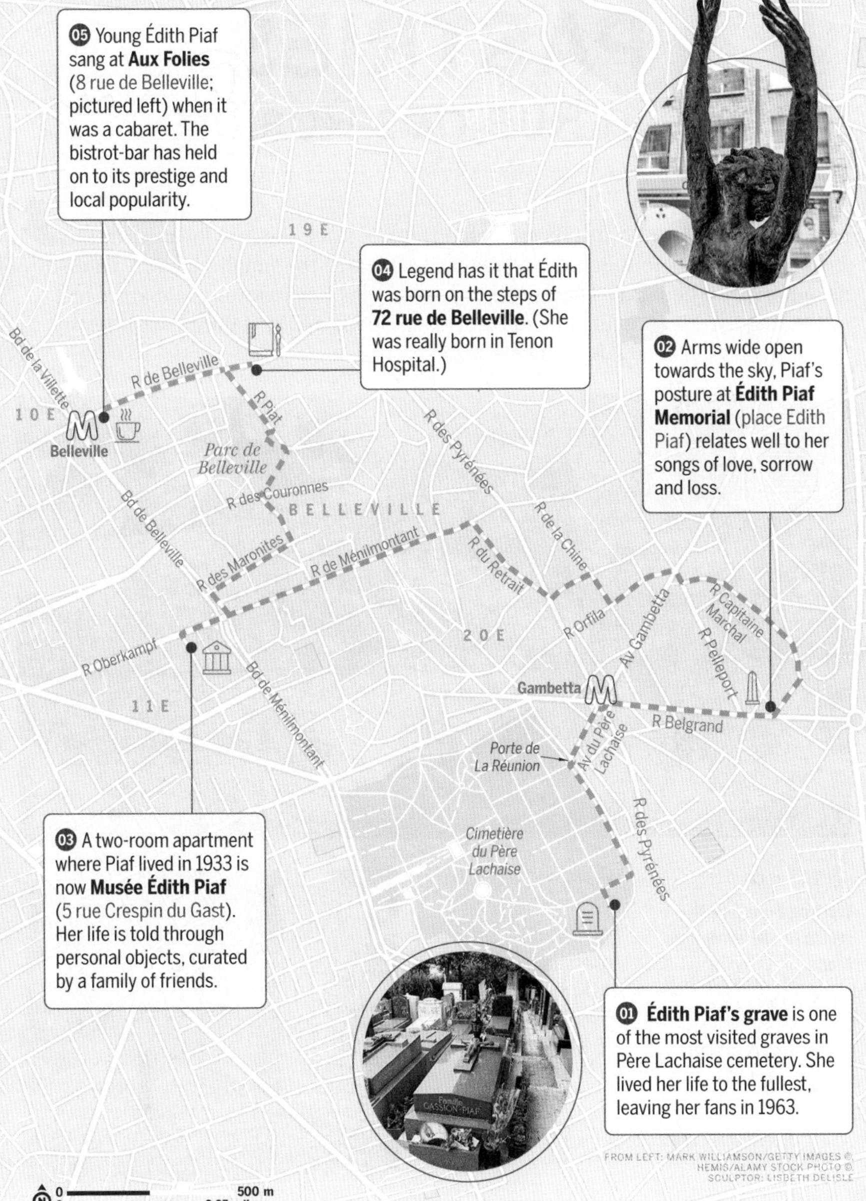

FROM LEFT: MARK WILLIAMSON/GETTY IMAGES ©, HEMIS/ALAMY STOCK PHOTO ©, SCULPTOR: LISBETH DELISLE

18 PASTRIES in Rue des Rosiers

HISTORY I FOOD I CULTURE

Jewish communities have existed in Paris since the middle ages. In the 19th century, they founded the 'Pletzl' in Le Marais: the 'small place' in Yiddish, as opposed to the larger place des Vosges. Rue des Rosiers was the main street of the historic Pletzl quarter, and some of its shops and restaurants still testify to the neighbourhood's Jewish heritage.

ASYA NURULLINA/SHUTTERSTOCK ©

How to

Getting here Take the metro to St-Paul or Pont Marie.

When to go Every Sunday from 10am to 6pm (7.30pm in summer) most of Le Marais becomes a pedestrian-only zone.

Tip Le Marais' narrow streets aren't easy for traffic, especially on weekends, when the area can get very crowded as it's a favourite for shopping Parisians.

MASSIMO BORCHI/ATLANTIDE PHOTOTRAVEL/GETTY IMAGES ©

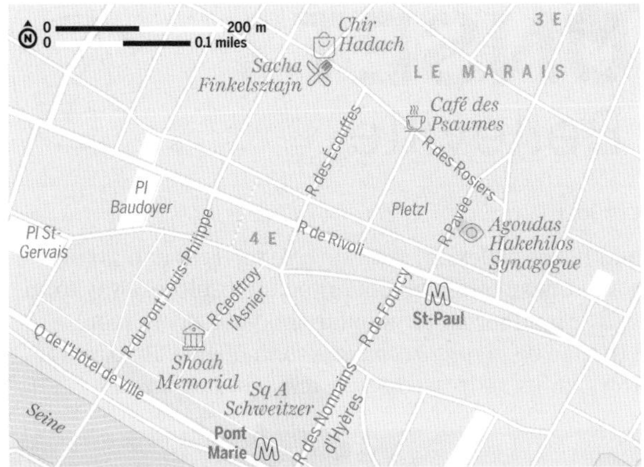

Top left Pastries, Le Marais **Bottom left** Dogwalker outside Sacha Finkelstajn's

The Last Jewish Quarter

Nowadays, Ashkenazi Jews from Eastern Europe and Sephardi Jews from Northern Africa live together in the neighbourhood. Although Paris has one of the largest Jewish communities in Europe, only a few Jewish families still live in Le Marais today.

The Pletzl's Visible Heritage

In rue des Rosiers, stop at **Sacha Finkelstajn's** little yellow shop: feast your eyes on the cheesecakes, Polish and Austrian strudels and poppy seed rolls...and make your choice! Across the street, have a look at **Chir Haddach's bookshop** and its often-entertaining pieces in the window. A bit further along the street, you'll notice **Café des Psaumes**, a place of discussion and exchange where both religious and non-religious Jewish people are welcome.

War Traces & Stories

The area holds strong memories of the tragic events of WWII: **rue des Ecouffes**, one of the poorest streets at the time, was the most raided in 1942. At **No 17 rue des Rosiers**, there's a hidden synagogue, where a miracle took place during the *Vel d'Hiv* raid: although the authorities knew about the place and people were hiding inside, they overlooked it, sparing dozens of lives. A few minutes' walk from rue des Rosiers towards the Seine, the **Shoah Memorial** (rue Geoffroy l'Asnier) offers an elegant yet discreet space to remember the history of the area.

An Art Nouveau Synagogue

On rue Pavée, the **Agoudas Hakehilos Synagogue** is the only religious building designed by Parisian architect Hector Guimard. A significant figure in art nouveau, he is mostly known for the traditional 19th-century entrances to metro stations, only two of which have survived until today. He originally built the synagogue for his wife, who was Jewish. The façade's undulating and vertical lines show the influence of the art nouveau movement inspired by nature. It is one of six synagogues in the neighbourhood, with another located just behind place des Vosges.

19 SUNSET in Belleville

GARDENS I HISTORY I STREET ART

The steep streets and hills of Belleville, with its cafe terraces and family-run restaurants, make this an atmospheric neighbourhood to explore, away from the most visited landmarks. For another more popular and, let's say it, more relaxed side of Paris, head to the 20e *arrondissement* – to the Belleville park for a sunset picnic or simply through its staircased alleys and winding streets.

THIERRY OUGEN/GETTY IMAGES ©

How to

Getting here Take the metro to Couronnes (lower) or Pyrénées (upper).

When to go In spring and summer for the greenery, but more generally on clear sunny days, to watch the sunset from the top of the hill.

Opening hours From 8am Monday to Friday; from 9am Saturday and Sunday; closing hours vary depending on the time of year and season.

Hilly area The Parc de Belleville is the highest park in Paris from top to bottom.

CHRISTIAN MUELLER/SHUTTERSTOCK ©

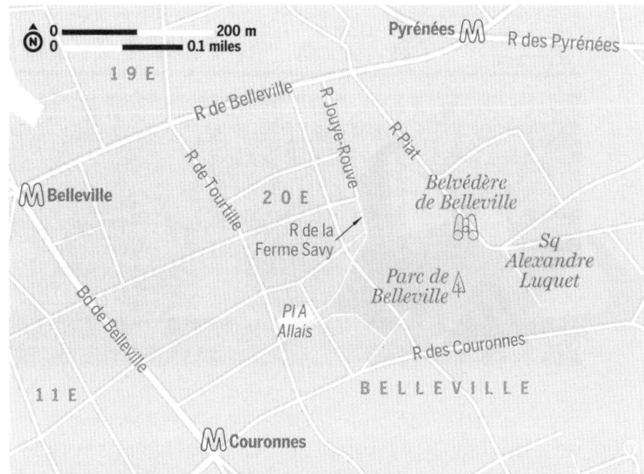

On Top of the City's Highest Hills

The highest point above sea level in Paris is not Montmartre, it's actually the top of the Belleville park. Until the 19th century, Belleville used to be mainly farmland and vineyards. Hard to believe now, but farm animals once grazed on the slopes of Belleville. There was a cattle farm just below metro Belleville – discreet signs of it are still visible on rue de la Présentation.

Sunset Belleville Boulevard

It's a totally different atmosphere now and Parc de Belleville is the perfect place to exercise, either by going up its steps or taking a slow walk under the shadow of the levelled trees, until you meet the waterfall. Children will love the boat-like climbing playground – adults may regret not being allowed there! Don't miss the Belvédère de Belleville on rue Piat, decorated with many street art murals. It's 'the most beautiful view of Paris', according to locals. Your sunset awaits...

The Paris Commune Mural

Worth mentioning since you're already there: look for the human-size mural commemorating the Paris Commune on rue de la Ferme Savy, on the lower exterior walls of the park. The 72-day revolt culminated in bloodshed on the streets of Belleville – a tragic but iconic event which has left its mark on the local rebellious spirit.

Top left View from Belvédère de Belleville **Bottom left** Steps, Parc de Belleville

A Refuge for All

Belleville people like to believe that Belleville is not Paris, and never has been. The area is marked with a long history of working-class people and immigration, which has shaped its landscape, economic life and spirit. What I like the most about Belleville is the way it has stayed popular and, to some extent, a refuge for all. I designed a tour to discover the Belleville Chinese community, but also the heritage of the Paris Commune in Belleville, and Belleville in songs and music... And soon, I will also make one about Mediterranean Belleville. Don't ever forget: Belleville is Belleville!

Donatien Schramm *is a long-time Belleville resident and self-taught tour guide.*

Belleville's 100 Nationalities

A BRIEF HISTORY OF IMMIGRANT COMMUNITIES IN BELLEVILLE

It is said that there are 100 different nationalities in Belleville. Arriving at Belleville metro station, it's obvious that the energy of the neighbourhood is quite different from some other areas in Paris. But how did it become so diverse?

From left Chinese food shop, rue de Belleville; Market in Belleville; Parc des Buttes-Chaumont

WILL SALTER/LONELY PLANET ©

Until the early 20th century, Belleville was not as diverse as we know it today. As a matter of fact, most families living in the neighbourhood were from working-class families born and raised in and around Paris. The great works of Baron Haussmann had chased some poorer families out of more central locations and the proximity of the main industries had attracted workers from further away. All in all, cheap housing had made it a place of choice for industry workers.

It is these circumstances that attracted a new foreign population in the 1920s. After WWI, mostly Polish, Turkish–Armenian, Belgian and Italian migrants came to live in Belleville. Then the 1930s marked the development of 'Yiddish Belleville' and its shoe-making industry, with the arrival of the Ashkenazi Jews from Eastern Europe. At that time, both Belleville and Le Marais were Jewish quarters. Belleville still bears traces of this heritage through several synagogues close to the perimeter of Belleville park. They are now shared with the Sephardi Jews, who arrived later in the 1960s, mainly from Tunisia.

The Making of an Immigration Quarter

The 1950s and '60s marked a turning point in Belleville's history of immigration. The combination of low rent, a need for a bigger labour force in the aftermath of WWII, and later in 1962, the end of the Algerian War led to important waves of immigration from North African countries. Very present in the commercial landscape and benefiting from a strong linked network, those communities became so visible that until the 1980s, the neighbourhood was mostly considered Arab.

PAUL MAGUIRE/SHUTTERSTOCK ©

DAN TIEGO/SHUTTERSTOCK ©

Despite the way some *Bellevillois* felt at the time, it's interesting to note that this didn't push away the descendants of other communities. In fact, what happened in Belleville is often what happens in areas where there are large migrant communities: when the second or third generation becomes more well-off, they leave the cheaper areas that had welcomed their parents. Other populations in need of cheap housing then come and inhabit the area.

> Strong community infrastructure – including game circles, cultural groups and activities, and health networks – encouraged immigrant populations to stay put.

The Rise of Chinese Belleville

History repeats itself. In the 1980s, people of Chinese origin came to Belleville, along with communities from African countries and the West Indies, attracted by cheap accommodation, though the area had fallen into disrepair. The Chinese impact on Belleville is obvious today. Relying on a strong community infrastructure – including shops, restaurants, game circles, cultural groups and activities, and health networks – they created an appeal for the rest of the community, which in turn encouraged people to stay put when previously immigrants would have stayed only temporarily.

More recently in the 1990s, people from Pakistan and the former country of Yugoslavia arrived in Belleville. Walking up rue de Belleville is like diving into a melting pot: Chinese shopkeepers, pizzerias, and Parisian cafes all coexist in a bustling, multilingual atmosphere.

From Quarries to Gardens

The area behind Belleville used to be called *Amérique*. However, it had nothing to do with the United States of America, although legend has it the limestone extracted from the quarries used to be shipped to the other side of the Atlantic. The name is likely to have come from the fact that the place was far away and not easily accessible to workers. It is now home to a 10-hectare atypical garden: the **Parc des Buttes-Chaumont**, inaugurated in 1897. It is a strange but charming combination of neoclassical and oriental inspirations, meant to satisfy a desire for the 'picturesque'.

20 Visit the Garden CEMETERY

ART I HISTORY I NATURE

Originally designed like an English garden by neoclassical architect Alexandre Brongniart, Père Lachaise cemetery is not only the largest graveyard in Paris today, but it's also one of the most important reserves of biodiversity in the city, with more than 3000 trees and 500 animal species.

VALERIYA/GETTY IMAGES ©

How to

Getting here Take the metro to Philippe Auguste (line 2), Père Lachaise (lines 2, 3) or Gambetta (line 3).

Main entrance Get off at metro Philippe Auguste to start your visit from the main avenue of the cemetery.

Take a map Maps of the cemetery are often available at the entrance.

Be respectful Although designed as a park, it is first and foremost a place of remembrance, so be respectful.

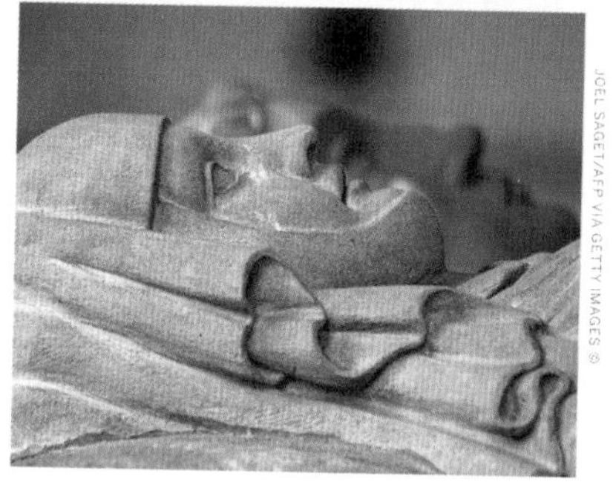

JOËL SAGET/AFP VIA GETTY IMAGES ©

Top left Mausoleum and headstones, Père Lachaise **Bottom left** Tomb of Héloïse and Abélard **Near left** Resting place of Théodore Géricault

Mindful of Nature

When Napoléon Bonaparte declared the right of every citizen to be properly buried in 1804, he started the Père Lachaise cemetery project. Influenced by the romantic movement, it was designed with curved alleys, a layered structure and an abundance of nature. So abundant that some tombs are being swallowed by giant roots today!

The Oldest Is the Most Romantic

A bush of maple trees partly covers the oldest, 'romantic' section, where many romantic artists rest, for example Chopin and Géricault. However, they're accompanied by older remains – the neogothic tomb of cursed medieval lovers Héloïse and Abélard – and younger ones, such as Jim Morrison's.

Look for symbolic trees as you go: on the main avenue leading to Bartolomé's impressive memorial to his wife, you'll see green oaks, a symbol of longevity. Walk left in the direction of iconic 19th-century novelist Honoré de Balzac's sepulture, under yew trees, which symbolise immortality. In spring, you'll see wildflowers between paved stairs, flying butterflies and even red squirrels, who love yew trees.

Scattered Ashes

For people who want to be cremated and still belong with nature but without a grave, there are two places in the cemetery: the **Crematorium** with a green wall that can also integrate urns, and the **Prairie** for people who wish to have their ashes scattered among nature.

Fake Skeletons or Real Ghosts?

Like many graveyards, the Père Lachaise cemetery has its share of myths and supernatural stories. However, one tomb is related to a real ghost story: look for a grave ornate with skulls, carrying the name 'Etienne-Gaspard Robertson'. An abbot, but also a painter, illustrator, physicist and keen balloonist, he became an influential developer of phantasmogaria – an ingenious art show that used lanterns to create ghostly apparitions. His shows, in which he used magic lanterns to project skeletons and demons onto walls, was extremely popular in the Tivoli Gardens (now St-Lazare).

Listings

BEST OF THE REST

Belleville's Chinatown

Chez Alex Wenzhou €

A highly recommended restaurant, with a warm welcome, specialising in dishes from Wenzhou, a city near Shanghai. Try fried buns, sautéed aubergines and the *xiao long bao* ('soup dumplings').

Guo Xin €

A family-run restaurant with some of the best, fresh homemade dumplings in Paris. Fillings vary from minced pork with vegetables, celery and beef, egg and shrimp, or simply vegetables only.

Chez Trois €

For lovers of spicy soups. This Chinese restaurant serves dishes from the north of Beijing, and is generous with chilli. Conveniently located around the corner from Aux Folies.

Best Tofu €

A shop serving traditional, silky tofu. Opt for takeaway as the shop is always full of locals lining up to get their daily fresh tofu.

Green Spaces

Joseph Migneret Garden

A hidden haven off rue des Rosiers, with bird houses and vines, a sign of the historical Jewish presence. Its name commemorates a school director who tried to hide Jewish children during WWII to keep them safe.

Gardens of the National Archives

Few people know that these gardens – among the most beautiful in Paris – are actually free of charge, although located within the National Archive Museum.

Pierre Emmanuel Natural Garden

A tiny garden dedicated to wildflowers, which could be seen across the city when Paris was less urbanised. The garden adjoins Père Lachaise cemetery, on the southern tip.

Cake Shops & Tearooms

Le Loir dans la Théière €€

A very popular cake shop, at the heart of Le Marais, with a large selection of pies and fruit tarts. Go for its extraordinary lemon tart: the meringue layer will be at least four times as high as the curd!

Une Glace à Paris €€

Founded by two pastry chefs with a passion for ice cream, this excellent ice-cream parlour is also a creative shop where ice cream is constantly reinvented into cakes.

Bontemps La Pâtisserie €€

An elegant, flowery tearoom with an almost countryside feel. The ingredients are inventive and the combinations of flavours bold. Try the *sablé* biscuits (shortbreads) and seasonal tarts.

Gardens of the National Archives

Cocktails & Lively Bars

Sherry Butt

Expert mixologists will enjoy this trendy cocktail bar in Le Marais. Dive into your cocktail in a dimmed atmosphere. Often crowded in the evening.

La Bellevilloise

A very popular venue for dancing, drinks and Sunday jazz brunches. La Bellevilloise welcomes concerts, exhibitions, conferences and even balls.

Le Perchoir Ménilmontant

Great for sunny after-work drinks, this party rooftop was a first-of-its-kind in the area. It's now appreciated by locals too, and although spacious, it fills up fast on beautiful days.

La Sardine

Located on a small village-like square, this bar is perfect for people-watching with an early evening drink and 'reinventing the world', as the French say, through passionate conversation.

Museums & Galleries

Museum of Hunting and Nature

This museum is a space to reflect on nature, animals and our relationship to them. Located in an immense restored mansion in Le Marais.

Maison Européenne de la Photographie (MEP)

An exhibition venue, with a library and auditorium, dedicated to photography. It's one of the largest specialised libraries in Europe.

Crafts & Shopping

Village St-Paul

A hidden labyrinth of alleys and small courtyards. These jewellers, craft shops and small restaurants keep the shopkeeping tradition of Le Marais alive.

Performer, La Bellevilloise

Papier Tigre

A creative stationery brand that doesn't just make simple notebooks but also 'stationery tools' for thinkers and artists. Its collection is renewed every season.

LGBTIQ+

Tata Burger €

A fun restaurant where you can be served very suggestive burgers by more than extroverted waiters, and that's all good! You're always in for a good time and tasty drinks.

Le Freedj

A small gay bar/nightclub, recommended for a younger crowd, but anyone is welcome. Two levels of good music with a highly festive atmosphere.

Duplex Bar

Highly recommended for a chilled evening, with an artsy touch as paintings are often exhibited on the walls. A welcoming and friendly place.

BASTILLE & EASTERN PARIS

CRAFT | FOOD | HISTORY

PiPOUNÉ
32 €/KG
Fouchtra
DE CHÈVRE
30 €/KG
FUMAISON
DE BREBIS
le kg 35€
REBLOCHON
FERMIER
26 €/KG.
ARAMITS
de CHÈVRE
36 €
Cacouyard
3,90€ le demi
LE PETIT
SAINT-POINT
24 €/KG.
REBLOCHON de SAVOIE
LE PETIT ST-POINT
TRAPPE
ECHOURGNAC

BASTILLE & EASTERN PARIS

Trip Builder

TAKE YOUR PICK OF MUST-SEES AND HIDDEN GEMS

With a strong heritage of artisanship, the 11e and 12e *arrondissements* around Bastille have retained their popular and village-like atmosphere, welcoming artists and new shopkeepers. Local communities are very active, bringing a lively feel to the district's charming restaurants, bars and workshop yards.

Neighbourhood Notes

Best for The nightlife and convivial dinners, secret courtyards and soothing strolls in urban gardens.

Transport Metro Bastille or Charonne.

Getting around It's always better to be on foot so you don't miss any alleyways or courtyards you'd like to pop into.

Tip Head to bars and cafes north of place de la Bastille – around Parmentier – for a more chilled local taste.

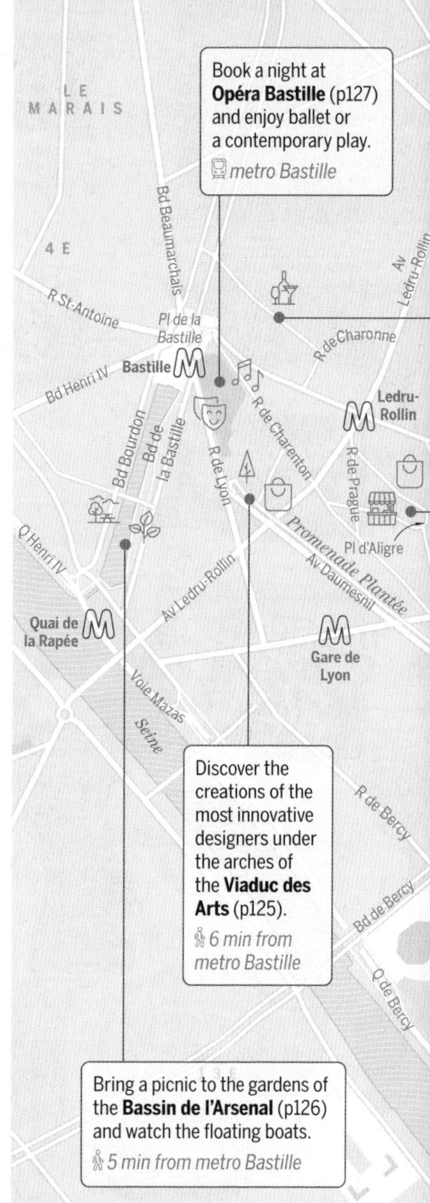

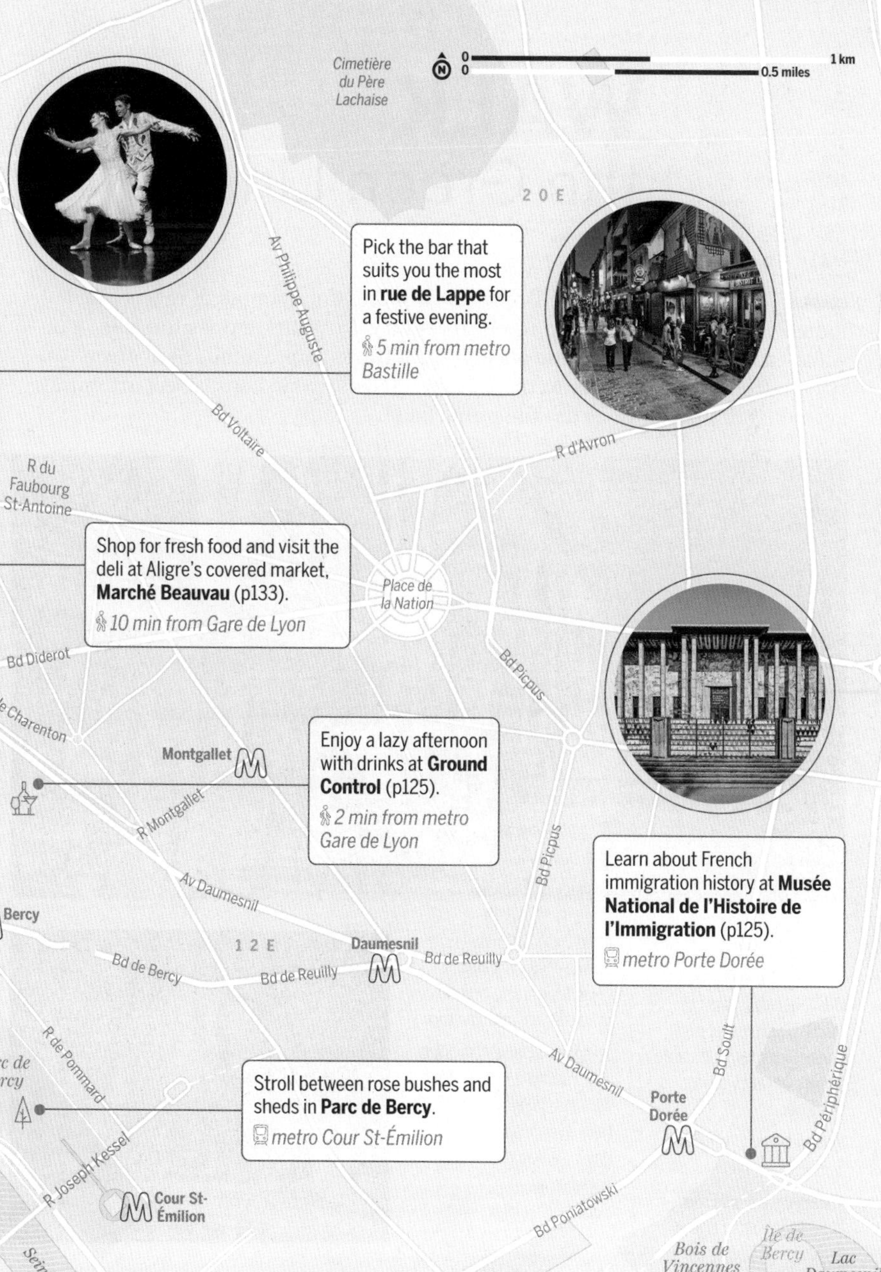
Cimetière
du Père
Lachaise
0
0
1 km
0.5 miles
20E
Av Philippe Auguste
Pick the bar that suits you the most in **rue de Lappe** for a festive evening.
5 min from metro Bastille
Bd Voltaire
R d'Avron
R du Faubourg St-Antoine
Shop for fresh food and visit the deli at Aligre's covered market, **Marché Beauvau** (p133).
10 min from Gare de Lyon
Place de la Nation
Bd Diderot
Bd Picpus
R de Charenton
Montgallet
Enjoy a lazy afternoon with drinks at **Ground Control** (p125).
2 min from metro Gare de Lyon
R Montgallet
Bd Picpus
Learn about French immigration history at **Musée National de l'Histoire de l'Immigration** (p125).
metro Porte Dorée
Av Daumesnil
Bercy
12E
Daumesnil
Bd de Bercy
Bd de Reuilly
Bd de Reuilly
R de Pommard
Parc de Bercy
Av Daumesnil
Bd Soult
Stroll between rose bushes and sheds in **Parc de Bercy**.
metro Cour St-Émilion
Porte Dorée
Bd Périphérique
R Joseph Kessel
Cour St-Émilion
Bd Poniatowski
Seine
Bois de Vincennes
Île de Bercy
Lac Daumesnil

21 WALK the Green Line

WALK I GARDENS I STREET ART

The Coulée Verte René-Dumont is a successful example of regenerated industrial infrastructure from the 19th century. Parisians and visitors alike can walk – and partly cycle – these ancient train tracks: a peaceful 4.5km green stretch from the city centre to the suburbs. Artists' workshops, street-art murals and collaborative gardens dot the promenade.

BRUNO DE HOGUES/GETTY IMAGES ©

How to

Getting here From metro Bastille (west end) or Porte Dorée (east end). There are many possible points of entry along the line.

When to go Spring and summer.

Opening hours From 8am Monday to Friday, from 9am Saturday and Sunday: closing hours vary depending on the time of year and season.

Jogging space Although it is mainly destined for walkers, joggers tend to take over. Go on a weekday to enjoy the Coulée Verte slowly.

ALAIN KUBACSI/GAMMA-RAPHO VIA GETTY IMAGES ©

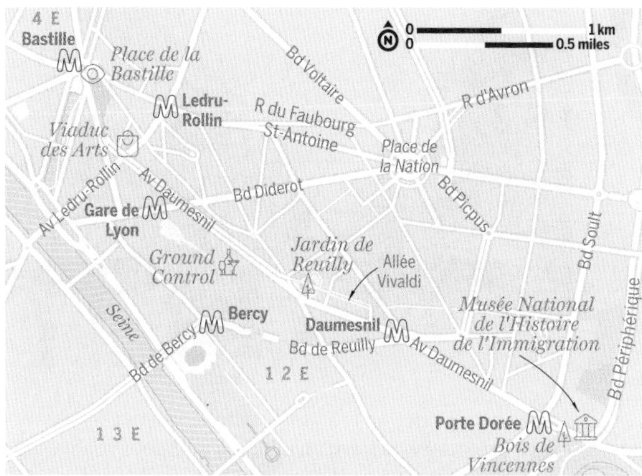

The Coulée Verte was created on an ancient train line. Opened in 1993, it is the world's first elevated park walkway.

Viaduc des Arts

The gardens were initially a 19th-century viaduct and you'll be above ground for the stretch between the Bastille and the **Jardin de Reuilly**. The arches have been converted into a series of workshops, known as the **Viaduc des Arts**, so don't hesitate to head down – and up again – to discover trendy designers and artists, including glass-blowers.

Train Memories

The section between the Jardin de Reuilly and **Square Charles Péguy** is the part where you can see some traces of the gardens' heritage as a train line. Slightly off allée Vivaldi, notice the building with turquoise shutters: an old train station. After a couple of tunnels decorated by commissioned street art, look out for an old green-and-white building with a hexagonal roof – this old water tower was where steam trains used to stop to replenish their water.

The Circular Ring

Other abandoned tracks were transformed into gardens: the **circular ring** is still being regenerated by the City of Paris. It's easy to miss, but the Coulée Verte hits another promenade at the ancient junction of both lines. The southernmost branch leads to the **Musée National de l'Histoire de l'Immigration**, and the other one to the Bois de Vincennes, where you can row boats on **Lac Daumesnil**.

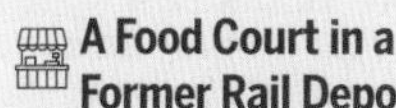
Top left Viaduc des Arts **Bottom left** Coulée Verte

A Food Court in a Former Rail Depot

Don't miss **Ground Control** if you're passionate about revamped industrial places. Located in a former rail depot belonging to the French national railway services, this is an immense space behind Gare de Lyon, now hosting food stalls, art exhibitions, pop-up stores, cultural events and DJs. Ground Control supports actions to avert the climate crisis, with a focus on the local, ethical and sustainable. Go there for drinks early in the evening to find seats, before the place becomes crowded and you need to line up to get a hot cone of crispy French fries.

The Many Lives of Bastille

TIME TRAVEL ON ONE OF PARIS' MOST FAMOUS SQUARES

Many historic layers overlap on place de la Bastille. Destroyed and rebuilt several times, this French Revolution landmark is today a historical centre with a strong cultural pulse. To the observant traveller, it will reveal more than just one chapter of Paris' history.

LL/ROGER VIOLLET VIA GETTY IMAGES ©

From left Rue St-Antoine c. 1910; Bassin de l'Arsenal; Colonne de Juillet

This is an instruction manual for the time traveller wishing to explore Paris from an unusual perspective. To help you, use a map and a little imagination.

Location: Place de la Bastille

Assume a central position on the square. Now partly pedestrianised and used by skateboarders who enjoy its flat spaces, the area where you're standing now hasn't always looked this way: before the 16th century, it looked nothing like a square. The Bastille prison used to stand on the westernmost part, overlooking the Arsenal canal. Water used to flow outside where the place de la Bastille was built. The canal linking the Bassin de l'Arsenal to the Canal St-Martin is now subterranean, still running under your feet and below the central Colonne de Juillet. Face west, towards rue St-Antoine.

Position 1. Rue St-Antoine (14th–18th centuries)

Nothing remains today of the Bastille fortress, as Baron Haussmann's large-scale renovations radically transformed Paris. In the 14th century, a medieval fortress stood here to protect the city gates. It was declared a state prison in 1417. On 14 July 1789, the Bastille was stormed by French revolutionaries. Only a plaque with the silhouette of the ancient prison is still visible at No 3 place de la Bastille. Rotate 80 degrees and face towards the southwest.

Position 2. Bassin de l'Arsenal (16th–19th centuries)

From the 16th to the 19th century, an arsenal existed here, protecting Paris from invaders. After the Revolution, the Bassin became a commercial port which was later

JEROME LABOUYRIE/SHUTTERSTOCK ©

JEAN MARC ROMAIN/GETTY IMAGES ©

turned into a leisure port in 1983, flanked by a public garden where it's common to picnic today. Rotate 180 degrees and face north.

Position 3. Colonne de Juillet (18th–19th centuries)

This monument commemorates the revolution of July 1830. What would stand at the centre of place de la Bastille had been the object of much debate and although it never came to pass, Emperor Napoléon Bonaparte's idea was the most ambitious. He intended a gigantic elephant fountain, made of bronze, to be erected. The remains of the project served as the basis of the Colonne de Juillet. Note the lions' heads on the pedestal, initially designed for water to flow through their mouths. Rotate 100 degrees and face southeast.

> Nothing remains today of the Bastille fortress, as Baron Haussmann's large-scale renovations radically transformed Paris.

Position 4. Opéra Bastille (19th century–present)

Your last stop. You are looking at what used to be a train station up until 1969. For a whole century, workers would arrive here from the surrounding villages. On weekends, people from the surrounding Faubourg St-Antoine would travel the other way to party in *guinguettes* (popular riverside cafes where they could listen to music and dance) upstream. The train station was demolished and construction of the Opéra Bastille started in 1984. It is now a cultural powerhouse for ballet and plays. Behind it, an extension for a space dedicated to theatre is expected by 2023.

An Anachronistic Revolution

Travellers have little time to admire the 2000 painted ceramic tiles as they rush out of the metro. So the huge mural depicting the French Revolution – on the line 1 platform to La Défense at Bastille station – is often overlooked. Chances are that no one ever noticed that artists Odile Jacquot and Liliane Belembert made several characters wear modern glasses, which is completely anachronistic for the time. What's the message behind these glasses? Do they hint at the blindness of kings and queens versus the clear sight of the people? Or are they just a wink at metro travellers who are too busy to see?

22 The Artisans' COURTS

WALKING TOUR I ARTISANSHIP I ARCHITECTURE

From the 15th century, the people living in the St-Antoine district started a long tradition of artisanship. First, woodworkers and furniture makers, then boilermakers and people working with earthenware. In narrow alleys and courtyards, the craftspeople perfected their art. Today, many workshops remain and are gradually being invested in again by modern makers and artists.

BRUNO DE HOGUES/GAMMA-RAPHO VIA GETTY IMAGES ©

How to

Getting here Take the metro to Bastille (lines 1, 5, 8); finish at Ledru-Rollin (line 8).

When to visit Many of the old craftspeople's workshops are closed on weekends so pick your day wisely or you may find doors are shut!

Be discreet You will be visiting private alleys, some residential and some with actual workshops, so try to keep your pictures and Instagram poses unobtrusive.

The Bastille Victors' Hometown

Mainly inhabited by working-class populations, the district of St-Antoine has been the hearth of civil unrest. Each time a revolt is sparked, barricades spring from the ground in the neighbourhood. When the Bastille fell in 1789, almost 70% of the rebels were workers from that area.

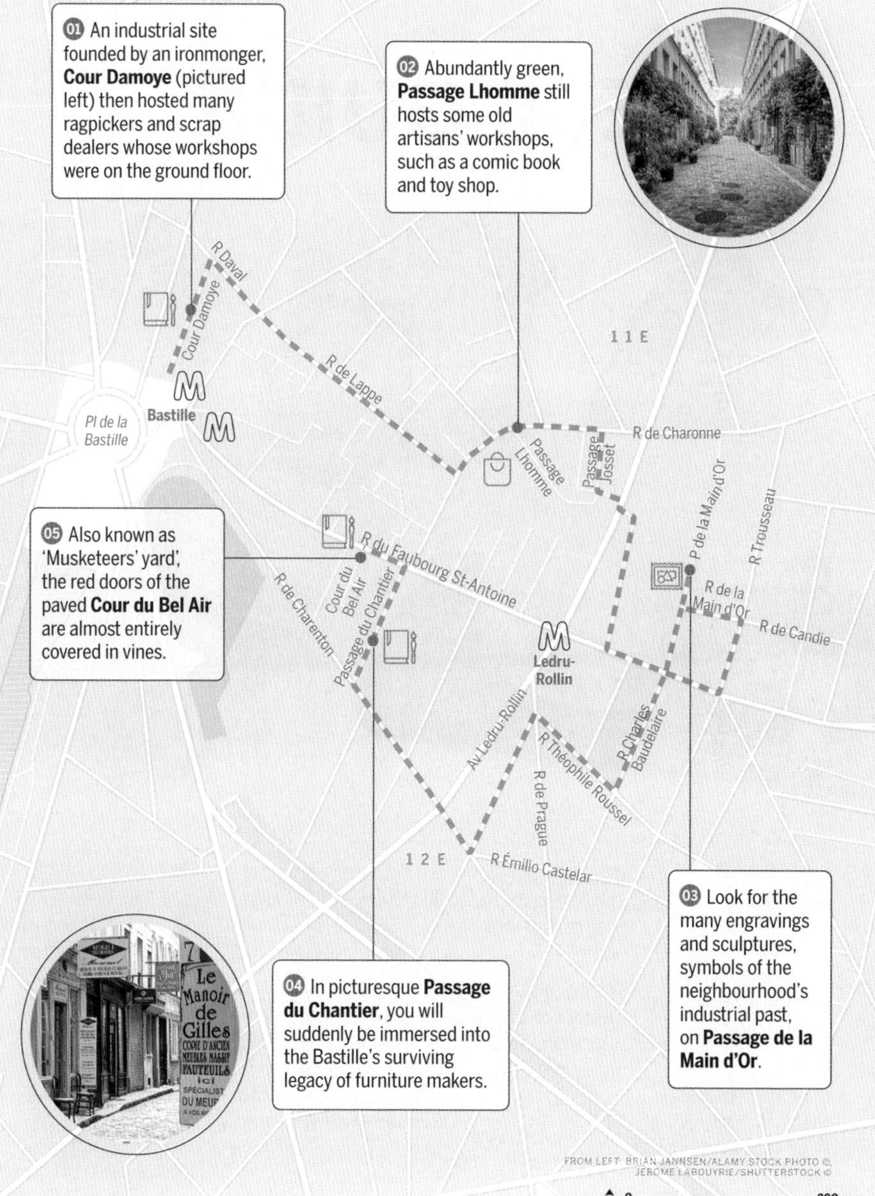

FROM LEFT: BRIAN JANNSEN/ALAMY STOCK PHOTO ©, JEROME LABOUYRIE/SHUTTERSTOCK ©

A Brief
CHEESE GUIDE

01 St-Nectaire
Originally made by women, a soft cow's milk cheese from the volcanic Auvergne region. Has a slight hazelnut taste.

02 Maroilles
Quite a strong-smelling cheese from the north of France, made from cow's milk. Tastes of spices and hazelnut – the smell can be stronger than the taste!

03 Crottin de Chavignol
A goat's cheese from the Loire valley. It becomes more crumbly as it ages.

04 St-Félicien
A creamy cow's milk cheese from the Rhône-Alpes region. Cousin of St-Marcellin, a smaller town in the same area.

05 Mont d'Or
Produced 700m above sea level in Haut-Doubs. Strapped into a spruce box, it's served cold or warm with white wine.

06 Tomme de Savoie
A cheese with an ancient history made from cow's milk in the French Alps region. Tomme from other regions exists.

07 Mimolette
Orange-paste cheese from the north made from cow's milk, originally inspired by Edam

cheese. More salty and crumbly as it matures.

08 Roquefort
A blue cheese made from sheep's milk. Perfect with nuts, or spread on a fresh baguette. Stronger alternative: Bleu de Bresse.

09 Munster
A strong-smelling cow's milk cheese made in the Vosges mountains. Some eat it with cumin seeds.

10 Comté
From the Jura mountains, made from unpasteurised cow's milk. Delicious on a cheese board or melted, its taste is described as 'fruity'.

11 Morbier
Soft cow's milk cheese from the Jura mountains Sometimes used as an alternative to *raclette*.

12 Reblochon
A soft and creamy cow's milk cheese from Savoie. Famous in France for its use in the winter dish *tartiflette*.

13 Brillat-Savarin
A triple cream cow's milk cheese produced in Burgundy. Named after an 18th-century French gourmet.

23 Eat It All in ALIGRE

FOOD TOUR I DRINKS I CULTURE

Aligre market is referred to as the 'soul of the district'. Almost every morning, food vendors open their stalls at the covered Marché Beauvau, and there are three other sections too: a more popular one outside in rue d'Aligre, along with the organic food area, and sellers of antiques and everything else on the semicircular square.

BRUNO DE HOGUES/GETTY IMAGES ©

How to

Getting here Take the metro to Ledru-Rollin, Gare de Lyon or Bastille.

Opening hours 7.30am to 1.30pm Tuesdays to Fridays, to 2.30pm Saturdays and Sundays.

French food souvenirs Besides delicious fresh produce, there are many tasty French food souvenir options on offer in the market, such as olive oil, cheese, mustard and spices.

CHRISTINEGATES/GETTY IMAGES ©

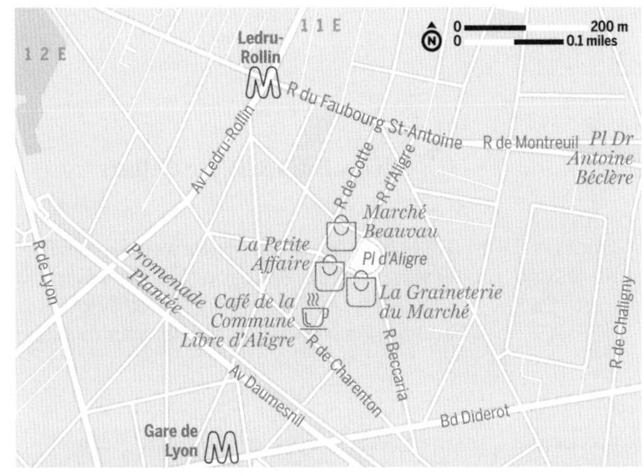

Top left Street market, Aligre **Bottom left** Bread, Parisian market

Breakfast Shopping at Aligre

From 7.30am onwards, Aligre is the perfect neighbourhood for foodies who want to taste and feel the local vibe of Faubourg St-Antoine.

People-Watching with Croissants

Start your early food tour with a croissant or any other baked goods you like. Sit at a terrace for an early coffee around **place d'Aligre**, and people-watch for a while, like Parisians love to do. Then finally walk into the orange-tiled **Marché Beauvau**. The building was classified as a historical monument in 1982.

Not Just a Covered Market

After immersing yourself in food, don't leave without taking a look at the stalls on the semicircular area outside: antiques, African masks, books and jewels...call the vintage shopper in you! This tradition dates back to a royal edict allowing the poor to come and sell whatever they wanted on place d'Aligre .

But that's not all: don't overlook the surrounding shops and cafes. The green shop **La Graineterie du Marché**, selling grains and beans, is probably one of the last of its kind in Paris. Already noon? Eat a crêpe...or couscous. Foodies, you're in for a good day.

Alternative Aligre

Aligre is not just an area, it's a whole community. Beyond giving the impression of a village, the super-local Commune Libre d'Aligre (Free Aligre Commune) association organises cultural and solidarity initiatives in the quarter. Named after the Paris Commune, they have a community cafe in rue d'Aligre, but opening times are unreliable. In the same street, other local shops such as La Petite Affaire – a small supermarket known for encouraging the sale of close-to-best-before-date products at much lower prices – continue with a mindset of solidarity that's characteristic of the Aligre area, with its strong working-class heritage.

Listings

BEST OF THE REST

Cakes, Brunch & Coffee

Passager €

A cafe with a sweet selection of pancakes, ideal for chilled brunches, with tartines and bagels too. Located back-to-back with traditional paved alleyways.

Aujourd'hui Demain €€

A vegan restaurant with excellent cakes and vegan brunches. It's also a vegan concept store with deli, fashion, beauty care and stationery. Basically, your ethical flagship store.

La Briée €

A shop specialising in French brioche from all regions. Come to eat in or take away. You will be able to see the baking process in the open workshop.

La Cave à Dessert €€

Wine or dessert...why choose? Aurore's team loves (and sells) both. Their cakes are all creative and inspired by people they know. Some even carry their names!

Crafts & Shops

Les Fleurs

In an old workshop tucked in one of the small industrial alleys, this charming design shop has a good selection of toys, accessories, jewels, homeware, clothing and stationery.

Mapoésie

Created by a designer in love with patterns and fabric, this shop sells colourful and geometrical clothes, scarves, accessories and decorations.

Lively Bars & Wine Cellars

Le Troll Café

For beer connoisseurs. There's always a friendly atmosphere in this bar, which offers over 100 different types of beer. Appreciated by locals and can get crowded, so plan for your rounds.

Le Gamin

In busy rue de Lappe, this bar specialises in whiskies and rums, with a selection of over 300 bottles. Chill in the early evening, it can become festive as it goes.

Agrology

A deli specialising in Mediterranean products, with a tasty selection of natural wines and spirits. It's both a bar and a wine cellar, in a cosy venue off the Aligre market.

Small Kitchens

Mokonuts €€

This family-run kitchen serves breakfast and refined fusion food for lunch (reservation highly recommended). You'll be charmed by Omar and Moko's warm welcome and talent.

Mokonuts

The Friendly Kitchen €

Try Fanny's vegan organic seasonal recipes, with Middle Eastern inspirations. There's lunch, dinner, brunch and gluten-free cakes. People also love how pretty everything looks.

Aï Hsu Table €€

A very small, exclusive address, with a limited menu. Aï serves refined Japanese family dishes, sometimes complemented with surprising ingredients. Reservation recommended.

Le Grand Bréguet €

An organic, local canteen and bar. Spacious and welcoming, it's also a venue for workshops and local events. Open all day; a great place to stop and refresh.

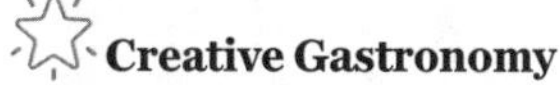

Creative Gastronomy

Table €€€

A discreet one-star Michelin restaurant near the Aligre market. The chef's motto: 'The way we eat decides the world we live in.'

Privé de Dessert €€

An original concept where you eat dessert first, or almost: with artful trompe-l'oeil, the chef designs entrées and main courses in the shape of desserts, and vice versa.

French Cuisine & Bistros

A l'Ami Pierre €

A traditional bistro recommended for its authenticity by locals, where everybody is welcome. Serves French dishes such as snails and *andouillette* (tripe sausage).

Café de l'Industrie €

Two spacious restaurants and a wine bar with a simple but tasty menu that rarely changes: a safe bet for French food with a twist. Excellent service.

Bofinger

Bofinger €€

An iconic brasserie, serving Alsatian dishes. Go for the atmosphere and the art nouveau decor. With its mirrored walls and glass dome, it's a time-travel experience.

Arts & Digital Culture

L'Atelier des Lumières

A venue dedicated to digital art, located in a 19th-century renovated foundry. The space is often used for immersive light and sound exhibitions, taking advantage of its endless walls and ceilings.

La Cinémathèque

An often-overlooked museum in Parc de Bercy, dedicated to the history of cinema, that has become an important archive collection.

Live Music

Les Disquaires

Live music bar with an eclectic program. Best for its jazz, soul and funk, African-Caribbean and Brazilian nights. Conveniently located just a few minutes' walk from rue de Lappe.

THE ISLANDS

FOOD | CULTURE | HISTORY

THE ISLANDS
Trip Builder

TAKE YOUR PICK OF MUST-SEES AND HIDDEN GEMS

In the middle of Paris, on the Seine River, lie two islands: Île de la Cité, the historic heart of the city, and Île St-Louis, an alluring island where life seems to take on a delightful, slower pace. These two islands are a must for history buffs, Francophiles and all who want to experience the *joie de vivre.*

Neighbourhood Notes

Best for Exploring like a *flâneur,* revisiting history and mingling with locals.

Transport Take line 4 to Cité, line 7 to Pont Marie, or the RER B or RER C to St-Michel Notre Dame.

Getting around Explore the islands on foot.

Tip Carve out half a day to visit the islands as they are small but dense.

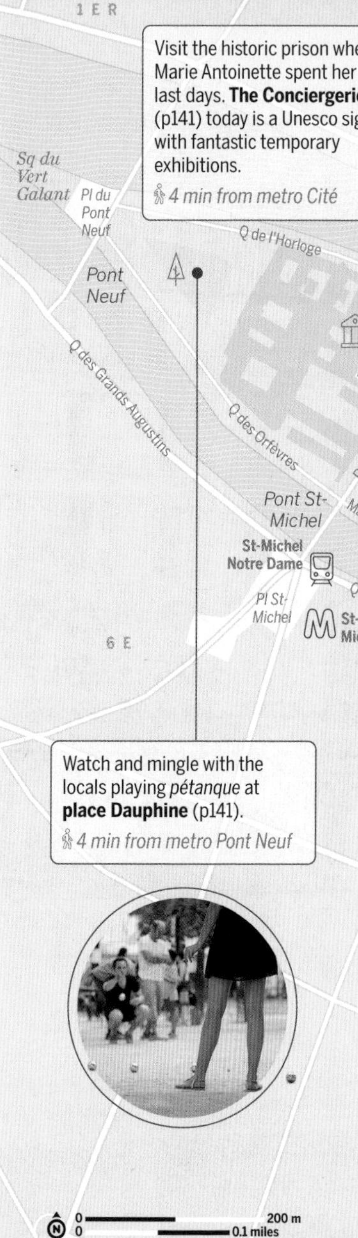

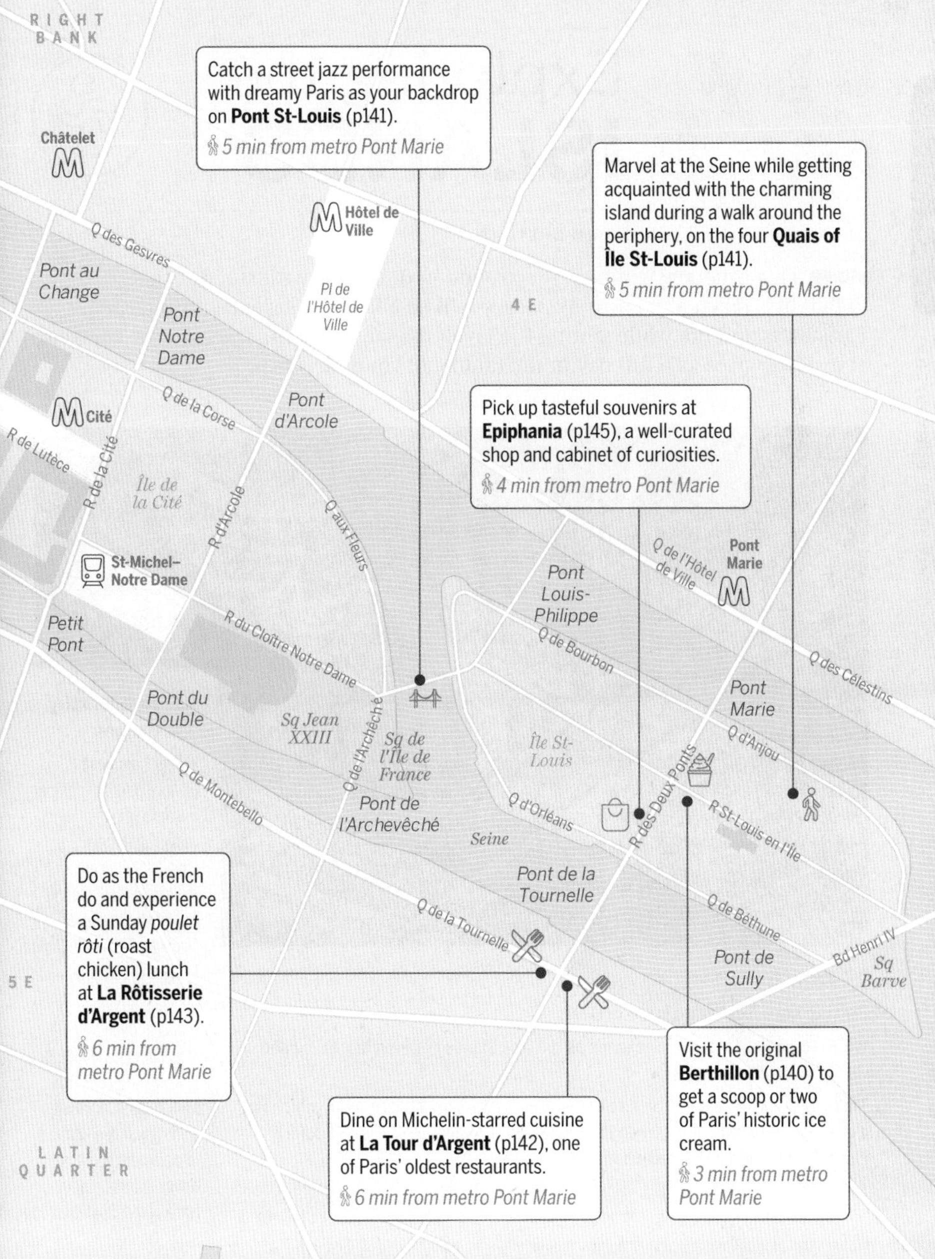
RIGHT BANK
Catch a street jazz performance with dreamy Paris as your backdrop on **Pont St-Louis** (p141).
5 min from metro Pont Marie
Marvel at the Seine while getting acquainted with the charming island during a walk around the periphery, on the four **Quais of Île St-Louis** (p141).
5 min from metro Pont Marie
Châtelet
Hôtel de Ville
Q des Gesvres
Pont au Change
Pl de l'Hôtel de Ville
4E
Pont Notre Dame
Cité
Q de la Corse
Pont d'Arcole
Pick up tasteful souvenirs at **Epiphania** (p145), a well-curated shop and cabinet of curiosities.
4 min from metro Pont Marie
R de Lutèce
R de la Cité
Île de la Cité
R d'Arcole
Q aux Fleurs
St-Michel–Notre Dame
Q de l'Hôtel de Ville
Pont Marie
Pont Louis-Philippe
Petit Pont
R du Cloître Notre Dame
Q de Bourbon
Q des Célestins
Pont du Double
Sq Jean XXIII
Q de l'Archevêché
Sq de l'Île de France
Île St-Louis
Pont Marie
Q d'Anjou
R des Deux Ponts
Q de Montebello
Pont de l'Archevêché
Q d'Orléans
Seine
R St-Louis en l'Île
Pont de la Tournelle
Do as the French do and experience a Sunday *poulet rôti* (roast chicken) lunch at **La Rôtisserie d'Argent** (p143).
6 min from metro Pont Marie
Q de la Tournelle
Q de Béthune
Pont de Sully
Bd Henri IV
Sq Barye
5E
Visit the original **Berthillon** (p140) to get a scoop or two of Paris' historic ice cream.
3 min from metro Pont Marie
Dine on Michelin-starred cuisine at **La Tour d'Argent** (p142), one of Paris' oldest restaurants.
6 min from metro Pont Marie
LATIN QUARTER

24 Exploring the ISLANDS

LOCAL LIFE | WALKING TOUR | CULTURE

This itinerary will take you around both islands with stops at the highlights. Taken at a leisurely pace, you'll be able to experience the charm of Parisian island life while getting the lay of the land. The itinerary can be enjoyed at a slower pace as a full day in the middle of your Paris trip.

Noteworthy Homes

Hôtel Lambert (1 quai d'Anjou) Once inhabited by Voltaire in the 18th century, this Île St-Louis mansion has hosted influential people such as Salvador Dalí.

Hôtel de Lauzun (17 quai d'Anjou; pictured above) Club de Hashishins meetings – where members, including Victor Hugo and Alexandre Dumas, experimented with drugs – took place here in the 1840s.

How to

Getting here Take metro line 4 to Cité.

When to go Best to avoid weekends as the tiny islands get even more crowded with locals out and about.

Tip Many shops and cafes on Île St-Louis also sell Berthillon ice cream, which is a great option for the days when the original Berthillon (29-31 rue St-Louis) is closed. Just look for the Berthillon logo!

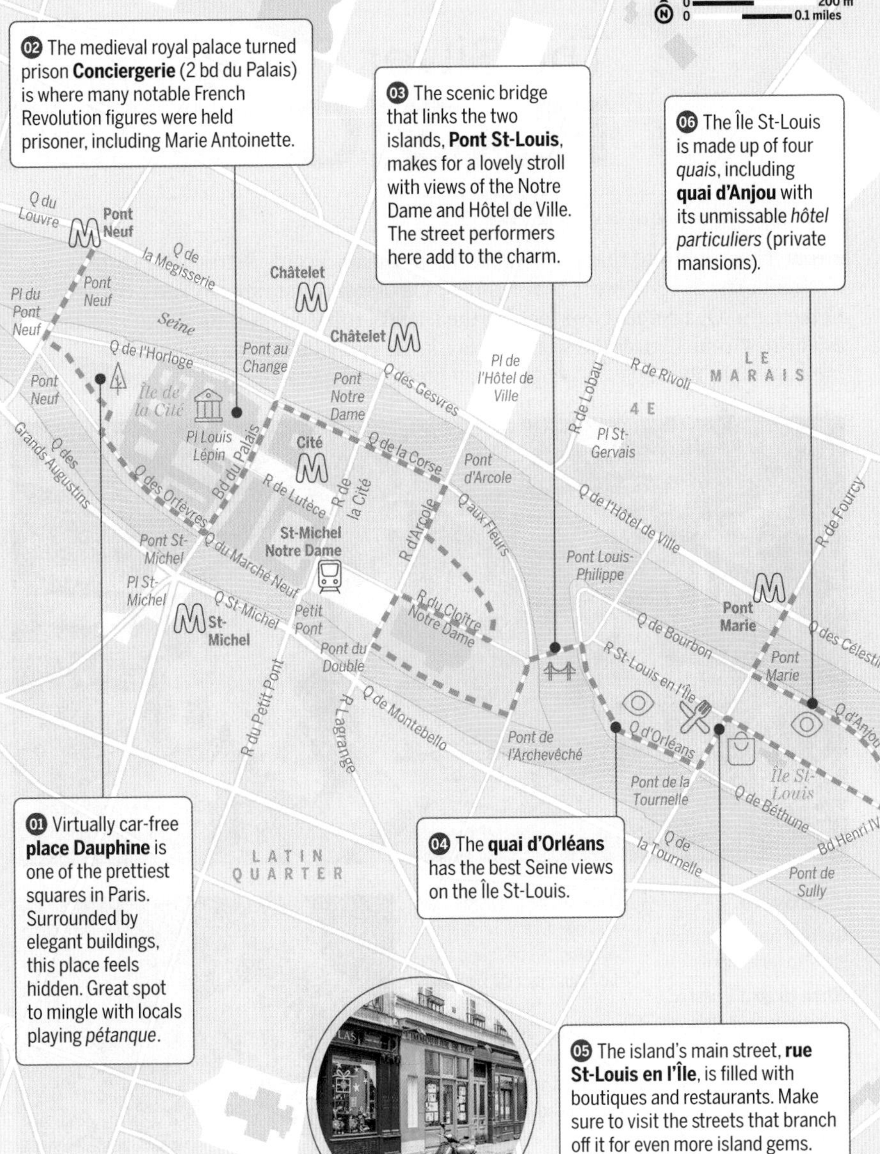

01 Virtually car-free **place Dauphine** is one of the prettiest squares in Paris. Surrounded by elegant buildings, this place feels hidden. Great spot to mingle with locals playing *pétanque*.

02 The medieval royal palace turned prison **Conciergerie** (2 bd du Palais) is where many notable French Revolution figures were held prisoner, including Marie Antoinette.

03 The scenic bridge that links the two islands, **Pont St-Louis**, makes for a lovely stroll with views of the Notre Dame and Hôtel de Ville. The street performers here add to the charm.

04 The **quai d'Orléans** has the best Seine views on the Île St-Louis.

05 The island's main street, **rue St-Louis en l'Île**, is filled with boutiques and restaurants. Make sure to visit the streets that branch off it for even more island gems.

06 The Île St-Louis is made up of four *quais*, including **quai d'Anjou** with its unmissable *hôtel particuliers* (private mansions).

25 The Silver Tower MAGIC

HERITAGE | GASTRONOMY | HISTORY

The restaurant that inspired scenes in Disney Pixar's *Ratatouille,* La Tour d'Argent (The Silver Tower), is also one of the oldest restaurants in Paris. Situated in the Latin Quarter and overlooking the islands, it has fed royalty, dignitaries and celebrities from all over the world. Today, it has expanded into a mini-empire along the quai de la Tournelle, so people on all budgets can experience the magic.

MARTIN BUREAU/AFP VIA GETTY IMAGES ©

How to

Getting here Take metro line 7 to Pont Marie.

When to go It's best to come here for lunch so you can take in the views during daylight hours.

Tips All the provisions you need for your island picnics can be found at Le Boulanger de La Tour and La Petite Épicerie de la Tour. Reservations for the restaurants are required at least one week in advance.

MAURICE ROUGEMONT/GAMMA-RAPHO VIA GETTY IMAGES ©

MARTIN BUREAU/AFP VIA GETTY IMAGES ©

Far left Yannick Franques and staff **Near left** Main course, La Tour d'Argent **Bottom left** Wine cellar, La Tour d'Argent

La Tour d'Argent €€€

This legendary Michelin-starred restaurant located on the 6th floor of its own building offers the best bird's eye-view of the islands and monuments, including Notre Dame. At the helm of the kitchen is chef Yannick Franques, a Meilleur Ouvrier de France, and his 'Chef Imagination' course at lunch and dinner is an adventurous way to experience all the menu has to offer. However, the three-course lunch is the most affordable option and is a great way to experience dining in the brightly lit room. The wine list comes in a book that is over 400 pages long, showcasing over 320,000 bottles in the cellar that survived WWII. Make sure you ask the staff throughout the meal about the special history of the place!

La Rôtisserie d'Argent €€

This casual and homely rôtisserie is the bistro of La Tour d'Argent. At the heart of the menu is the roast chicken, but there are also other classic French dishes like beef filet with *sauce au poivre* (peppercorn sauce). Like La Tour d'Argent, la Rôtisserie serves duck from Challans but at a fraction of the price in two servings, in two different ways. In the warmer months, the terrace right by the Seine offers great views of Île St-Louis.

Le Boulanger de La Tour €

La Tour d'Argent's bakery supplies bread for its restaurants but is also open to the public. You'll find larger versions of the baguettes it serves in its Michelin-starred restaurant, classics pastries, as well as sandwiches, like its famed Jambon Beurre, that won't break the bank.

La Tour d'Argent Menu Highlights

Pike Quenelles André Terrail Named after the current owner's grandfather, who purchased the restaurant in 1911, this is a must-try entrée that comes with mushrooms and a delicious buttery, browned brioche.

Duckling Frédéric Delair This is one of the restaurant's specialities. Diners who order the duck receive a postcard with the bird's serial number, which also gets logged by the restaurant.

Cheese The selection exclusively highlights cheeses from the Île-de-France region.

Crêpes Mademoiselle The servers make the dessert in front of you in the dining room on a cart. It's a performance you shouldn't miss.

Listings

BEST OF THE REST

Island Bites

Poget & De Witte €€

Named after the owners, the head of the seafood department at Galeries Lafayette Paris and an oyster fisherman, this tiny seafood shop on Île St-Louis has the best oysters in town.

Ha Noi 1988 €

Travel to Hanoi at this vibrant Vietnamese restaurant on the Île de la Cité. The menu here highlights Northern Vietnamese cuisine. Their Vietnamese coffee is a must.

Les Deux Colombes €

This charming restaurant on Île de la Cité, with gorgeous views of the Seine and Hôtel de Ville, offers delicious comfort foods using high-quality ingredients. The lunch *formules* (fixed-price menus) are affordable and filling.

Le St-Régis €€

This legendary Île St-Louis institution is the picture-perfect example of an iconic Parisian bistro. Even if you don't eat here, stop by for a drink to at least experience the St-Régis.

Le Sergent Recruteur €€€

Chef Alain Pégouret, who trained under Joël Robuchon, has helped make Île St-Louis a must-visit destination for fine dining enthusiasts with his Michelin-star restaurant.

KHANA €

This Afghan restaurant on Île St-Louis serves up traditional dishes with modern touches. The portions are generous and the service is warm.

Epicurean Gems on Île St-Louis

Le Petit Grain €

This second location of the beloved sourdough bakery from the team at restaurant Le Grand Bain is on Île St-Louis. Although it's the size of a broom closet, it still offers quite the selection of bread, pastries (think sourdough croissants) and sandwiches.

Latiffe Foie Gras €

Latiffe has been supplying top chefs and gourmands all over the globe with foie gras for over 100 years. Its tiny Île St-Louis boutique offers a large selection of its products.

La Ferme Sain-Sabin €

This no-frills cheese shop on Île St-Louis is a great place to try and purchase French cheeses without feeling intimidated. The kind owner speaks English and will guide you in your selection.

Loutsa Torréfacteur – Paris Notre-Dame €

This coffee shop on Île de la Cité has a roasting machine on-site by the Lyon-based French roaster, Loutsa. With highly trained baristas,

Le St-Régis

they really have mastered the art of pulling espresso.

Fleuryan €

The island's one-stop shop for organic produce and ready-to-eat healthy meals, treats and juice on Île St-Louis. You can't miss their bright façade.

Peculiar Boutiques

Epiphania

This cabinet of curiosities opened in 2021 on Île St-Louis and is filled with well-curated souvenirs and trinkets sourced from all over the world, including some vintage finds.

Papeterie Gaubert

This *papeterie* has been a Parisian institution since 1830. The shop on the Île de la Cité is a bazaar for stationery lovers. It still sells the light blue Japanese paper that Colette sourced exclusively here by weight!

Librairie Ulysse

This bookshop on Île St-Louis is dedicated to travel and will inspire wanderlust for days. Here you'll find maps, travel guides, books, magazines, postcards and more from all over the world.

Opulence Luxury & Vintage

This high-end vintage shop on Île St-Louis sells designer goods in pristine condition at fair prices. You'll find a great selection of bags, fashion jewellery, accessories and clothing from brands like Hermès and Chanel.

Raphaël Bedos Antiquités

Visiting antique shops in Paris can be nerve-wracking but not here. This friendly gallery shop on Île de la Cité has an impressive museum quality collection of treasures dating back to the Middle Ages!

La Ste-Chapelle

Other Island Delights

Marché aux Fleurs – Reine-Elizabeth II

In 1808, Napoléon decided to build a flower market on the Île de la Cité. Here at one of the largest flower markets in the world, you'll find flowers, plants, garden decor, and a bird market on Sunday. Renovations are due to take place from 2023 until 2025, but the market will remain open.

La Ste-Chapelle

This Gothic chapel, built in the mid-13th century, is widely considered the finest in France. Many visitors come for the stained-glass windows that make up the walls.

Square du Vert-Galant

Located past Pont Neuf at the tip of Île de la Cité, this park is magical. The majestic weeping willows, plus the secluded feel, add to the appeal of this place.

26 A Day on THE SEINE

BOATS | MUSIC | SWIMMING

The many sightseeing cruises that run up and down the Seine are a popular tourist attraction, but there are many other, self-guided ways to get up close and personal with the majestic body of water that runs through the centre of Paris and its connected network of canals.

How to

Hire a boat From a kiosk on the quai de la Seine, Marin d'Eau Douce hires easy-to-manoeuvre electric boats, no licence required, for exploring the Bassin de la Villette and Canal de l'Ourcq at your own pace. They even rent *pétanque* sets so you can dock for a game of boules on the banks.

Tip Bring a picnic or add on a pre-packed picnic or *apéro* (predinner drinks) hamper when you book with Marin d'Eau Douce.

Play a Game of Pétanque

Pétanque is a popular activity along the **Canal de l'Ourcq**; each summer its banks fill with locals playing a game, often while sipping rosé. **BarOurcq**, a tiny dive on the quai de la Loire, loans deck chairs and *pétanque* sets to customers free of charge.

Take a Refreshing Dip

Each summer, **Paris Plages** appears along the river and canals to console those unable to escape for a beach holiday, but while it has deck chairs, palm trees and even sand, there's never been a place to swim.

In 2017, Parisians were able to plunge into the **Bassin de la Villette**, the

Top right Marin d'Eau Douce boat, Canal de l'Ourcq **Bottom right** Paris Plages

BRUNO DE HOGUES/GAMMA-RAPHO VIA GETTY IMAGES ©

Treasures from the Watery Depths

The Canal St-Martin is drained every 10 to 15 years for a thorough dredging. The last clean-up took place in 2016 and among the bizarre objects found on its bottom were more than 100 Vélib' bikes, a pistol, a rifle, a sewing mannequin, a wheelchair and one ski boot.

wide stretch linking Canal de l'Ourcq and Canal St-Martin, for the first time since the '20s. The free-admission pools return each summer and plans are underway to clean up the Seine so that it will also be swimmable in time for the 2024 Olympics.

Watch a Concert on a Boat

Many boats moored along Paris' waterways are floating bars, eateries or concert venues. **L'Improviste** is a *péniche* (narrowboat) jazz club, **L'Antipode** offers eclectic concerts and a restaurant, **Bateau Phare** is a chic lightship lounge with DJ sets and **Petit Bain** hosts indie and punk shows.

OLRAT/GETTY IMAGES ©

THE LATIN QUARTER

CINEMA | BOOKS | CULTURE

THE LATIN QUARTER
Trip Builder

TAKE YOUR PICK OF MUST-SEES AND HIDDEN GEMS

Named after the original scholars who flocked here from all over Europe and communicated in Latin, this neighbourhood on the Left Bank still remains the intellectual centre of Paris. Home to universities, bookshops and arthouse cinemas, the Latin Quarter is the best place to get a glance of the historically bohemian side of the city.

Neighbourhood Notes

Best for Wandering and visiting bookshops.

Transport Metro to Place Monge or Cluny–La Sorbonne.

Getting around The winding streets and alleyways of the Latin Quarter are best explored on foot.

Tip The best way to enjoy the narrow medieval streets is to meander.

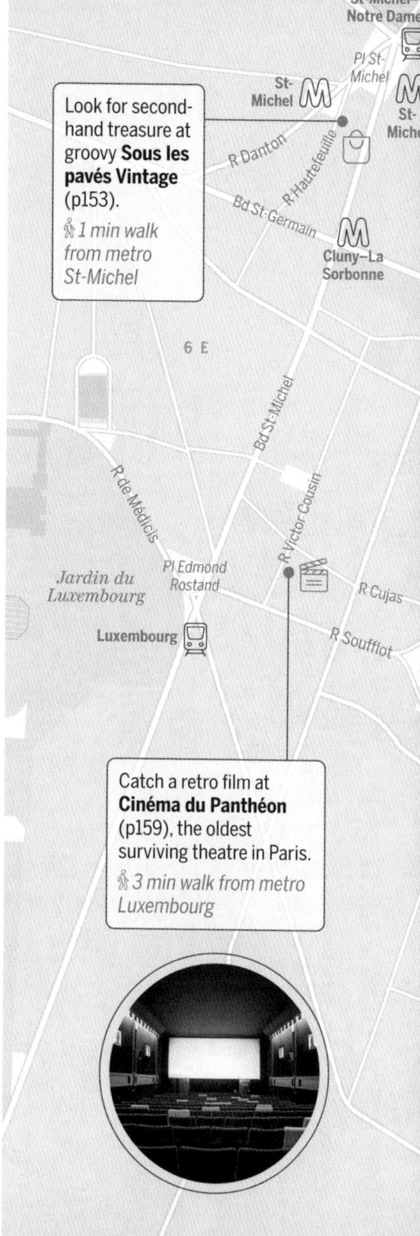

Look for second-hand treasure at groovy **Sous les pavés Vintage** (p153).
1 min walk from metro St-Michel

Catch a retro film at **Cinéma du Panthéon** (p159), the oldest surviving theatre in Paris.
3 min walk from metro Luxembourg

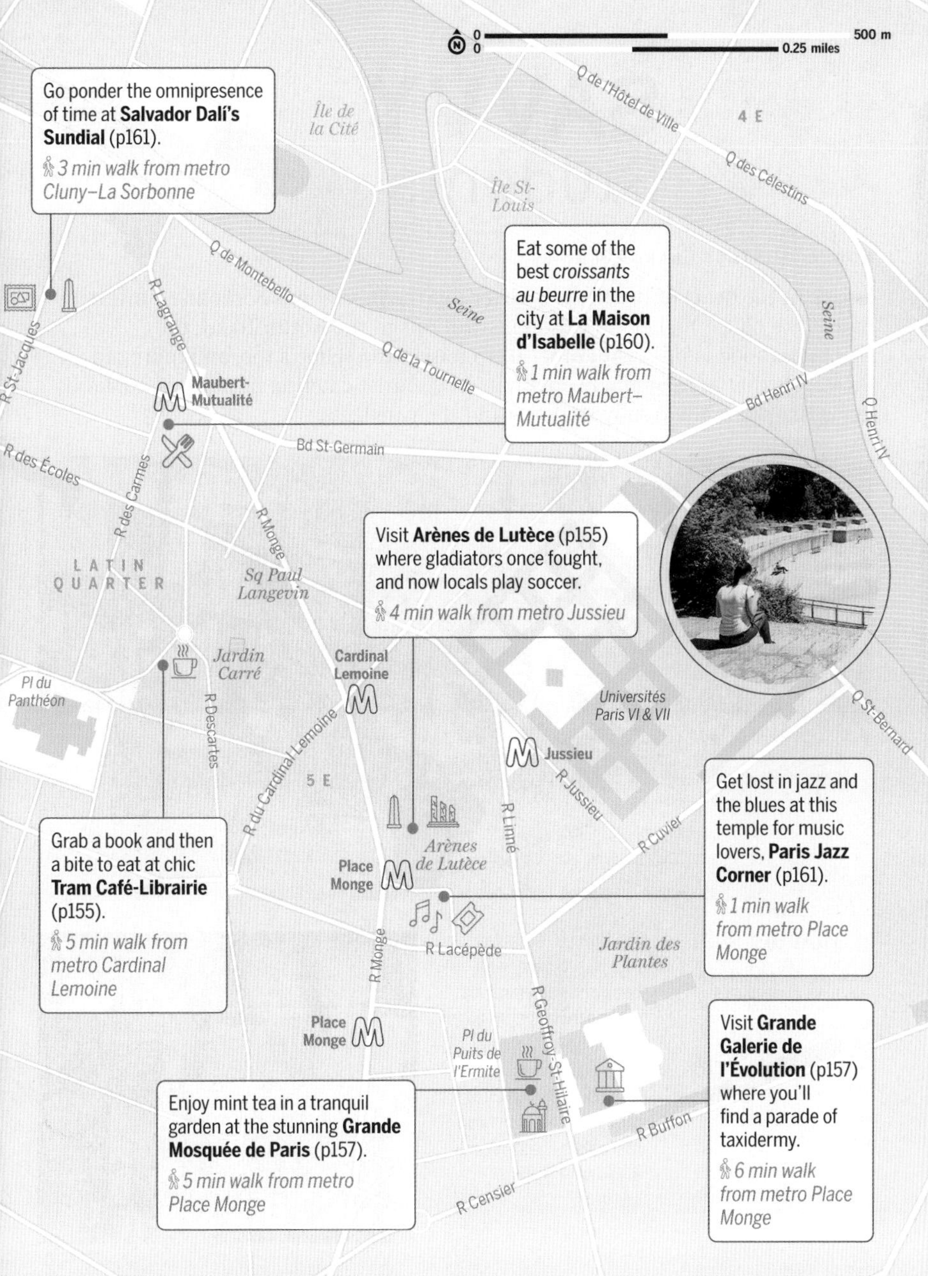
0 500 m
0 0.25 miles
Go ponder the omnipresence of time at **Salvador Dalí's Sundial** (p161).
3 min walk from metro Cluny–La Sorbonne
Eat some of the best *croissants au beurre* in the city at **La Maison d'Isabelle** (p160).
1 min walk from metro Maubert–Mutualité
Visit **Arènes de Lutèce** (p155) where gladiators once fought, and now locals play soccer.
4 min walk from metro Jussieu
Grab a book and then a bite to eat at chic **Tram Café-Librairie** (p155).
5 min walk from metro Cardinal Lemoine
Get lost in jazz and the blues at this temple for music lovers, **Paris Jazz Corner** (p161).
1 min walk from metro Place Monge
Visit **Grande Galerie de l'Évolution** (p157) where you'll find a parade of taxidermy.
6 min walk from metro Place Monge
Enjoy mint tea in a tranquil garden at the stunning **Grande Mosquée de Paris** (p157).
5 min walk from metro Place Monge
Île de la Cité
Île St-Louis
Q de l'Hôtel de Ville
4 E
Q des Célestins
Q de Montebello
Seine
Seine
Q de la Tournelle
Bd Henri IV
Q Henri IV
R St-Jacques
R Lagrange
Maubert-Mutualité
Bd St-Germain
R des Écoles
R des Carmes
R Monge
LATIN QUARTER
Sq Paul Langevin
Jardin Carré
Cardinal Lemoine
Pl du Panthéon
R Descartes
R du Cardinal Lemoine
Universités Paris VI & VII
Q St-Bernard
Jussieu
R Jussieu
5 E
R Linné
R Cuvier
Arènes de Lutèce
Place Monge
R Lacépède
R Monge
Jardin des Plantes
Place Monge
Pl du Puits de l'Ermite
R Geoffroy-St-Hilaire
R Buffon
R Censier

27 SAVVY Students

BOOKS | VINTAGE | BARGAIN BITES

At the heart of the Latin Quarter lies the prestigious Sorbonne University, one of the oldest higher education institutions in the world. Today, the neighbourhood is busy with other universities and schools too, and hiding in its streets that are seemingly dominated by tourist-catering businesses are local gems that serve the trendy students and their budgets.

CHRISTIAN MUELLER/SHUTTERSTOCK ©

How to

Getting here Metro to St-Michel or Cluny–La Sorbonne.

When to go This neighbourhood is busy all the time but feels super packed around lunchtime hours when the students are dismissed for lunch.

Tip Bring a reusable tote bag to carry your book and secondhand purchases as paper bags rip easily. A lot of the *bouquinistes* (booksellers) don't allow photography of their stands so make sure to ask nicely if you want to snap a memory.

EQROY/SHUTTERSTOCK ©

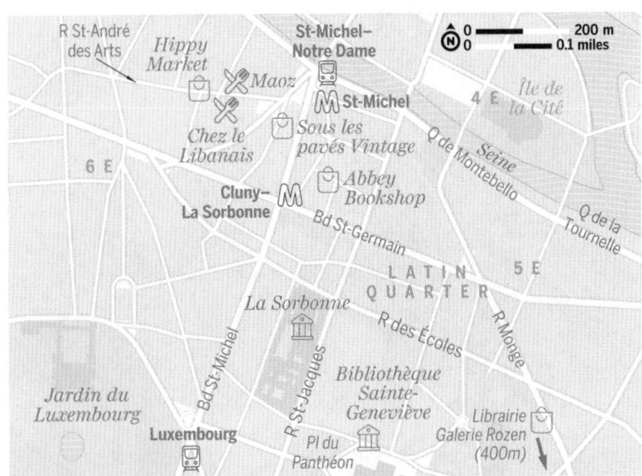

Top left Place de la Sorbonne **Bottom left** *Bouquiniste*'s stall

La Sorbonne Buildings belonging to France's oldest university are scattered around the vicinity. Place de la Sorbonne, at the centre of the original university grounds, is a good public place to imagine student life.

Bookshops It wouldn't be the Latin Quarter without its plentiful eccentric bookshops. Librairie Galerie Rozen is dedicated to art and culture with an amazing selection of vintage concert posters and art prints. Abbey Bookshop is a used English-language bookshop hidden in a pedestrian passage.

Les Bouquinistes These iconic open-air booksellers can be found along the banks of the Seine and are a Unesco World Heritage site. They are an important part of the Parisian landscape.

Bibliothèque Sainte-Geneviève The world's first independent public library is open to anyone over the age of 18. Ask staff for a tour of the alluring library.

Secondhand Trendy students have attracted some of the capital's best secondhand shops. Sous les pavés Vintage is two floors of higher-end pieces at reasonable prices. Hippy Market has racks of funky clothing and Kiliwatch Collector next door has a curated selection.

Rue St-André-des-Arts This ancient street is filled with historic buildings and affordable eateries that cater to students. The best places for a delicious meal under €10 are Maoz, a vegetarian felafel shop that makes everything but the pitta from scratch, and Chez le Libanais, a popular hole-in-the wall for Lebanese wraps.

Librairie des Loisirs

Although Librairie des Loisirs looks like an ordinary Boulinier – a chain of used bookshops in Île-de-France – this location is dedicated to *loisirs* (leisure). This is one of the local residents' best-kept secrets. Here, it's easy to come by rare art books, unique vintage cookbooks and other niche-specific titles at affordable prices. In front of the shop is the further discounted book selection where everything is €1. The employees put the rarer and better condition finds towards the back of the shop, mostly on the wall next to the till or in the window directly in front of the till.

28 Explore the Latin QUARTER

WALKING TOUR | HISTORY | GREEN SPACES

This is one of only a few areas in central Paris where narrow medieval streets and alleyways still remain. The best way to explore the Latin Quarter is to meander its winding streets, stopping at the important landmarks of the neighbourhood as you stroll.

How to

Getting here Metro to Place Monge.

When to go The best time to visit Marché Mouffetard is between 10am and noon as most vendors close up for the day at lunchtime.

Tip Wear comfortable walking shoes, apply sunscreen and bring a refillable water bottle to keep you hydrated throughout the day. The streets near place Monge are filled with speciality boutiques that are mostly frequented by locals. Let your eyes and curiosity lead you!

Arènes de Lutèce

Cherished by local residents and unknown to most tourists, the ruins of Arènes de Lutèce date back to the 2nd century, when Paris was named Lutetia. This Roman amphitheatre was discovered by accident in 1869 and is the city's oldest monument. Today, locals use the space where gladiators once fought as a public open space, mingling with neighbours, having picnics and playing ball games.

The Panthéon

Completed in 1789, the neoclassical dome of the Panthéon is part of the iconic Paris skyline. It is a mausoleum for some of France's greatest citizens, including Marie Curie, Simone Veil and Voltaire. The interior is decorated with mosaics, intricate frescoes and grand paintings of French history.

Sip & Read

Tram Café-Librarie is a chic coffee shop and bookshop near the Panthéon. On one side, you'll find a curation of French books and on the other, a cafe with homemade baked goods, warm drinks and the best croque monsieur (with truffle salt and Prince de Paris ham).

Top left Dome of the Panthéon **Bottom left** Jardin des Plantes (p156) **Above** Muséum National d'Histoire Naturelle (p156)

Rue Mouffetard

One of the oldest streets in Paris, **rue Mouffetard** – or 'La Mouffe' as the locals have dubbed it – is a vivacious, cobblestoned street lined with market stalls (except on Mondays), food shops, bars filled with university students and affordable restaurants. This street served as major inspiration for Victor Hugo when he was writing *Les Misérables*.

Natural Treasures

A collection of 13 different sites, **Muséum National d'Histoire Naturelle** is made up of zoos, museums, galleries and gardens throughout the Île-de-France region. The heart of the museum collection is in the Latin Quarter, comprised of its most prominent spaces: Jardin des Plantes, Grande Galerie de l'Évolution and Grandes Serres.

The 400-year-old **Jardin des Plantes** is a regal botanic garden that takes up 24 hectares

La Mouffe's Best Coffee Stops

Dose Get your caffeine fix at this hip coffee shop where they roast their own beans. There's a quick takeaway window where you can grab coffee and pastries to go but you can also dine in for brunch. The terrasse is sheltered under a covered passage with a direct view of the street – a prime spot for people-watching on La Mouffe!

Chinaski Located on an adjacent street, this restaurant named after Charles Bukowski's alter-ego is a coffee shop serving brunch on weekends and transforming into a savvy bistro by night. The owner is a well-known bartender so don't miss out on the cocktails!

where visitors can walk through and even study different plant species. It is France's main botanic garden and once served as a garden for medicinal plants under the authority of the king's physician.

In **Grande Galerie de l'Évolution**, you'll find an impressive parade of taxidermy animals, as well as skeletons and fossils. The building and renovated interior itself is stunning and the museum layout is brilliant. It's a common misconception that this is a museum for children, but it's enjoyed by all ages.

For a taste of the tropics, head to the **Grandes Serres**. These sleek greenhouse structures are made up of four spaces, each dedicated to a different ecosystem. For example, there's one greenhouse dedicated to the desert where visitors will find succulents from Mexico, the Sahara, the United States and Australia, whereas the Grand Deco structure is home to the jungle, and filled with orchids and banana leaves.

Art Deco Mosque

The stunning **Grande Mosquée de Paris** is an oasis. Open to the public, visitors can walk in and admire the gorgeous mosaics and tiles, experience the North African *hammam* (steambath; women only), and enjoy mint tea with flaky pistachio pastries and orange blossom desserts in the tranquil garden. Moderate dress is required for entry.

Left Cafe terrace **Below** Grande Mosquée de Paris

29 The Roving CINEPHILE

CINEMA | CULTURE | BOHEMIAN

In France, especially in Paris, going to the cinema to watch a film is an important part of weekly life for many. There are over a dozen cinemas, both mainstream and arthouse, concentrated in the Latin Quarter. Experiencing a classic or arthouse film in a historic cinema, with drinks before at an adjacent terrasse or a cafe, is a quintessential Latin Quarter experience.

DESIGNIUM/SHUTTERSTOCK ©

How to

Getting here Metro to St-Michel or Cluny–La Sorbonne.

When to go Check out film times and reserve your tickets in advance. Evening shows often sell out.

Tip In France, most arthouse cinemas will play films in 'VOSTF', the original language, with French subtitles. If you want to catch a French film, but don't know French, check out Lost in Frenchlation (lostinfrenchlation.com), an organisation that holds screenings in Paris for French films with English subtitles.

LOIC VENANCE/AFP VIA GETTY IMAGES ©

Le Champo Walking into the French New Wave HQ will give you the impression of following in the footsteps of François Truffaut or Claude Chabrol – a real pilgrimage to the cinema of filmmakers! It is a privilege to still be able to watch films in such a symbolic theatre. After the film, grab a coffee at Sorbonon on rue des Écoles and listen to the students debate (one of French people's favourite activities).

Reflet Médicis This is one of the only places in Paris where you can find a good film to watch before 2pm! Make sure to check out the art deco stained glass in room 3. And of course, there is a cafe called Le Reflet just in front, in case you want a glass of wine while keeping an eye on the queue...

Cinéma du Panthéon The oldest functioning cinema in Paris and home to the event **L'Inconnu du Ciné-Club**, where you can watch a secret film introduced by a secret guest. Upstairs in the salon, you'll find Café Nouvelle Vague with leather chairs, black-and-white pictures of famous French movie stars, and unique objects hunted down by Catherine Deneuve herself at the flea market. This is the best place to have a tea and leaf through *Les Cahiers du Cinéma,* a French magazine dedicated to film. Next door you'll find Librairie du Cinéma du Panthéon with a great selection of *cinélittérature* (books on cinema) and a jukebox that plays film tunes.

Top left Cinéma du Panthéon **Bottom left** Le Champo

Paris & Cinema

Paris is absolutely central when it comes to cinema history as the world's first public movie screening took place here in 1895. The concentration of cinemas in the Latin Quarter can be attributed to the fact that this neighbourhood was home to the 1950s Cineaste (filmmaker) movement. University students here also historically frequented the theatres in-between classes. The May 68 protests, led by the students, helped cement film as an art form and not just entertainment. Paris is today home to 88 cinemas in total, a third of which are still independently owned.

With thanks to Manon Kerjean, *founder of Lost in Frenchlation.* *@lostinfrenchlation*

Listings

BEST OF THE REST

All-Day Treats

La Maison d'Isabelle €

Winner of the 2018 Best Croissant of Paris, this modest bakery is dedicated to only using organic flour and butter. Its flaky croissants are truly among the best in the city and only cost €1.

Fromagerie Laurent Dubois €

Laurent Dubois is the first cheesemonger to receive the Meilleur Ouvrier de France (Best Craftsman of France). His shops offer a fantastic selection of cheese, including their own cheese pastry creations, a combination of their cheeses with other flavourful ingredients.

Plus82 €

This cute coffee shop sources its beans from a roaster in Jeju-do, South Korea, and serves Korean-inspired sweets. Its *bingsu* (Korean-style shaved ice) and matcha cookies, made by its own in-house, French-trained Korean pastry chef, are highlights.

Coutume Institut €

This gorgeous coffee shop with ample seating is located inside the Institut Finlandais. A great rest spot for delicious food and drink in the area.

Pierre Oteiza €

This artisan Basque producer has the best *jambon* (ham) and *saucisson* (dried pork sausage) the public can buy. It sells grocery goods to take home but also has fresh offerings: think sandwiches, individual charcuterie cones, and meat and cheese boards.

Memorable Meals

La Bête Noire €

Homey and creative neighbourhood eatery that serves as a cafe with baked goods, before and after lunch, and a bistro with an ever-changing lunch menu, driven by what's in season.

Han Lim €

One of the oldest Korean restaurants in the city that is still around today, located just a stone's throw away from the Panthéon. This family-run place opened in 1981 and is known for its old-school Korean fried chicken and Korean bone broth soup.

Kitchen Galerie Bis €€/€€€

The sibling restaurant of Michelin-starred Ze Kitchen Galerie, this modern restaurant serves up innovative French dishes with Asian touches. Think skilful additions of lemongrass bouillon and kimchi to classic French cooking.

Kodawari Ramen €

This ramen shop transports you to Japan with a reconstruction of Tokyo's vibrant alleyways. The ramen here is top-notch.

Fontaine St-Michel

Shu €€€

This intimate Japanese restaurant is a hidden gem that specialises in *kushiagué* (small bites of food on skewers). Its sashimi offerings are also excellent.

Other Neighbourhood Attractions

Institut du Monde Arabe

The Institut du Monde Arabe works to promote Arab culture and to cultivate Franco-Arab interchange. It offers a dynamic cultural program of temporary exhibitions and events, from film screenings to conferences, in a modern glass building. Don't miss the sweeping views of Paris from the roof terrace.

Fontaine St-Michel

The monumental Fontaine St-Michel is worth a quick visit before you enter or leave the neighbourhood as it's situated near the metro stations. Wall fountains are rare in Paris and this one, which depicts the struggle between good and evil, is considered the largest.

Salvador Dalí Sundial

There are 120 sundials scattered throughout Paris that often go unnoticed. This one is extraordinary because it was created and gifted by the surrealist artist Salvador Dalí himself. Dalí even attended the unveiling of the artwork, accompanied by his pet ocelot and a brass band.

Shoes, Books & Music

Carel

This shop for the iconic Parisian shoe brand is located near its original boutique that opened in 1952. Worn historically by stylish students in the area, Carel shoes are incredibly comfortable. Today, these shoes are representative of Parisian style and are a favourite of fashionable celebrities like Alexa Chung.

Shoes from Carel

Shakespeare & Company

Located across the street from Notre Dame, this legendary shop is named after the original Shakespeare and Company bookshop, the meeting point for Hemingway's 'Lost Generation'. A warning that this place gets incredibly busy. Its cafe next door offers healthy pastries, lunch and coffee.

The Red Wheelbarrow

The Jardin du Luxembourg is reflected on the windows at this charming *Librairie Anglophone* with sliding ladders on the walls, run by the kind founder, Penelope.

San Francisco Books Co.

This secondhand English-language bookshop near Odéon Theatre has an impressive selection of books on the city, with the best collected in a pile at the front of the store.

Paris Jazz Corner

Tucked away on a quiet and beautiful residential street, this record store is a temple for music aficionados. Here you'll find an impressive jazz and blues collection of used and new vinyls and CDs.

Scan to find more things to do in the Latin Quarter online

ST-GERMAIN & LES INVALIDES

HISTORY | FOOD | SHOPPING

Experience St-Germain & Les Invalides online

ST-GERMAIN & LES INVALIDES
Trip Builder

TAKE YOUR PICK OF MUST-SEES AND HIDDEN GEMS

This legendary part of Paris has attracted and nourished some of the world's most celebrated thinkers, artists, writers and musicians. Today it's a fashionable and upscale neighbourhood with a creative spirit. Come for the history and art, stay for the food and shopping, and leave a bit more cultured.

Neighbourhood Notes

Best for Following the footsteps of cultural icons, eating the capital's food highlights, and shopping.

Transport Take line 4 to St-Germain-des-Prés station.

Getting around Best experienced on foot (or bus for longer distances).

Tips If you've ever heard that how you dress matters in Paris, it applies here.

Q d'Orsay

Take in one of the world's most impressive art collections at the **Musée d'Orsay** (p173).

8 min walk from metro Rue du Bac

Esplanade des Invalides

Marvel at nature at Wes Anderson's favourite taxidermy shop, the historic **Deyrolle** (p174).

2 min walk from metro Rue du Bac

Discover new magazine titles at the best newspaper kiosk in the city, **Bogopresse** (p167).

6 min walk from metro Sèvres–Babylone

Bd de Vaugirard

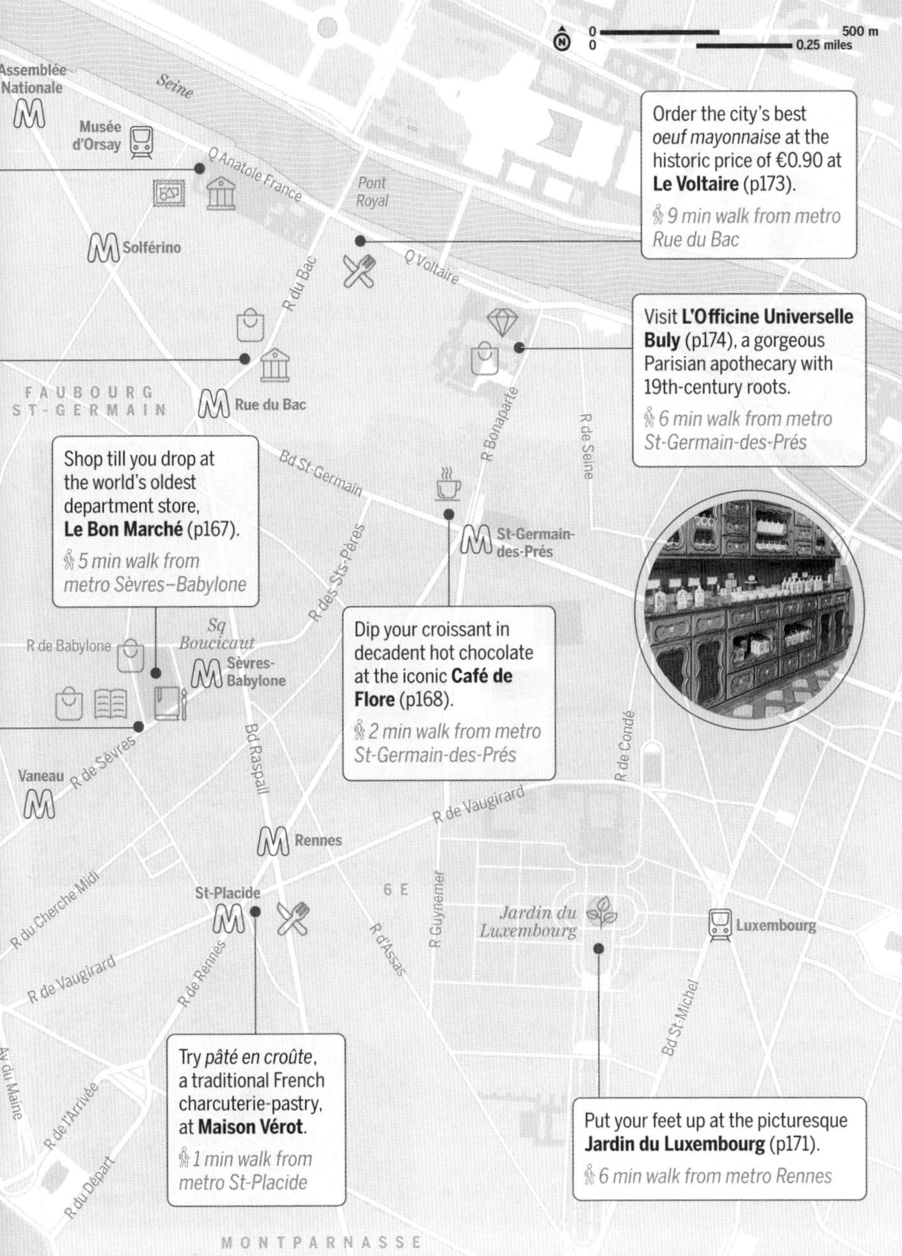
500 m
0.25 miles
Assemblée Nationale
Seine
Musée d'Orsay
Q Anatole France
Pont Royal
Solférino
R du Bac
Q Voltaire
Order the city's best *oeuf mayonnaise* at the historic price of €0.90 at **Le Voltaire** (p173).
9 min walk from metro Rue du Bac
Visit **L'Officine Universelle Buly** (p174), a gorgeous Parisian apothecary with 19th-century roots.
6 min walk from metro St-Germain-des-Prés
FAUBOURG ST-GERMAIN
Rue du Bac
R Bonaparte
R de Seine
Shop till you drop at the world's oldest department store, **Le Bon Marché** (p167).
5 min walk from metro Sèvres–Babylone
Bd St-Germain
St-Germain-des-Prés
R des Sts-Pères
Sq Boucicaut
R de Babylone
Sèvres-Babylone
Dip your croissant in decadent hot chocolate at the iconic **Café de Flore** (p168).
2 min walk from metro St-Germain-des-Prés
Bd Raspail
R de Sèvres
Vaneau
R de Condé
R de Vaugirard
Rennes
R du Cherche Midi
St-Placide
6E
R Guynemer
R d'Assas
Jardin du Luxembourg
Luxembourg
R de Vaugirard
R de Rennes
Bd St-Michel
Av du Maine
Try *pâté en croûte*, a traditional French charcuterie-pastry, at **Maison Vérot**.
1 min walk from metro St-Placide
Put your feet up at the picturesque **Jardin du Luxembourg** (p171).
6 min walk from metro Rennes
R de l'Arrivée
R du Départ
MONTPARNASSE

30 The Chicest SHOPPING

LOCAL LIFE | DESIGN | LUXURY

The neighbourhood of St-Germain-des-Prés is historically known for shopping, with streets lined with independent boutiques as well as major international-brand stores. It's also *the* place for style spotting, given it's home to some of Paris' best-dressed inhabitants. Shop till you drop and then sit down at an iconic cafe to admire chic Parisian style.

EQROY/SHUTTERSTOCK ©

How to

Getting here Take line 10 or 12 to metro Sèvres–Babylone.

When to go This neighbourhood is busy all the time, bustling with both tourists and locals. Le Bon Marché will often have *braderie* (clearance) sections during the government-mandated *soldes* or sale season (usually in January, February and June/July) where you can find past-season items for up to 70% off.

Tip During high season (between June and December), the more popular stores will have a queue to enter. Don't be scared off by long lines as they always move fast!

ULYSSEPIXEL/GETTY IMAGES ©

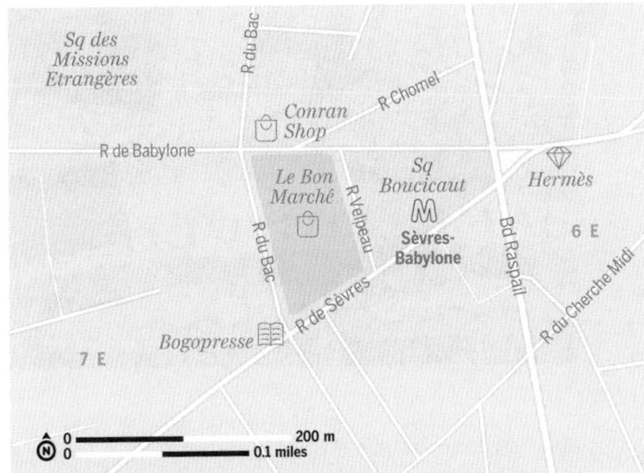

Top left Hermès flagship store
Bottom left Le Bon Marché

The Pick of the Shopping Crop

Le Bon Marché is a historic department store that is home to several floors of the most coveted brands from across the globe. The pieces it carries are impeccably curated and beautifully displayed. On the top floor, you'll find the famous **Rose Bakery's Tea Room**, a great place to catch a break or fuel up. Try its globally famous cakes or salad assortment and quiche that changes daily.

Housed in a building designed by Gustave Eiffel, the **Conran Shop** is dedicated to eclectic design, selling exquisite gifts and homewares. Here you can also feast your eyes on designer furniture. The shop is an epitome of the *savoir-vivre* (know-how on living) that Paris and Parisians are so celebrated for.

Located in front of Le Bon Marché, **Bogopresse** is a magazine kiosk that focuses on trendy, hard-to-come-by titles from all over the globe, curated by the brother duo that runs it. You'll find glossy fashion magazines (think *Purple*), artsy, food magazines like *Eaten*, as well as French titles.

Astier de Villatte is best known for its 18th- and 19th-century-inspired chic, colourless ceramics. It describes its brand as 'an incarnation of Parisian taste', and at its cosy Left Bank boutique, you can find just that. All its creations are made by artisans in its atelier in Paris.

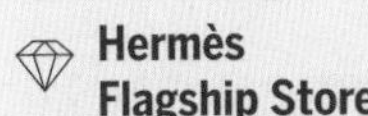

Hermès Flagship Store

The revamped Hermès flagship store is worth a visit even if this brand isn't your style. The beautiful shop has preserved the original art deco mosaic floor from the pool that was once there, which can be best observed with a bird's-eye view from the top floor. Pay close attention to all the details as there are hidden treasures tastefully dispersed across the store, including artworks from Émile Hermès' (President of Hermès) private collection, prints from the Hermès collection of contemporary photographs, as well as a special collection of exclusive objects, like the one-of-a-kind jukebox covered in an iconic Hermès print.

La Vie Café

THE RELEVANCE OF PARIS' STORIED CAFES

One of the allures of St-Germain-des-Prés is spending time at its iconic cafes. Dip your overpriced croissant in the most decadent hot chocolate you've ever experienced, or sip a *verre du vin* (glass of wine) while nibbling on olives and partaking in one of Paris' favourite pastimes: people-watching from the terrasse.

MAZIARZ/SHUTTERSTOCK ©

For many who have visited or studied Paris, thinking about St-Germain-des-Prés conjures up images and stories that took place at one of its cafes. Maybe it's envisioning Picasso in a dimly lit booth making simple doodles at **Café de Flore**, a vivid description of Hemingway's hearty meal of potato salad and one-too-many beers at **Brasserie Lipp**, or imagining your favourite literary and philosophy heroes, like Albert Camus and Simone de Beauvoir, conversing at **Les Deux Magots**.

Each of these three establishments, all located on the same street, has a legendary history that has filled and inspired books and attracted visitors for decades. But there are a few other reasons why they are thriving today, beyond history and Parisian cafe culture, with customers queuing up even in a pandemic.

First, they perfectly embody what Paris does best: marrying the past with the present and allowing all who step foot in them to experience the myths in person, in real life. With unfussy French waiters in classic black-and-white uniforms waltzing around with straightforward menus and trays of food and drinks, and historic memorabilia tastefully scattered around indoors, it feels as if you're stepping back in time. Visitors can come in with the myths they have heard but leave with their own personal memories.

Second, no matter how hectic these places get, there is something so welcoming about the ambience at all three. The cultural icons who frequented these cafes arrived early to work and then dined and revelled with

Left Café de Flore; Brasserie Lipp; Les Deux Magots

PETR KOVALENKOV/SHUTTERSTOCK ©

PETR KOVALENKOV/SHUTTERSTOCK ©

friends until dinner. They would often come back after dinner to keep the night going. In the words of Jean-Paul Sartre, 'We are at home at Café de Flore.' Although staying all day anywhere that isn't a co-working space is now frowned upon in Paris, anyone, Parisian or not, can come here to have a pleasant experience.

Moreover, Parisian cafes are open all day and designed to be enjoyed solo, with close-together tables where you can lean over to read what the stranger to your right or left is devouring. Most often, you are seated facing the street so you can look up from your book or phone and marvel at all the life taking place in front of you. People-watching from a terrasse is an art and the Parisians have mastered it. You never feel alone or out of place at a cafe.

There is something so empowering about the terrasse experience, where you dress up to just lazily lounge and observe

Lastly, Paris is a place to see and to be seen and the best place to start is at one of these three terrasses. There is something so empowering about the terrasse experience, where you dress up to just lazily lounge and observe, with an occasional sip or bite to eat in-between. When you're ready to rejoin the hustle and bustle of the city, you just have to pick up the bill and leave. Remember, you're paying for the experience.

La Crème des Cafés

Café de Flore and Les Deux Magots are located almost next to each other, only separated by the Louis Vuitton boutique, and have historically been rivals when their celebrated clients became loyal to one over the other. There are even historical records of the cafes becoming political! I always get asked: 'Where would you go if you could only go to one?' My answer is always, 'Try both', as people just gravitate more towards one even though they have similar menus, whether it's due to the decor or the ambience. When you do go and visit, make sure you explore indoors as well (I always suggest trying out the bathroom!).

Recommended by Eileen Cho, *a Paris-based writer and photographer from Seattle, Washington. @eileenwcho*

31 Left Bank MAGIC

WALKING TOUR | HISTORY | ARCHITECTURE

This itinerary will take you to all the beautiful and worthwhile landmarks in the St-Germain-des-Prés neighbourhood. You'll experience hundreds of years of history, from stunning royal gardens to a theatre that Marie Antoinette herself visited. Put on good walking shoes and prepare to fall in love.

The Drunken Boat

On **rue Férou**, a tiny street next to the St-Sulpice church, a photogenic wall is covered in Arthur Rimbaud's *Le Bateau Ivre*. The lovely poem is about an imaginary voyage at sea of a sinking ship, offering readers an escape. Rimbaud first recited the poem near this spot.

How to

Getting here Take line 4 or 10 to metro St-Sulpice.

When to go Start early so you can stop and enjoy the public spaces.

Tip Bring snacks, water, sun protection and a book to read at the Jardin du Luxembourg. Watch the locals play chess on the designated chess tables. Carve out extra time to visit the art galleries of St-Germain-des-Prés near rue de Furstemberg.

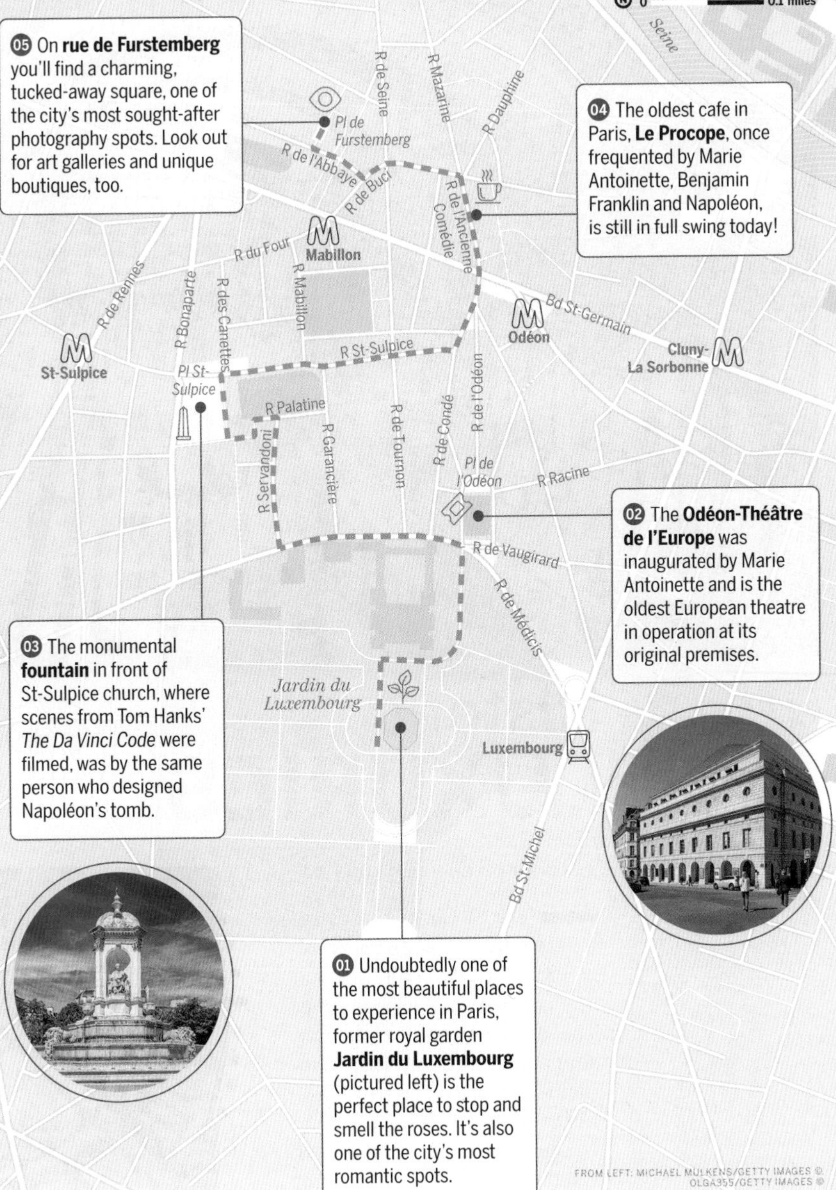

0
0
200 m
0.1 miles
Seine
05 On **rue de Furstemberg** you'll find a charming, tucked-away square, one of the city's most sought-after photography spots. Look out for art galleries and unique boutiques, too.
04 The oldest cafe in Paris, **Le Procope**, once frequented by Marie Antoinette, Benjamin Franklin and Napoléon, is still in full swing today!
R de Seine
R Mazarine
R Dauphine
Pl de Furstemberg
R de l'Abbaye
R de Buci
R de l'Ancienne Comédie
R du Four
Mabillon
R de Rennes
R Bonaparte
R des Canettes
R Mabillon
Bd St-Germain
Odéon
Cluny-La Sorbonne
St-Sulpice
Pl St-Sulpice
R St-Sulpice
R Palatine
R de l'Odéon
R de Condé
R de Tournon
R Garancière
R Servandoni
Pl de l'Odéon
R Racine
02 The **Odéon-Théâtre de l'Europe** was inaugurated by Marie Antoinette and is the oldest European theatre in operation at its original premises.
R de Vaugirard
R de Médicis
03 The monumental **fountain** in front of St-Sulpice church, where scenes from Tom Hanks' *The Da Vinci Code* were filmed, was by the same person who designed Napoléon's tomb.
Jardin du Luxembourg
Luxembourg
Bd St-Michel
01 Undoubtedly one of the most beautiful places to experience in Paris, former royal garden **Jardin du Luxembourg** (pictured left) is the perfect place to stop and smell the roses. It's also one of the city's most romantic spots.

32 Historic LUXURIES

SAVOIR FAIRE | HERITAGE | ART

The St-Germain-des-Prés neighbourhood is historically where many Parisian tastemakers and cultural icons spent time. This experience takes you to some of its cultural highlights, including an art museum, a historic restaurant that's still frequented by the who's who of celebrities, and speciality shops.

SALVADOR MANIQUIZ/SHUTTERSTOCK ©

How to

Getting here Take the metro to Rue du Bac.

When to go There are smaller crowds at the Musée D'Orsay between November and March. Many say that the museum is busier on Tuesdays and Sundays, and that the best time to visit is at lunchtime when the museum's crowd thins out.

Tips The Musée d'Orsay is closed on Mondays and remains open late on Thursdays (until 9.45pm). Reserving tickets online in advance is encouraged.

MARKORD/SHUTTERSTOCK ©

Musée d'Orsay

Paris' second most-visited museum (after the Louvre) is located in a former train station that could just as well be a palace given its beautiful beaux arts architecture. Although it is globally renowned for its impressionist collection, its permanent collection features all art forms, including sculpture and photography. Smaller than the Louvre, this museum can be comprehensively visited and enjoyed in one visit.

The museum's restaurant, **Café Campana**, is situated at the exit of the Impressionist Gallery in a large dining hall underneath elegant frescoes. The menu highlights French cuisine and is quick, delicious and affordable.

A Who's Who Restaurant

The historic restaurant **Le Voltaire** is situated right by the Seine in the same building where

MICHAEL WARWICK/SHUTTERSTOCK ©

Fine Arts Education

The prestigious **École des Beaux-Arts** (School of Fine Arts) is located on rue Bonaparte. With a history spanning 350 years, it's trained some of the world's most famous artists, from Renoir to Degas. Visitors can only access the temporary exhibitions and main courtyard – a must visit!

Top left Main hall, Musée d'Orsay **Bottom left** Musée d'Orsay clock **Above** Le Voltaire restaurant

Voltaire lived. Many come for the history and star-studded people-watching, but stay for the delicious food, including its *oeuf mayonnaise*, which is still on the menu for less than a euro.

Rue Bonaparte

The highest concentration of buildings registered as historic monuments in the 6e can be found on this street. The highly sought-after residential street is also home to historic shops. **Deyrolle**, a shop dedicated to taxidermy and entomology (the classification of species) that opened in 1831, is also a cabinet of curiosities and a museum. A favourite of filmmaker Wes Anderson, the whimsical shop is filled with perfectly preserved animals, from large mammals to insects, collected from all over the globe. You'll also find books, stationery, speciality clothing and sophisticated gift offerings. Note: photography is not allowed.

L'Officine Universelle Buly flagship is another must-visit shop on rue Bonaparte. This romantic apothecary brand was inspired by

Musée d'Orsay Insights

The audioguide is fantastic and necessary for a comprehensive visit of the museum.

Some of the museum's most famous pieces include Manet's *Le Déjeuner Sur l'Herbe* (Luncheon on the Grass), Van Gogh's self-portrait and Millet's *The Gleaners.*

On the 2nd floor, take a peek into the gorgeous *salle des fêtes,* a golden party room with chandeliers, if the doors are open. If not, you could kindly ask a security guard to let you in.

The large clock on the top floor is one of the best photo spots in the city, with panoramic views of Paris in the background.

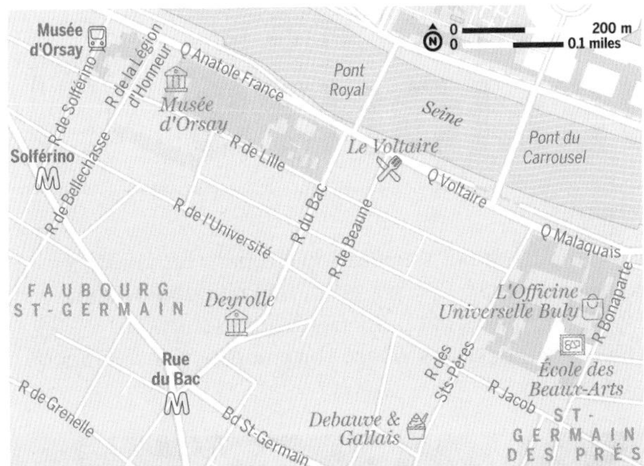

Left Self-portrait, Vincent van Gogh
Below 'Pistoles de Marie Antoinette', Debauve & Gallais

Honoré de Balzac's novel about a Parisian perfumer who was based on a real person, Jean-Vincent Bully. Bully started his apothecary business in 1803 and the brand today sells products using the reformulated original skincare recipes. The highly trained staff can help introduce the products to you, but fan favourites are minebari combs, historically used by the emperors of Japan, and hand creams.

Historic Sweets

The mythical chocolate shop **Debauve & Gallais** has been around since the 18th century when the founder helped mask the taste of Marie Antoinette's medications with his cocoa concoctions. These chocolate medallions, named, appropriately, 'Pistoles de Marie Antoinette', can still be purchased today in gorgeous boxes decorated with motifs of the queen.

This chocolatier was also the official chocolate supplier for Napoléon and several kings of France. In 1823, it invented a healthier chocolate treat using almond milk and orange blossom water. Today, the chocolate shop is still independently owned and family run. Visitors can pick and choose their chocolates at the counter or purchase packaged boxes.

33 A Gastronome's DELIGHTS

GASTRONOMY | ARTISAN | TERROIR

Home to the famous Ferrandi, one of France's top culinary institutes, there are many top food experiences to be discovered in this neighbourhood. Sabrina Goldin, one of the brilliant minds behind Paris' beloved Carbon restaurant, dishes out her favourite addresses where you can experience France's famous gastronomy and food history.

EQROY/SHUTTERSTOCK ©

How to

Getting here Take line 10 or 12 to metro Sèvres–Babylone.

When to go The area is always busy but avoid the pre-lunch or pre-dinner crowds at Poilâne and La Grande Épicerie.

Tips Make sure you check out the specially designed breads at Poilâne. This bakery once even collaborated with Salvador Dalí on a bread chandelier! Its *punitions* (shortbread cookies) make fantastic gifts. La Grande Épicerie offers a delivery service where you can get your purchases delivered to your Parisian address at a designated time.

EQROY/SHUTTERSTOCK ©

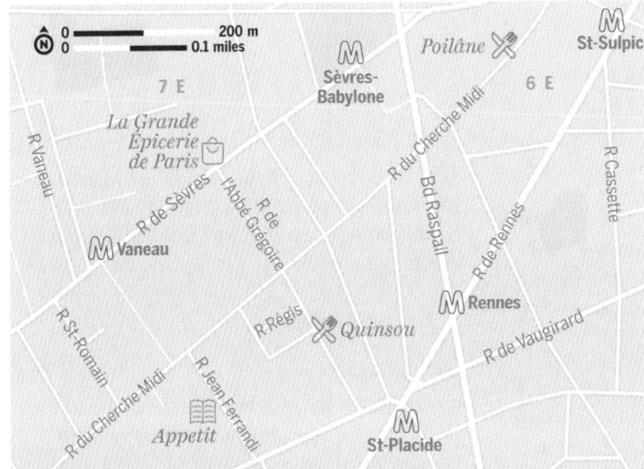

Top left Bread loaves, Poilâne
Bottom left La Grande Épicerie

The Michelin-starred **Quinsou** has the best of both worlds: upscale French-inspired cuisine and the new, conscious approach to sourcing products ethically. It's located on a small street that is important to French cuisine, across from **Ferrandi**. Whatever chef Antonin Bonnet is behind is of the utmost sensitivity and delicacy.

The history behind **Poilâne**, the legendary sourdough bakery, a family business, and the simplicity of the products are what make it so special. Here you'll find no-fuss food with consistent quality and a piece of history in every bite.

Going to **La Grande Épicerie** is the equivalent to the joy some people experience in going luxury shopping. Everything here is fancy and chic – the perfect spot to buy food products for a special occasion or to take back home! You'll find endless rows of food items from all over the globe, carefully arranged by country or region. The prepared foods at the upscale deli in the back and pastries in the front make a great option for a quick meal. The savviest locals do their grocery shopping here.

Appetit is Paris' go-to cookbook bookshop. Parisians still honour the ritual of buying books from independent bookshops and this is an epicurean's paradise. You'll also find kitschy items a gourmand would love!

Quinsou Insights

Its lunch course is the most affordable way to experience the Quinsou magic, but reservations need to be made well in advance online. Its bread is made in-house and chef Antonin Bonnet goes above and beyond to ethically source his produce. Here, the French-inspired menu often highlights Korean flavours as a nod to the chef's family. Chef Bonnet, who is fluent in both English and French, comes out to thoughtfully explain your dishes. Pay attention to all the details of the restaurant, including your silverware! In the summer, the window walls are opened, bringing in a light, sweet breeze.

With thanks to Sabrina Goldin, *a Paris-based Argentinian restaurateur and hospitality consultant. @studio.carbon.paris*

Listings

BEST OF THE REST

Fine Meals

Ralph's €€€

Ralph Lauren's posh American restaurant is located inside his flagship store in the 6e and has excellent burgers, steaks and salads. Finish the meal at Ralph's Coffee out front.

Yen €€

One of the best places in the city for Japanese food can be found in the 6e. Its speciality is handmade soba (buckwheat noodles) but its sashimi and wagyu offerings are also excellent.

Le Relais de L'Entrecote €€

A favourite of locals and tourists, this chain only serves one dish: walnut salad followed by *steak-frites*. Here at the oldest location, all you have to do is tell the waiter how you want your steak cooked.

Dupin €€

This restaurant near Le Bon Marché offers affordable and tasty meals using the best French ingredients. Its chocolate soufflé is an absolute must.

Colorova €€

Whether you're going for lunch, brunch or tea, Colorova near Le Bon Marché is always a good idea. Its innovative menu, plus a chef who has a penchant for pastries, make for a memorable meal in a cosy setting.

Aux Prés €€

French celebrity chef Cyril Lignac rose to fame thanks to television but his businesses offer consistently excellent food. Here you'll find cocktails and his favourite dishes, like crispy salmon sushi and lobster rolls.

Le Bon Saint Pourçain €€€

This small French restaurant on a tiny and romantic street in the 6e offers an intimate dining experience with views of the kitchen no matter where you sit.

Small Bites

Beaupassage €/€€

From Pierre Hermé's tearoom-like cafe to the trendy coffee spot Arabica to Thierry Marx' bakery, you'll find everything you need to satisfy your snack cravings at this shopping arcade and courtyard space.

Le Chocolat Alain Ducasse €

Only good things happen when France's most prized chef decides to venture into chocolate. With two shops in the neighbourhood, you're never far from some of the best chocolate creations in Paris.

Ten Belles €

This bakery roasts its own coffee and its Rive Gauche outpost offers a smaller selection of baked goods and drinks with its prized beans. The chocolate rye cookie and changing, seasonal Danishes are highlights.

Commemorative coin, Monnaie de Paris

Mori Yoshida €

Japanese chef Mori Yoshida's pastry shop is located near Invalides and offers French pastries with a Japanese flair. Matcha, black sesame, cherry blossom and yuzu flavours are the norm here.

Chez Nous €

This inviting and chic wine bar near the Seine is a great place to experience wines and charcuterie plates. The servers are outgoing and friendly without being overwhelming when it comes to wines.

Fruttini by Mo €/€€

This ice-cream shop's speciality is ice cream frozen in fruits and vegetables. Its offerings are seasonal and can range from a tiny fig to a whole melon.

Barthélémy Cheese €

Shop owner Nicole has been in business for over 50 years and has some of the best suggestions for what's in season. Her beautiful shop and display alone are worth the visit.

More Museums

Musée du Luxembourg

This historic museum was the first museum to open to the public in France. Today, it hosts several popular exhibitions throughout the year and is also home to the popular Mademoiselle Angelina tearoom.

Musée Rodin

This museum, created by the sculptor Auguste Rodin in his mansion surrounded by gardens, is now home to many of his creations as well as his art collection. Temporary exhibitions are often blended with the permanent collection.

Monnaie de Paris

France's oldest institution is owned by the French government and is responsible for creating France's coins. The institution hosts contemporary art exhibitions in its historic building.

MICHAEL THALER/SHUTTERSTOCK ©

Institut de France

Other Cultural Highlights

Galerie Kamel Mennour

Kamel Mennour is a well-known gallery owner who has locations in both Paris and London. His main space is located in St-Germain-des-Prés in a large *hôtel particulier* (private mansion). Here you can see some of the work from the contemporary artists he represents for free.

Silencio des Prés

The exclusive and legendary nightclub Silencio has opened a new nightlife hotspot in St-Germain-des-Prés. Taking over the last available independent cinema, this new space is a 360-degree cinema-and-restaurant-in-one.

Institut de France

The 'Protector of Arts, Literature and Science', this French institution is housed in the 6e in a gorgeous building. It's made up of five of France's academies, including the Académie Française, which is responsible for protecting the French language.

Scan to find more things to do in St-Germain & Les Invalides online

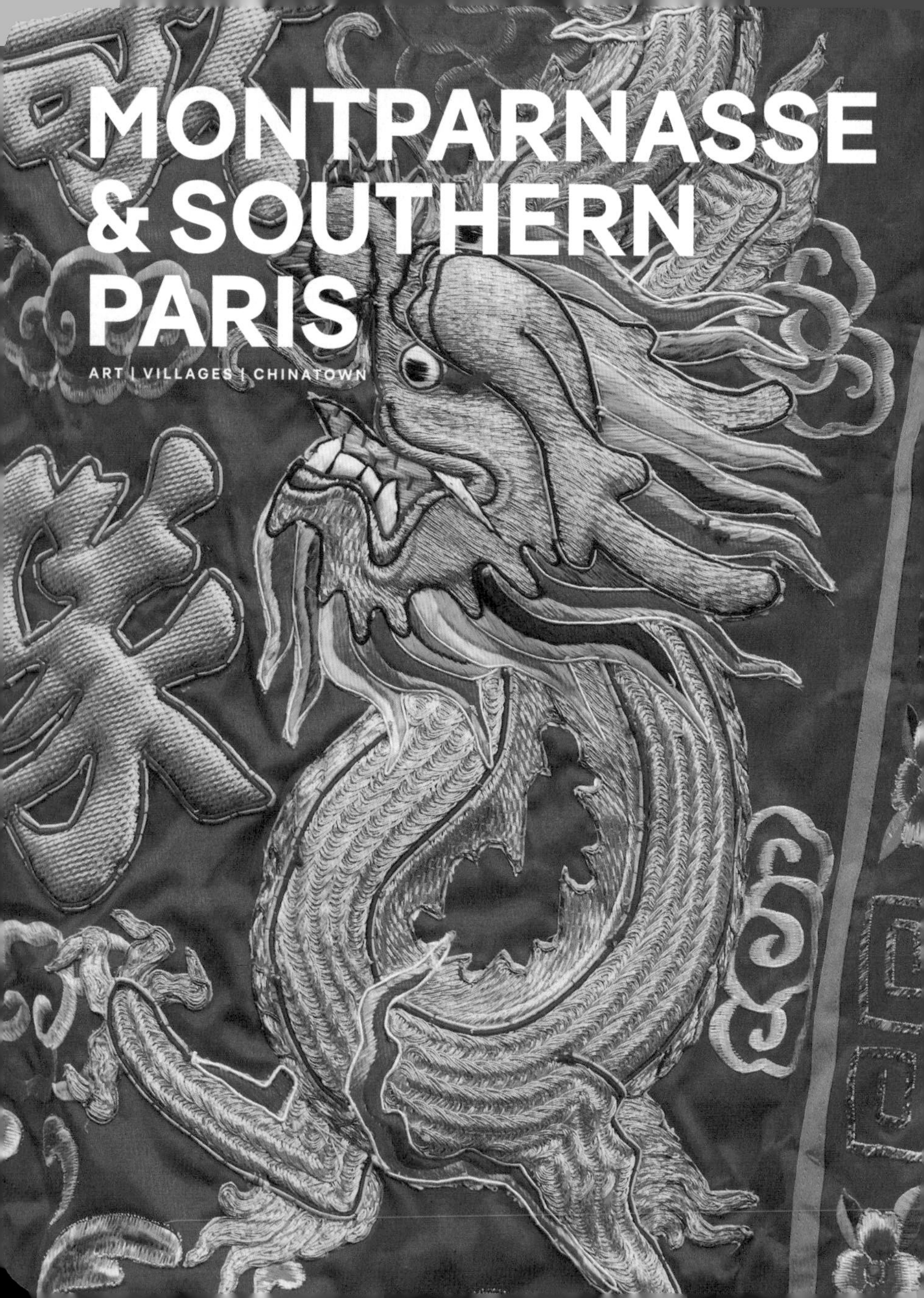
MONTPARNASSE
& SOUTHERN
PARIS
ART | VILLAGES | CHINATOWN

MONTPARNASSE & SOUTHERN PARIS

Trip Builder

TAKE YOUR PICK OF MUST-SEES AND HIDDEN GEMS

This vast swath of southern Paris is full of surprises and discoveries and is a perfect place to explore if you're looking for a local experience. Unpretentious yet seductive, gritty yet full of good vibes, it's a happy mix of typical village-like areas, edgy street art, vast parks and striking contemporary architecture.

Neighbourhood Notes

Best for Picturesque neighbourhoods, cutting-edge architecture and vast parks.

Transport Montparnasse Bienvenüe is the metro hub for Montparnasse and the 15e. Bibliothèque François-Mitterrand and Place d'Italie are convenient 13e stops.

Getting around Walk, ride or use the metro.

Tip Hop on the T3 tram to whizz around Paris' perimeter.

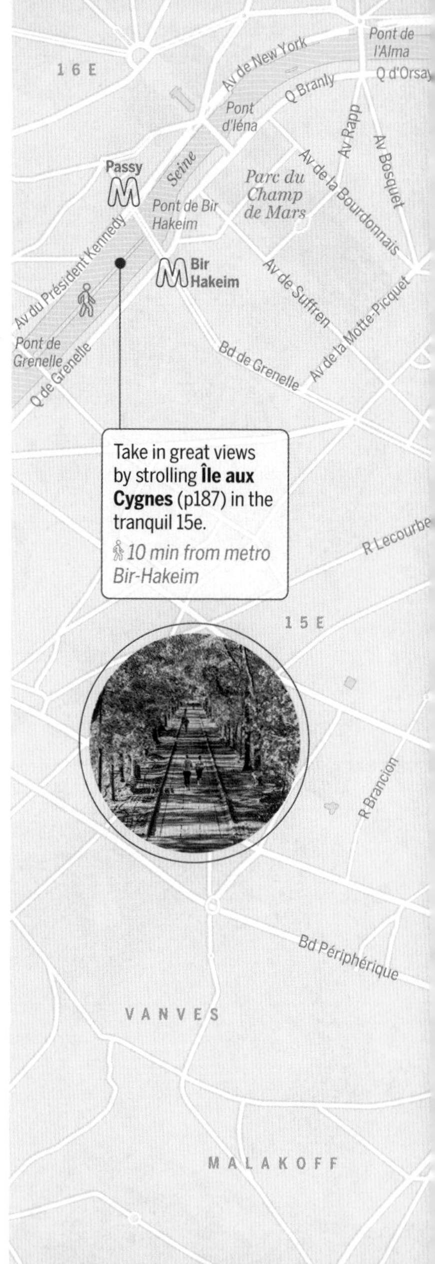

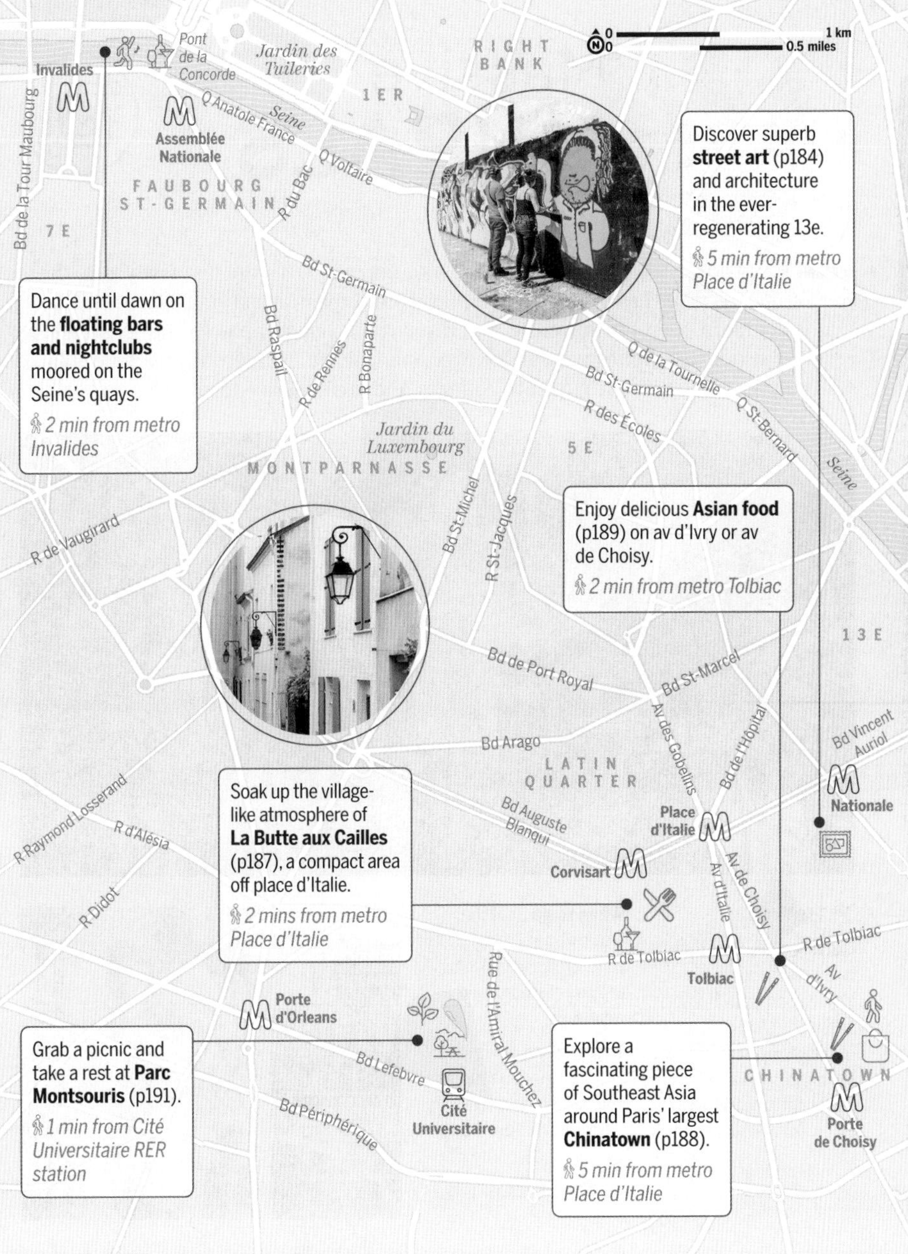
Discover superb **street art** (p184) and architecture in the ever-regenerating 13e.
5 min from metro Place d'Italie
Dance until dawn on the **floating bars and nightclubs** moored on the Seine's quays.
2 min from metro Invalides
Enjoy delicious **Asian food** (p189) on av d'Ivry or av de Choisy.
2 min from metro Tolbiac
Soak up the village-like atmosphere of **La Butte aux Cailles** (p187), a compact area off place d'Italie.
2 mins from metro Place d'Italie
Grab a picnic and take a rest at **Parc Montsouris** (p191).
1 min from Cité Universitaire RER station
Explore a fascinating piece of Southeast Asia around Paris' largest **Chinatown** (p188).
5 min from metro Place d'Italie
0 1 km
0 0.5 miles
Invalides
Pont de la Concorde
Jardin des Tuileries
RIGHT BANK
1ER
Assemblée Nationale
Q Anatole France
Seine
Q Voltaire
FAUBOURG ST-GERMAIN
R du Bac
Bd de la Tour Maubourg
7E
Bd St-Germain
Bd Raspail
R de Rennes
R Bonaparte
Q de la Tournelle
Bd St-Germain
R des Écoles
Q St-Bernard
Seine
Jardin du Luxembourg
MONTPARNASSE
5E
Bd St-Michel
R St-Jacques
R de Vaugirard
13E
Bd de Port Royal
Bd St-Marcel
Av des Gobelins
Bd de l'Hôpital
Bd Vincent Auriol
Bd Arago
LATIN QUARTER
Nationale
Place d'Italie
Bd Auguste Blanqui
R Raymond Losserand
R d'Alésia
Corvisart
Av d'Italie
Av de Choisy
R Didot
R de Tolbiac
R de Tolbiac
Tolbiac
Av d'Ivry
Rue de l'Amiral Mouchez
Porte d'Orleans
Bd Lefebvre
Bd Périphérique
Cité Universitaire
CHINATOWN
Porte de Choisy

34 Massive MURALS

ART | CULTURE | WALKING

Paris doesn't limit itself to iconic monuments. Over the last few years, the 13e *arrondissement* has emerged as a playground for international street artists and is a superb open-air museum. Wherever you go east of place d'Italie, street art has become a familiar part of the urban landscape. Numerous façades and walls are embellished with graffiti, collages and striking masterpieces.

How to

Getting here Take metro line 6 to Place d'Italie station and walk along bd Vincent Auriol. A map of the various murals can be found online – very useful for locating the lesser-known murals.

When to go Beat the crowds by planning your stroll mid-morning or mid-afternoon on weekdays.

Tours It's not a bad idea to take a guided tour (in English) of the district – **Street Art Tour Paris** (streetarttourparis.com) comes recommended.

JULIEN JEAN ZAYATZ/SHUTTERSTOCK ©

Far left Mural by Hush, bd Vincent Auriol **Bottom left** *Les Trois Âges* by Borondo, rue du Chevaleret **Near left** La Felicità

Mural-Spotting in the 13e

A Giant Street-Art Scene Over 30 monumental murals enliven streets and thoroughfares in an area between av de France, rue de Tolbiac and bd Vincent Auriol, with more being added every year. Moseying past a few of these cheery murals is a great way to explore less-visited neighbourhoods.

Favourite Frescoes Highlights include a colourful **fresco** (13 rue Lahire) by famous artist Inti, **Bach** (57 rue Clisson), the elaborate **Sun Daze** (167 bd Vincent Auriol), created by the talented twins How and Nosm, and, on an adjacent building, a splendid portrait of a **geisha-like woman** (169 bd Vincent Auriol) by British artist Hush, **Le Chat** (cnr bd Vincent Auriol and rue Nationale) and monumental **La Marianne** (186 rue Nationale) by Shepard Fairey, which represents the symbol of the French Republic.

Other great works to look for include the strikingly expressive **Turncoat** (190 rue Nationale) by D*Face (who is from London), and the equally stunning **Rise Above Level** (cnr bd Auriol and rue Jeanne d'Arc), another massive mural by Shepard Fairey. On the opposite side of bd Vincent Auriol, it's impossible to miss the awesome **Dancer** (98 bd Vincent Auriol), with a strapline (*'Et j'ai retenu mon souffle'* – 'And I hold my breath'), by the collective Faile. More information (and an interactive map) can be found on boulevardparis13.com.

Artistic Immersion

Most colourful mural The giant *Mona Lisa* by Okuda.

Restaurant with murals La Felicità, inside an old train depot.

Most meaningful mural The one by SPY, because of his conceptual approach that stands out from the others.

Best perspective Several amazing murals can be seen between the Place d'Italie and Quai de la Gare metro stations (line 6).

Most secret mural Spot 13, a graffiti hotspot below Lavo//matik gallery.

Most interesting street for murals Bd Vincent Auriol.

Most poignant The work of Borondo, showing the three ages of life.

Most elegant The poetic and chic work of Pantonio.

Tips by Kasia Klon, *artist and tour guide in Paris.* *@streetarttourparis*

35 Secret VILLAGES

PICTURESQUE | AUTHENTIC | OFF THE BEATEN TRACK

From Butte aux Cailles in the 13e to Île aux Cygnes in the 15e, you're going to experience little-known, pocket-sized neighbourhoods that scream village life. With small houses, flowered gardens, very few cars and no noise, they all feature a welcoming bucolic atmosphere, far from the hustle and bustle you'd expect from a city this size.

JEROME LABOUYRIE/SHUTTERSTOCK ©

How to

Getting here Place d'Italie (13e), Denfert-Rochereau (14e), Pernety (14e) and Javel-André Citroën are the most convenient metro stations.

Getting around Use the metro (line 6) to get from one *arrondissement* to the next.

When to go Weekdays are very peaceful.

Hidden spot Explore a section of the former Petite Ceinture du 15e steam railway line, which stretches for 1.3km, with biodiverse habitats including forest, grassland and prairies.

ROMAN MALANCHUK/SHUTTERSTOCK ©

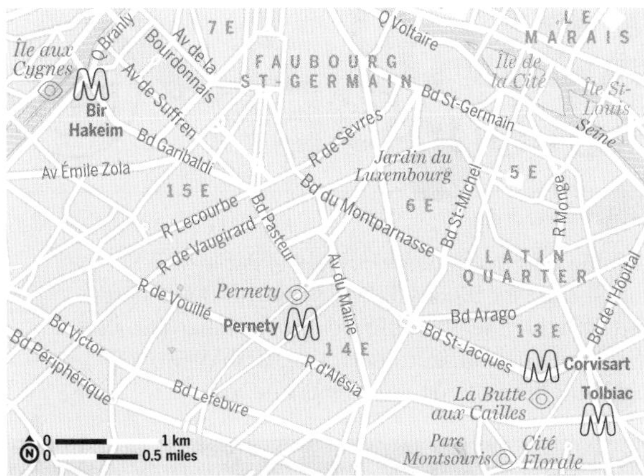

Choose Your Neighbourhood

Paris' Best-Kept Secret A stone's throw east of Parc Montsouris, the micro-neighbourhood of the **Cité Florale** is a gem to wander in. Built in the 1920s, the 'Floral City' comprises five streets all named after flowers and flanked by small houses whose façades are covered with ivy, wild vines and flowers.

Village Life The **Butte aux Cailles** is a compact area off place d'Italie, where cobblestoned streets are lined with quaint houses. It has plenty of fabulous dining options and bars popular with students and locals.

Island Life Paris' little-known third island, the artificial **Île aux Cygnes**, was formed in 1827 to protect the river port and measures just 850m by 11m. On the western side of the Pont de Grenelle is a soaring one-quarter-scale Statue of Liberty replica, inaugurated in 1889. Walk east along the tree-lined walkway that runs the length of the island for knockout Eiffel Tower views.

Bohemian Atmosphere Nestled on the outskirts of the Montparnasse train station, the **Pernety** district has retained its intimate character. With its pedestrian lanes and charming brick buildings, it's entirely different from the Haussmannian architectural style that characterises much of the rest of Paris.

Step Back in Time Paris' traditional village atmosphere thrives along **rue Daguerre**, 14e. Tucked just southwest of the Denfert-Rochereau metro station, this narrow street is lined with florists, cheese shops, bakeries, greengrocers, delis and classic cafes. Sunday mornings are especially lively.

Top left Cité Florale **Bottom left** Statue of Liberty replica, Île aux Cygnes

Atmospheric Streets & Squares

In the Pernety area (14e), look for **rue des Thermopyles**, where you can sample authentic, simple village life. In the 15e, **rue St-Charles** (between av Émile Zola and Rond-Point St-Charles) is *the* place to shop like a real Parisian. Here you'll find traditional bakeries, groceries, pastry shops, cheesemongers and delis. In the 13e, **rue de la Butte aux Cailles** has numerous traditional restaurants, including Le Temps des Cerises. It also features some great street art by Miss.Tic. Also in the 13e, **Square des Peupliers** is one of the few places in Paris where you can see individual houses with private gardens.

Mélanie Després *is a historian and tour guide in Paris. Facebook: @visitesaufildelart*

36 ASIAN Flavours

CHINATOWN | STROLLING | RESTAURANTS

Southeast of place d'Italie and near rue de Tolbiac is Paris' largest Chinatown. Don't let the massive tower blocks dating from the 1960s deter you from exploring this district, which feels so different from other Parisian neighbourhoods. It's a fascinating piece of Southeast Asia, with plenty of surprises, including culinary delights, colourful festivals and art.

LP2 STUDIO/SHUTTERSTOCK ©

How to

Getting here Take metro line 6 to pl d'Italie station.

Getting around Walk along av d'Ivry, av de Choisy, rue Baudricourt and adjacent streets.

When to go Chinatown is liveliest on weekends.

Green spot Parc de Choisy, a soothing park off av de Choisy.

Hidden spots South of rue de Tolbiac, passage Bourgoin and passage National are two lovely paved roads flanked with private houses.

DANIEL THIERRY/GETTY IMAGES ©

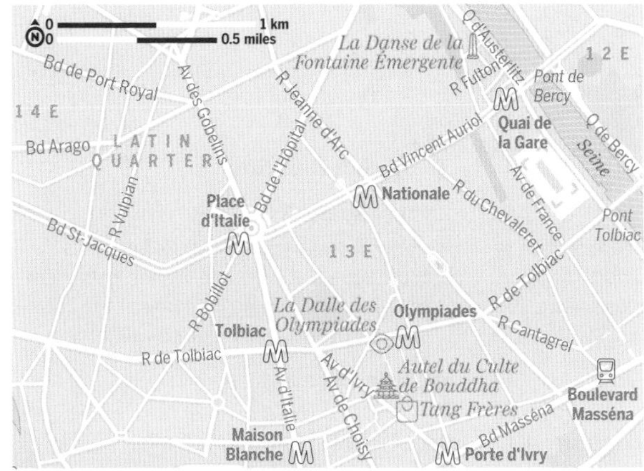

Top left Chinese New Year parade
Bottom left Autel du Culte de Bouddha

Glimmers of Asian Cultures

Art & Culture If you're a fan of underground cultures, head to **La Dalle des Olympiades**, off rue de Tolbiac. This vast concrete esplanade with platformed pedestrian zones surrounded by towers has become the focal point for local K-Pop dancers and skateboarders. On rue Paul Klee, **La Danse de la Fontaine Émergente** (Dance of the Emerging Fountain) is a large fountain built of stainless steel, plastic and glass, designed by French-Chinese sculptor Chen Zhen. Completed in 2008, it looks like a giant stylised dragon winding its way across the square, emerging and submerging from the concrete pavement. High-pressure water flows inside the sculpture. The most unusual sacred site in Paris must be the **Autel du Culte de Bouddha** (37 rue du Disque). This small yet colourful Buddhist temple is hidden in an underground car park beneath a tower block.

Food & Shopping For any Asian food you can imagine as well as many decorative and household items, shop at **Tang Frères** (48 av d'Ivry), the biggest Asian store in Paris (and possibly Europe). Nestled beneath the towers on avs d'Ivry and de Choisy you'll find great Vietnamese *pho* (noodle soup) bars, family-run restaurants serving homemade dumplings and spicy soups, as well as traditional Chinese pastry shops. Some of them have terraces that are great for a bout of people-watching.

Chinese New Year

The best time to immerse yourself in Chinatown is during Chinese New Year (also known as Spring Festival), usually in late January or February. With about 2000 participants and more than 200,000 spectators, it's one of the most spectacular events in the city. Celebrations typically last about two weeks and feature colourful parades as well as lion and dragon dances. Expect brightly lit red lanterns, firecrackers and performances by ribbon dancers, drummers, cymbal players and acrobats wearing traditional costumes. It kicks off in front of Tang Frères supermarket on av d'Ivry. For exact dates, check mairie13.paris.fr/culture.

Listings

BEST OF THE REST

Exciting Neobistros

Simone Le Resto €€

A generous smattering of pavement terrace tables flags this vibrant neobistro north of place d'Italie. Inventive, tempting menus are created in the open kitchen from high-quality products.

Le Sévéro €€

Steaks served with sensational *frites* (fries) are the mainstay of this upmarket bistro not far from Montparnasse; other meat specialities include black pudding and pigs' trotters.

Le Beurre Noisette €€

This eatery with a convivial chocolate-toned dining room in the heart of the 15e prepares meat dishes served with *beurre noisette* (brown butter sauce, named for its hazelnut colour).

Legendary Brasseries

La Closerie des Lilas €€

Hemingway, Picasso and Samuel Beckett patronised the 'Lilac Enclosure' (opened 1847), which features an upmarket restaurant and a lovable brasserie with a pavement terrace.

La Rotonde €€

Around since 1911, elegant La Rotonde stands out from the Montparnasse 'historic brasserie' crowd for its superior food, including meat from Parisian butcher extraordinaire Hugo Desnoyer and extravagant seafood platters.

Le Dôme €€€

A 1930s art deco extravaganza of the formal white-tablecloth and bow-tied-waiter variety, Le Dôme is one of the swishest places around Montparnasse for shellfish platters.

Asian Delights

Camly – Bo Bun 2 Go €

Halfway between place d'Italie and Bibliothèque Nationale de France, this great little restaurant serves up some of the 13e's best Vietnamese cuisine in a sleek interior.

Pho Bành Cúon 14 €

This small, buzzy restaurant (also known as Pho 14) right in Chinatown is wildly popular with in-the-know locals for its super-fresh and astonishingly cheap *pho*.

Thieng Heng €

This takeaway joint in the heart of Chinatown dishes up giant *banh mi* (Vietnamese stuffed baguettes), which have earned Thieng Heng a cult following.

Stylish Swimming Pools

Piscine de la Butte aux Cailles

Built in 1924, this art deco swimming complex – a historical monument – has a spectacular vaulted indoor pool and, since 2017, Paris' only Nordic (open-air) pool. Near place d'Italie.

La Rotonde

Piscine Joséphine Baker

Floating on the Seine off Bibliothèque Nationale de France, this striking swimming pool named after the 1920s American singer is popular in summer when the roof slides back.

Green Spaces

Parc Montsouris

South of the 14e, this sprawling lakeside park planted with horse-chestnut, yew, cedar, weeping beech and buttonwood trees is a delightful picnic spot and has endearing playground areas.

Parc Georges Brassens

This park in the 15e has a large central pond bordered by lawns, and gardens featuring roses and medicinal and aromatic plants. The sloping hill is home to a vineyard.

Parc André Citroën

In this park west of the 15e, the central lawn is flanked by greenhouses, dancing fountains, an elevated reflecting pool and smaller gardens.

Arts & Galleries

Galerie Itinerrance

Testament to the 13e's ongoing creative renaissance, this gallery showcases graffiti and street art, and can advise on street-art tours of the neighbourhood. South of the 13e.

Fondation Cartier pour l'Art Contemporain

Designed by Jean Nouvel, this stunning glass-and-steel building in Montparnasse hosts temporary exhibits on contemporary art in a diverse variety of media.

Les Docks

Framed by a wave-like glass façade, this transformed Seine-side warehouse off Bibliothèque Nationale de France houses the French fashion institute. Other draws include huge riverside terraces and a popular Australian rooftop bar.

RRRAINBOW/GETTY IMAGES ©

Parc Montsouris

La Fab

French fashion designer and art collector agnès b. opened this gallery in a striking new building in 2020. Her collection of contemporary works is presented in themed exhibitions. Near Bibliothèque Nationale de France.

Wine, Beer & Music

Poinçon

Half trendy bar and half slick bistro bathing in a warm atmosphere, Poinçon occupies a delightfully restored 1867-built railway station that was part of the Petite Ceinture.

Félicie

This unpretentious neighbourhood cafe in the 14e with a big heated pavement terrace, fun-loving staff and a laid-back vibe is a quintessentially Parisian spot to hang out any time of day.

Bateau El Alamein

Strung with terracotta pots of flowers, this deep-purple boat has a Seine-side terrace for sitting amid tulips and enjoying live bands. Off Bibliothèque Nationale de France.

DAY TRIPS
FESTIVITIES | WINE | NATURE

Bonus Online Experience

▸ **See Monet's Art in Bloom**

DAY TRIPS
Trip Builder

TAKE YOUR PICK OF MUST-SEES AND HIDDEN GEMS

Although you could spend years in Paris without running out of things to see and do, there's also a wealth of sights and activities just a short train ride away. Escape hectic city life for a day to explore magnificent châteaux, Champagne cellars, medieval cathedrals, tranquil forests and chic seaside resorts.

Trip Notes

Best for Grand palaces, wine tasting and getting back to nature.

Transport & getting around Most places are easy to reach by train. Hiring a bike can be a pleasant option for getting around and a car can give access to otherwise hard-to-reach side stops.

Tips Châteaux and gardens are often closed on Mondays.

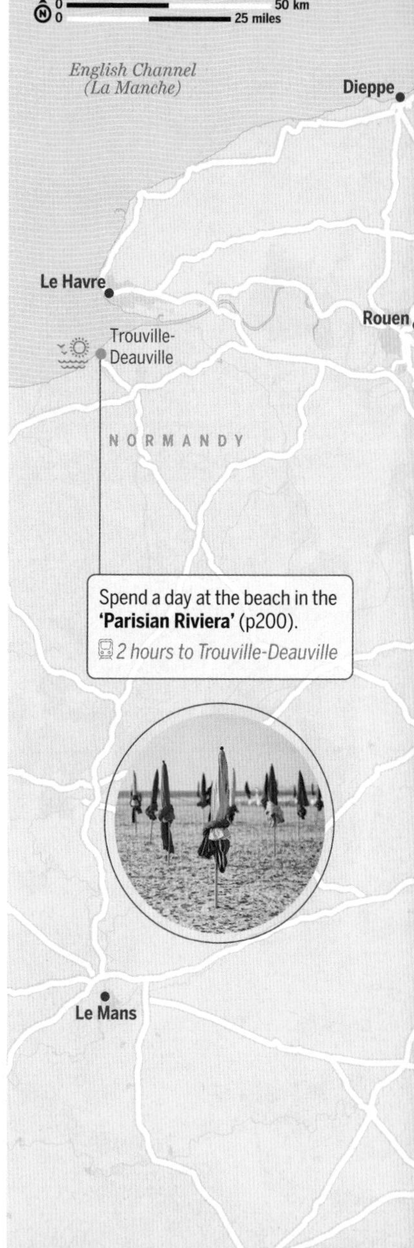

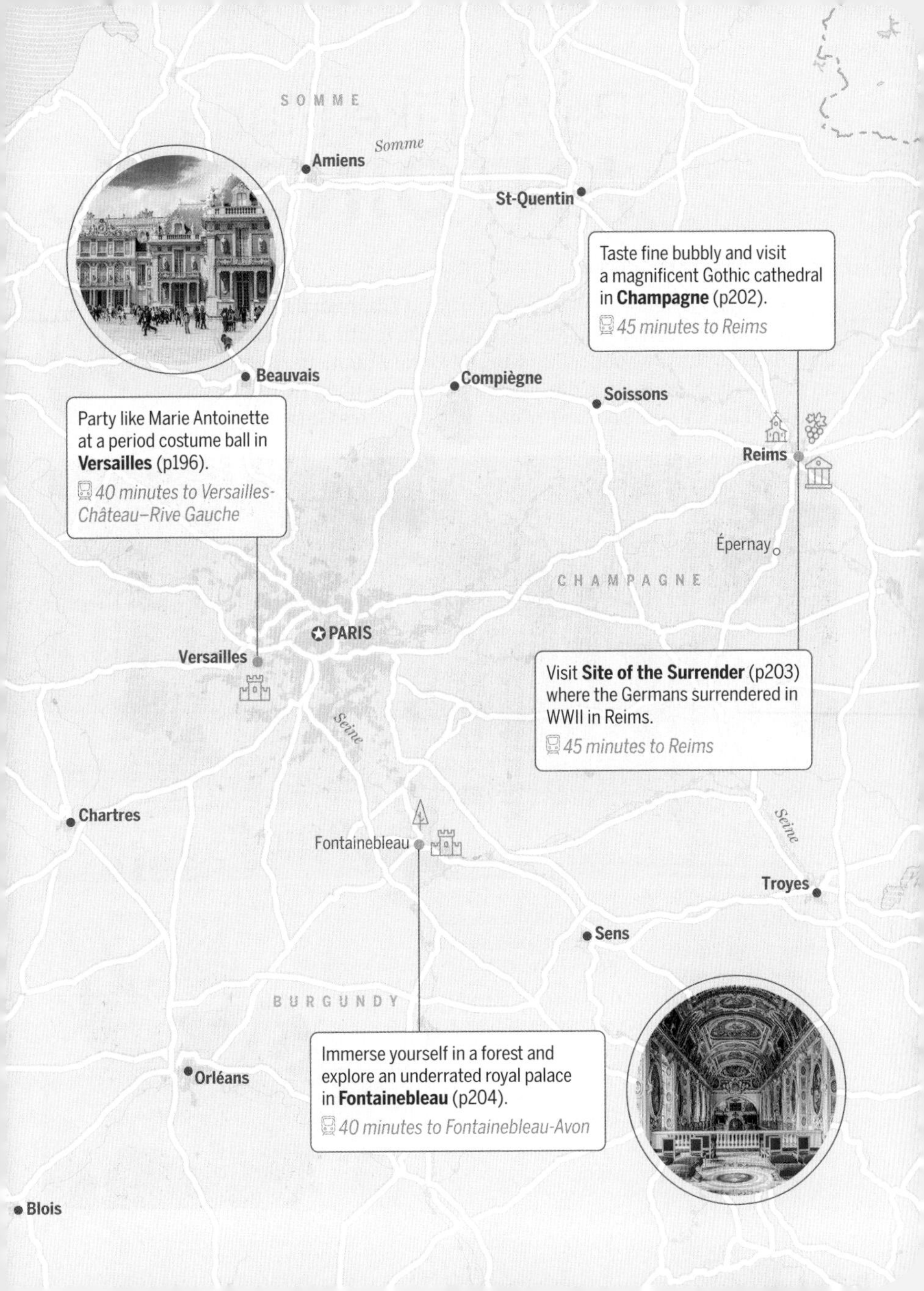

Party like Marie Antoinette at a period costume ball in **Versailles** (p196).

40 minutes to Versailles-Château–Rive Gauche

Taste fine bubbly and visit a magnificent Gothic cathedral in **Champagne** (p202).

45 minutes to Reims

Visit **Site of the Surrender** (p203) where the Germans surrendered in WWII in Reims.

45 minutes to Reims

Immerse yourself in a forest and explore an underrated royal palace in **Fontainebleau** (p204).

40 minutes to Fontainebleau-Avon

SOMME

Somme

Amiens

St-Quentin

Beauvais

Compiègne

Soissons

Reims

Épernay

CHAMPAGNE

PARIS

Versailles

Seine

Chartres

Fontainebleau

Seine

Troyes

Sens

BURGUNDY

Orléans

Blois

37 Party Like Marie ANTOINETTE

HISTORY I PALACES I DANCE

As you wander through the extravagant **Château de Versailles**, it's fun to imagine what it might have been like to attend lavish formal balls there in the time of the Sun King or Marie Antoinette. But there's no need to limit yourself to daydreaming – for one night each year, you can travel back in time and experience it at the **Fêtes Galantes**.

TAKASHI IMAGES/SHUTTERSTOCK ©

How to

Getting here & around RER line C to Versailles Château – Rive Gauche, approximately 40 minutes, then a 10-minute walk.

When to go The ball is held yearly on a Monday in late May/early June and runs from 7pm to midnight.

How much There are several ticket levels, ranging from €155 to €530.

Tips A quality, period-appropriate costume is required. The last RER back leaves before midnight, so you'll need to hire a car or spend the night to catch the entire event.

LUDOVIC MARIN/AFP VIA GETTY IMAGES ©

Far left Hall of Mirrors, Château de Versailles **Bottom and near left** Guests, Fêtes Galantes

As one of the most-visited attractions in France, the awe-inspiring Château de Versailles receives nearly 10 million visitors every year. Unsurprisingly, it's usually a very crowded and chaotic place. But there's a way to experience Versailles in an intimate, magical way that few tourists ever do.

Each year since 2015, the Fêtes Galantes costume ball has been held at the palace in the late spring. The ball is always centred around a theme, such as 'Marie Antoinette and Fashion', and the evening is immersive, with presenters and attendees in full, elaborate 18th-century costume.

The participants, who come from around the world, are allowed to visit some palace rooms that are not usually open to the public, such as the private apartments of Madame du Barry and Madame de Pompadour. The evening includes live baroque music concerts, demonstrations of period entertainment and games and even dancing lessons – in case you're not already well-versed in the minuet. After a buffet of dainty hors d'oeuvre and bite-sized sweets, guests head to the dazzling **Hall of Mirrors** for the grand ball to try out their new baroque dance moves.

Once the ball draws to a close, the evening ends with a spectacular fireworks show, viewed from the Hall of Mirrors through its floor-to-ceiling windows.

Go for Baroque: Event Tips

I've been to this exceptional event several times; here is my advice for the best experience. It's worth investing in a high-quality, historically accurate costume and accessories, either high-end hire or from a professional costume designer. Arrive early in the afternoon so you'll have time to enjoy the beautiful gardens of Versailles and take photos there in costume. Ideally, reserve a hotel room near the château so you can get dressed there in comfort and then arrive on foot. Book tickets well in advance – it's a very popular event!

Olympe de Bagatelle *is a costume maker, 18th-century fashion expert and wig designer. @decorum_et_bagatelle*

RAZVAN/GETTY IMAGES ©

Fontainebleau Forest

THE BIRTHPLACE OF NATURE TOURISM

Vast Fontainebleau national forest encompasses more than 20,000 hectares of oak, pine and beech trees as well as gorges and striking rock formations. A popular weekend destination for Parisians escaping for some fresh air, it's also rich in history.

Up until the 17th century, this expansive woodland was known as the Forêt de Bière – not because its fountains once flowed with ale, but from the word *bruyère* (heather). From the 10th century, it was a hunting ground for the kings of France, and the Château de Fontainebleau was primarily a seasonal lodging where French royalty stayed during the autumn hunting season. Later the forest's natural resources were utilised for industrial purposes – its sandstone was used to make paving stones for the streets of Paris and wood from its oaks was formed into barrels for ageing wine.

In 1839, an ex-soldier named Claude-François Denecourt started writing guidebooks describing walks and interesting sights in the former royal estate and, in 1842, he created the world's first marked walking trails there, pioneering hiking as a leisure activity. The network of more than 100km of forest paths that he designed, the *sentiers bleus,* are still marked today by blue lines painted on trees and rocks and known as the Denecourt-Colinet trails. Along the winding trails he constructed, he also built monuments, stairways, grottoes and fountains. Atop a hill, a stone observation tower, also named after Denecourt, was inaugurated by Napoléon III in 1853.

In 1861, more than 10 years before Yellowstone became the first national park in the United States, part of Fontainebleau Forest became the world's first nature preserve.

From left Fontainebleau Forest; Horse rider, Fontainebleau Forest; Musée des Peintres de Barbizon (Barbizon Museum of Painters)

PHOTOFORT 77/SHUTTERSTOCK ©

PACK-SHOT/SHUTTERSTOCK ©

Bouldering, Cycling and More

The forest is also a renowned destination for bouldering and rock-climbing and has been since the 19th century when it was used by French alpinists as a training ground for Himalayan mountain climbs. Today there are hundreds of bouldering and rock-climbing routes in several different areas, including **Trois Pignons** and the **Gorges d'Apremont**.

Claude-François Denecourt created the world's first marked walking trails in Fontainebleau Forest, pioneering hiking as a leisure activity.

Other popular activities in the forest include horseback riding and mountain biking, with designated paths for each. Many equestrian centres are located around the forest and offer rides with or without an instructor, while several businesses in surrounding towns, including Avon and Fontainebleau, offer cycle hire and guided cycling tours in the forest.

Another possibility is hiring a horse-drawn carriage, departing from the Château de Fontainebleau, for a two-hour ride through the forest. For a more unusual way to explore the forest, you can opt for a hike with donkeys or even dog sledding – though snow in the forest these days is rare, so the dog team pulls a wheeled cart rather than an actual sled.

The Forest as Muse

In the 19th century, a group of painters, including Corot, Millet and Rousseau, set up shop in the village of **Barbizon**, on the edge of the forest, and found inspiration for their landscapes in the forest's rich scenery. Known as the Barbizon school, they paved the way for the impressionists, such as Monet, Sisley and Renoir, who later also visited the Forest of Fontainebleau to paint woodland scenes in *plein air*.

38 Stroll the Parisian RIVIERA

BEACHES I FOOD I HISTORY

Normandy's seaside resorts of **Deauville** and **Trouville-sur-Mer**, known as the 'Parisian Riviera', are the closest beach towns to Paris. Chic Deauville, where Coco Chanel opened her first boutique in 1913, is known for its racecourse and film festival while lower-key Trouville has handsome villas, literary connections and fantastic seafood.

SIEMPREVERDE22/GETTY IMAGES ©

How to

Getting here & around Direct trains from Gare St-Lazare to Trouville-Deauville take just over two hours. Last returns are between 6pm and 8pm, depending on the day. Both towns are easily navigated on foot.

When to go The beaches are best in summer, but spring and autumn are less crowded. Pre-book trains and restaurants in early September, when the American Film Festival of Deauville takes place.

Markets Trouville's outdoor market is every Wednesday and Sunday morning, while Deauville's market hall runs daily until 1.30pm.

ROSSHELEN/GETTY IMAGES ©

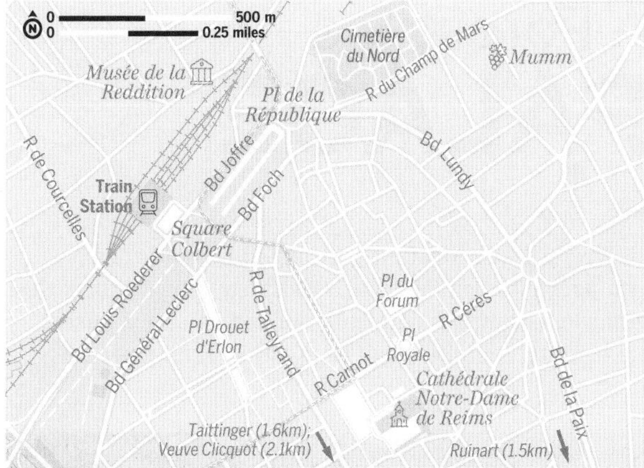

Top left Cathédrale Notre-Dame de Reims **Bottom left** Cellar, Veuve Clicquot

The ground deep below the towns of Reims and Épernay is full of ancient Gallo-Roman chalk quarries, connected by a network of tunnels. It was Nicolas Ruinart, in the 18th century, who first converted these quarries into Champagne production cellars. Today you can visit many of these *caves* (cellars) for guided tours and tastings. Reims is closer to Paris than Épernay – 45 minutes by train as opposed to an hour and a half – and has much to offer besides bubbly, including WWII memorials and a stunning medieval cathedral.

Tours and Tastings

Many of the best-known names in Champagne are here, including Ruinart, Veuve Clicquot, Mumm and Taittinger, offering guided or self-guided visits of their cellars followed by tastings. Some smaller houses, such as Charles de Cazanove, are also open for visits, but most of the smallest, independent producers are located outside of town and can only be visited by either hiring a car or joining an organised tour.

A Striking Cathedral

The ornate 13th-century **Cathédrale Notre-Dame de Reims** is a breathtaking example of Gothic architecture with an important place in French history. Twenty-five kings of France were crowned here over more than 600 years, from Louis VIII in 1223 to Charles X in 1825. Severely damaged during WWI, the cathedral was later rebuilt; several of its stained-glass windows are modern, designed by Marc Chagall in the 1970s. Every summer, free night-time sound and light shows are projected on the cathedral façade on weekends and holidays.

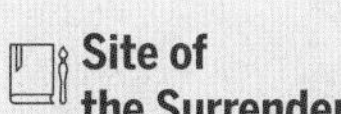

Site of the Surrender

While it's mostly known for Champagne and coronations, Reims also played an important role in WWII history. It was here that the Germans surrendered to the Allies on 7 May 1945, in the headquarters of General Dwight D Eisenhower. The room where the unconditional surrender was signed, with the original battle maps still affixed to its walls, is now the **Musée de la Reddition** (Museum of the Surrender). It's located inside a high school just north of the train station and features exhibits of memorabilia and artefacts as well as a short film in multiple languages.

40 A Forest & a PALACE

NATURE I PALACES I HISTORY

While the Château de Versailles is constantly thronged by hordes of visitors, there's another royal palace just outside Paris that's equally grand, with the added benefits of being far less crowded – and surrounded by an expansive forest. Hop on the train and head to Fontainebleau for a day of grandeur and peaceful rambling in nature.

MISTERVLAD/SHUTTERSTOCK ©

How to

Getting here & around Transilien R Montargis or Montereau train from Gare de Lyon to Fontainebleau-Avon (40 minutes), then line 1 Les Lilas bus to the château (10 minutes). A Navigo day pass for zones 1–5 is the most cost-efficient option as it includes metro, train and bus.

When to go The château is open daily except for Tuesdays. Château admission is free on the first Sunday of every month; pre-booking is recommended.

Tip Bring a picnic lunch for the hike.

V_E/SHUTTERSTOCK ©

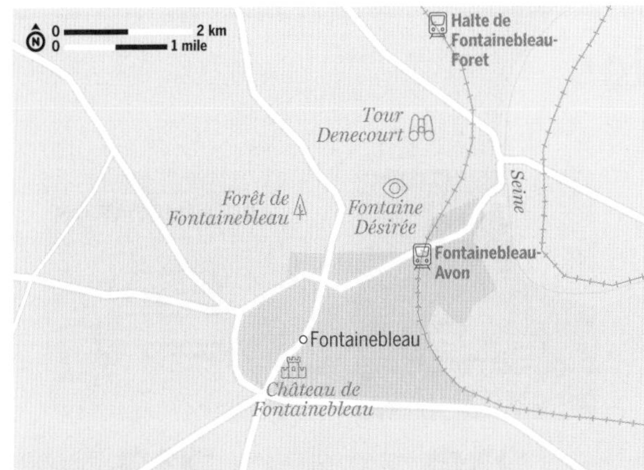

Top left Château de Fontainebleau
Bottom left Salon Louis XIII, Château de Fontainebleau

Get Some Fresh Air in a Tranquil Forest

Fontainebleau Forest has more than 400km of well-marked hiking trails ranging from easy to strenuous. As you exit the Fontainebleau-Avon station, you can turn left and walk straight up into the forest in less than five minutes. From the forest's edge, you can follow the blue Denecourt-Colinet No 2 trail signs up to the **Tour Denecourt** lookout tower for a scenic view. This moderate route of about one hour passes several 19th-century fountains and one of them, the **Fontaine Désirée**, has a stone table and benches – the perfect stopping point for a picnic lunch. Note that no forest maps are sold at the train station, so it's best to download offline hiking routes before arriving. On Saturday and Sunday mornings, some of the Montargis trains stop in the forest (**Halte de Fontainebleau-Forêt**) approximately 4km from Fontainebleau-Avon, if you want to get off earlier and hike down through the forest to the town.

Explore a Château That's Rich in History

While not nearly as well-known as Versailles, the **Château de Fontainebleau** holds a more important place in French history as it was inhabited by every French monarch for nearly 800 years, since its beginnings in the 12th century. With more than 1500 rooms, the sprawling complex is a fascinating melange of different architectural styles, from medieval and Renaissance to rocaille and neoclassical. Famous residents include Thomas Becket, Catherine de' Medici, Louis XIV, Marie Antoinette and Napoléon.

Historic Gardens

The château's extensive gardens and park also deserve a visit, and admission to them is free. Covering more than 120 hectares, they include a grand canal; an extensive formal 17th-century French garden created by André Le Nôtre, who also designed the gardens of Versailles; and an informal, English-style garden built in 1812. The grounds can be visited either on foot, aboard the miniature train that runs through the estate or by horse-drawn carriage. The train rides include an audioguide in several languages. You can also hire small rowboats for excursions on the large carp pond.

Practicalities

Right Av des Champs-Élysées

EASY STEPS FROM THE AIRPORT TO THE CITY CENTRE

Most international airlines fly to Aéroport de Charles de Gaulle, 28km northeast of central Paris. In French it is commonly called 'Roissy' after the suburb in which it's located. Inter-terminal shuttle services are free. The airport is linked to the city by rail, buses and taxi services.

AT THE AIRPORT

SIM CARDS

You'll get a better deal buying a SIM in the city. It's also hard to find advice on best packages and set-up at the airport. To buy one immediately, get a local SIM *(mobicarte)* at a Relay shop (in each terminal).

MONEY

ATMs are located throughout the terminals. They accept foreign cards and have multiple language options. International currency exchange *(bureaux de change)* services are located in the Arrivals areas of each terminal, although you'll probably get better rates at banks in the city centre.

DEEP PIXEL/GETTY IMAGES ©

WI-FI At the airport, wi-fi is available for free *(gratuit)*; there are faster premium services for an extra charge.

CHARGING STATIONS Lockable charge boxes are free and available throughout the airport. Don't forget your phone afterwards!

MORE INFORMATION The website parisaeroport.fr has details of airport facilities and transport services.

CUSTOMS REGULATIONS

Limits from non-EU countries include: 16L of beer, 4L of wine, 1L of spirits over 22% ABV or 2L not exceeding 22% ABV, 200 cigarettes, 50 cigars or 250g of tobacco. Total value cannot exceed €430 (plane or ferry arrivals; €300 by car, train or other arrivals). From EU countries, limits only apply for excessive amounts; see douane.gouv.fr.

GETTING TO THE CITY CENTRE

Train RER B €12.50, one hour, every 15 minutes; central Paris stops include Gare du Nord, Châtelet–Les Halles and St-Michel–Notre Dame. From T1, take the free CDGVAL shuttle-train to the station at T3. Buy tickets using cash or credit cards from ticket machines (English-language option) or ticket counters.

Bus Roissybus €13.70, to Paris-Opéra, 60 to 90 minutes, every 15 to 30 minutes 5.15am to 12.30am. Buy tickets from all three terminals' bus stops, the driver or airport train stations.

Noctilien night buses N140 and N143 to Gare du Nord and Gare de l'Est, €8, 60 to 90 minutes, every 30 to 60 minutes 12.30am to 5.30am.

HOW MUCH FOR A...

Local buses
Cheaper but slower daytime services are Bus 350 to Porte de la Chapelle (€6, 70 minutes) and Bus 351 (€6, 80 minutes).

Ride-share
Uber services cost around €49; rates can be much higher during surge periods. Follow pick-up instructions as directed on your app.

Taxi Allow 40 to 80 minutes to central Paris, depending on traffic. Take an official taxi from the clearly marked ranks at each terminal's Arrivals level. Taxis charge a fixed price of €53 to the Right Bank and €58 to the Left Bank; fares increase by 15% from 7pm to 7am and on Sundays. Credit cards accepted.

OTHER POINTS OF ENTRY

Aéroport d'Orly Paris' second airport, Orly, is located 19km south of central Paris. The easiest transport options are the Orlybus to Paris' place Denfert–Rochereau (€9.50, every 15 to 20 minutes 6am to 12.30am) or taxi (Right/Left Bank €37/32; fares increase by 15% 7pm to 7am and on Sundays).

Aéroport de Beauvais Serving some low-cost airlines, Beauvais airport is 75km north of Paris. Shuttle buses to Paris' Porte Maillot (€17) meet flights.

Gare du Nord The terminus for northbound domestic trains as well as several international services. Located in northern Paris and linked to Paris' metro/RER and bus network. The London–Paris **Eurostar** (eurostar.com) line runs to/from St Pancras International; voyages take 2¼ hours. **Thalys** (thalys.com) trains pull into Paris' Gare du Nord from Brussels, Amsterdam and Cologne.

Other mainline train stations Paris is the central point in the French rail network, SNCF. In addition to Gare du Nord, Gare d'Austerlitz, Gare de l'Est, Gare de Lyon, Gare Montparnasse and Gare St-Lazare train stations handle traffic to different parts of France and Europe. Each is well connected to the Paris public-transport system.

TRANSPORT TIPS TO HELP YOU GET AROUND

With its broad boulevards, charming backstreets and beautiful Unesco World Heritage–listed riverbanks, Paris is ideal for walking. Thanks to largely flat terrain and expanding bike lanes, cycling is an increasingly popular way to get around. The city's efficient, inexpensive public-transport network also makes it easy to explore far and wide.

TAXI & RIDE-SHARE

Find taxis at official stands or via companies such as **Taxis G7** (g7.fr). The *prise en charge* (flagfall) is €2.60 (€4 to order immediately, €7 in advance); minimum journey cost is €7.30. Per kilometre tariffs are €1.09 to €1.61, depending on the time of day; there are supplements for a fifth passenger and luggage. Alternatively, use **Uber** (uber.com/fr/cities/paris).

BICYCLE

The **Vélib'** (velib-metropole.fr) bike-share scheme has over 20,000 bikes, both classic (green) and electric (blue) at 1400 stations citywide. Buy a subscription online (EU credit cards only) or at docking stations. There are single-trip, day and multiday pass options (from €3), with rates charged in 30-minute increments (from €1).

TROTTINETTE

App-based electric *trottinettes* (kick-scooters) typically cost €1 to unlock and €0.15 to €0.23 per minute. **Lime** (li.me) is the most common. Rider regulations apply.

BUS

With no stairs, buses are widely accessible. Normal rides (one or two bus zones) cost one metro ticket. Noctilien buses operate at night.

BOAT

Combining scenery and convenience, the Batobus (batobus.com; 24-hour pass €19) is a handy hop-on, hop-off service stopping at nine key destinations along the Seine.

RATP

Paris' integrated public-transport system, which includes the metro, RER suburban trains and buses, is operated by Régie Autonome des Transports Parisiens (RATP; ratp.fr).

METRO & RER ESSENTIALS

Metro and RER network The fastest option for getting around, Paris' underground rail network, consists of two separate but linked systems: the metro and the Réseau Express Régional (RER). Paris' metro has 14 numbered lines (currently being expanded to 18 as part of the Grand Paris Express project) and the RER has five main lines (though visitors usually only need to use A, B and C).

Operating hours Services usually run from around 5.30am to between 12.35am and 1.15am (2.15am on Friday and Saturday).

Maps and journey planner Download free transport maps from ratp.fr, which also has a journey planner.

Zones There are five concentric transport zones radiating from Paris (zone 5 being the furthest); if you travel from Charles de Gaulle Airport to Paris, for instance, you will need a ticket for zones 1 to 5.

Tickets Paris is phasing out paper tickets. A Navigo Easy contactless card (€2, valid for 10 years) allows infrequent transport users, including visitors, to prepay for journeys (single t+ tickets €1.90, banks of 10 €14.90) by topping up the card. Navigo Easy can be used on the metro, RER (within the applicable zones), buses, trams and the Montmartre funicular. Airport buses Roissybus (€12) and Orlybus (€8.50) can be added on (cheaper than buying without the card). Navigo cards and top-ups are sold at metro/RER station ticket windows, RATP-affiliated outlets (eg tobacconists) and Charles de Gaulle Airport train stations.

Day passes A Forfait Navigo Jour (unlimited-use day pass) can be loaded onto Navigo Easy cards. It costs €7.50 for two zones and €17.80 for five zones.

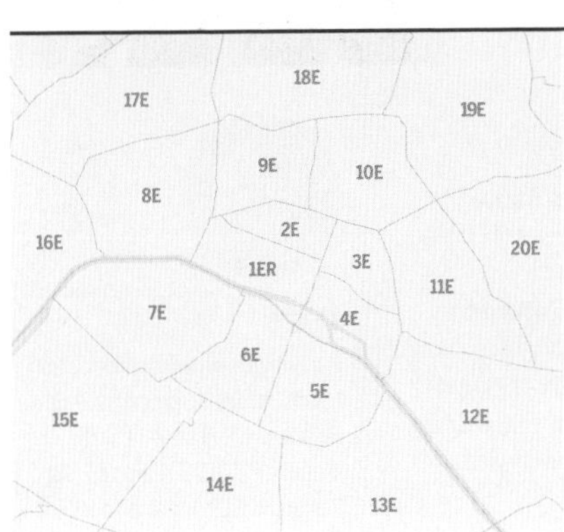

ARRONDISSEMENTS

Within the *périphérique* (ring road), Paris' 20 *arrondissements* (city districts) are numbered clockwise from the centre and form part of all Parisian addresses.

Above RER train, Charles de Gaulle–Étoile

KIEV.VICTOR/SHUTTERSTOCK ©

UNIQUE AND LOCAL WAYS TO STAY

Paris' accommodation options span hip hostels, B&Bs, apartments and charming inexpensive hotels to boutique gems, lifestyle hotels and opulent palaces. Generally, any savings from staying outside central Paris are often negated by travel time and costs – choose lodgings in Paris' arrondissements to instantly soak up Parisian life.

Find a place to stay in Paris

HOSTELS

Paris is home to some state-of-the-art, new-generation hostels such as Generator, near Canal St-Martin, and, close by, two by St Christopher's Inns. Only Hostelling International (HI) *auberges de jeunesse* (youth hostels) require membership cards.

B&BS

Bed-and-breakfast (B&B) accommodation (*chambres d'hôte* in French) offers an immersive way to experience the city. Paris' tourist office maintains a list of B&Bs.

APARTMENTS

As well as home-share sites like Airbnb, Paris has a number of *résidences de tourisme* (serviced apartments, aka 'aparthotels'), such as the chain Citadines. Rental agencies like Paris Attitude list pre-inspected furnished residential apartments for short to medium stays.

HOTELS

In Paris, hotel rooms are typically small by international standards, and cheaper properties may not have lifts or air-conditioning. Upper midrange and top-end hotels often have restaurants and bars on-site (but breakfast is rarely included in the price).

BOOKING

Accommodation is in high demand in Paris, particularly during peak times (April to October, as well as public and school holidays). Reservations are essential at these times, but are also recommended year-round.

Prices are invariably cheaper online, especially on the hotels' own websites.

Booking websites:

lonelyplanet.com/france/paris/hotels Reviews of Lonely Planet's top choices.

en.parisinfo.com/where-to-sleep-in-paris Search accommodation by categories of interest.

parisattitude.com Vetted apartments, professional service and reasonable fees.

TAXES

Paris levies an accommodation tourist tax per person per night. Palaces: €5; 5 stars: €3.75; 4 stars: €2.88; 3 stars: €1.88; 2 stars: €1.13; 1 star and B&Bs: €1; unrated/unclassified: €2.88.

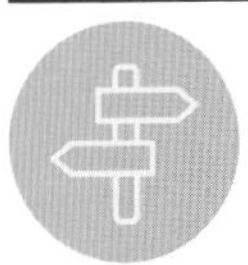

WHERE TO STAY, IF YOU LOVE...

Monuments, museums and elegant streetscapes Eiffel Tower & Western Paris (p30) Upmarket residential area with limited nightlife close to Paris' iconic tower and museums.

→ **Parisian icons and superb shopping** Champs-Élysées & Grands Boulevards (p46) Luxury hotels, flagship boutiques and department stores, gastronomic restaurants, glamorous nightlife.

Artistic treasures and epicurean treats The Louvre & Les Halles (p58) Epicentral location, excellent transport links to all parts of Paris, major museums, fashion and food shopping galore. Midrange to high-end properties are the mainstay.

↓ **Lofty views and lively multicultural quarters** Montmartre & Northern Paris (p76) Hilly streets, village charm and multicultural communities. Good budget options; many places to look out over Paris.

Hip boutiques and buzzing nightlife Le Marais, Ménilmontant & Belleville (p100) History-steeped streets and secret squares; some standout museums; copious drinking and dining choices. The hub of Paris' premier LGBTIQ+ scene. Very central.

Bustling markets and creative spaces Bastille & Eastern Paris (p120) Vibrant local neighbourhood blending tradition and innovation. Loads of restaurants, drinking and nightlife venues, small shops. Diverse accommodation offerings.

Heart-of-Paris location and architectural masterpieces The Islands (p136) The Île de la Cité is dominated by Notre Dame; limited high-end accommodation centres on the peaceful, romantic Île St-Louis.

Jazz clubs, literary connections and late-opening bookshops The Latin Quarter (p148) Energetic student area with scores of eating, drinking and entertainment options. Good mix of accommodation styles.

Stylish shopping and sophisticated dining St-Germain & Les Invalides (p162) Quintessentially Parisian neighbourhood close to the Seine with proximity to the Jardin du Luxembourg. Accommodation skews to the high end.

Street art, expansive parks and Paris' largest Chinatown Montparnasse & Southern Paris (p180) Villagey pockets, lots of green space. Some areas out of the way. Good-value accommodation.

Far left Citadines **Left** Sacré-Cœur (p94) **Above** Galeries Lafayette Haussmann (p53)

SAFE TRAVEL

In general, Paris is a safe city – streets are mostly well-lit and random street assaults are rare. Travellers should watch for petty theft and scams, be alert when using ATMs and avoid being caught up in street protests.

PETTY THEFT Always be on your guard for pickpockets and take precautions: don't carry more cash than you need, and keep credit cards and passports concealed. On cafe and restaurant terraces, avoid leaving your jacket containing your wallet or handbag over the back of your chair, and don't leave your phone unattended on the table.

SCAMS Common 'distraction' scams employed by pickpockets include fake petitions, scammers pretending to 'find' a gold ring (after subtly placing it on the ground), dropping or spilling items, or tying friendship bracelets on your wrist. Such scams are particularly prevalent where there are crowds of tourists, such as around Sacré-Cœur and the Eiffel Tower.

METRO SAFETY Stay alert for petty theft at stations and onboard trains. Metro stations best avoided late at night include Châtelet–Les Halles, Château Rouge, Gare du Nord, Strasbourg St-Denis, Réaumur Sébastopol, Stalingrad and Montparnasse Bienvenüe. Marx Dormoy, Porte de la Chapelle and Marcadet–Poissonniers can be sketchy day and night.

Medical services A local *pharmacie* (chemist) can help with minor health concerns. For serious problems, go to *urgences* (A&E) departments at Paris' *hôpitaux* (hospitals; aphp.fr/urgences). Call 15 for ambulance (SAMU) services.

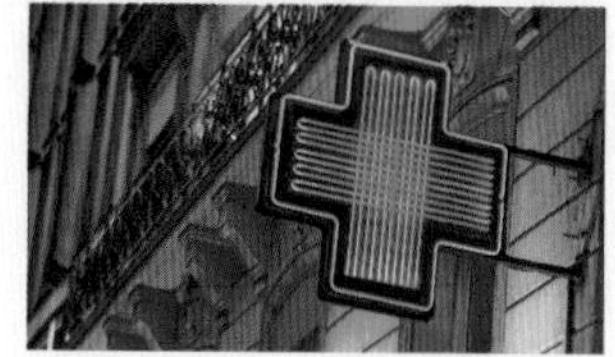

Street protests *La manif* (an abbreviation of *manifestation*) is a common occurrence in France. Visitors should take care if encountering one as they can turn violent.

COVID-19
The COVID-19 health situation in France continues to evolve: for updated information in English about the current requirements for visitors before travelling and after your arrival, visit gouvernement.fr/en/coronavirus-covid-19.

INSURANCE
Travel insurance covering theft, loss and medical problems is vital. EU, Switzerland, Iceland, Norway and Liechtenstein citizens get free or reduced-cost, state-provided healthcare with the European Health Insurance Card (EHIC).

QUICK TIPS TO HELP YOU MANAGE YOUR MONEY

CREDIT CARDS Visa/Carte Bleue is the most widely accepted credit card in Paris, followed by MasterCard (Eurocard). Amex cards are only accepted at more upmarket establishments. Some non-EU-issued cards can't be used at automated machines (eg at a metro station or museum) – ask your bank for advice before you leave.

ATMS
ATMs (*distributeur automatique de billets* in French) are widespread. Check if/how much they charge for international cash withdrawals with your bank before you travel.

DYNAMIC CURRENCY CONVERSION
The local-currency payment option (DCC; dynamic currency conversion) is always cheaper for credit-card transactions and ATM withdrawals.

CURRENCY

Euro

HOW MUCH FOR A...

baguette
around €1.20

glass of wine
from €2.50

two-course bistro *menu*
from €17

TIPPING

Taxis Round up to the nearest €1.

Restaurants Bills include a service charge; leave a few extra euros for good service.

Bars/cafes For table service, tip as you would in a restaurant.

Hotels Tip bellhops €1 to €2 per bag. Not expected for concierge, cleaners or front-desk staff.

TVA France's value-added tax (VAT), known as TVA *(taxe sur la valeur ajoutée)*, is 20% on most goods and services. Prices are generally TTC (*toutes taxes comprises;* 'all taxes included').

CASH
Cash isn't a good way to carry money; it can be stolen and you often won't get the best exchange rates. French vendors rarely accept bills larger than €50.

CURRENCY EXCHANGE
Check the latest exchange rates on websites such as xe.com. In Paris, *bureaux de change* are usually more efficient, open longer hours and give better rates than banks.

TAX REFUNDS

Non-EU residents over 16 who are visiting France for less than six months can often claim a TVA refund, provided the purchase amount is over €100 and made over a maximum of three days at a retailer that offers tax-free shopping (present your passport for eligibility). The retailer will provide a slip with a barcode that can be scanned at PABLO electronic terminals prior to check-in at the departure port. For more information, visit douane.gouv.fr/fiche/eligibility-vat-refunds.

RESPONSIBLE TRAVEL

Positive, sustainable and feel-good experiences around the city.

CHOOSE SUSTAINABLE VENUES

Dine farm to fork at Le Perchoir Porte de Versailles (leperchoir.fr/en/location/le-perchoir-porte-de-versailles) at Europe's largest urban rooftop farm, the 14,000-sq-metre, biodiverse Nature Urbaine.

Chart your own course and explore Paris' waterways by renting an electric-powered boat (no licence required) from Marin D'Eau Douce (boating-paris-marindeaudouce.com).

Take an upcycling workshop at eco-conscious cultural centre La Recyclerie (larecyclerie.com) in a repurposed former steam-train station, whose cafe utilises produce from its own urban farm on the tracks.

Look out over Paris from 150m up in the air aboard the helium-filled Ballon de Paris (ballondeparis.com). Tethered in the Parc André Citroën, this aerial sightseeing balloon monitors Paris' air quality.

Above right We Love Green festival **Far right** Velib' bikes

DAVID WOLFF - PATRICK/REDFERNS VIA GETTY IMAGES © LIGANKOV ALEKSEY/SHUTTERSTOCK ©

GIVE BACK

Catch zero-waste, renewable-energy-powered festival We Love Green (welovegreen.fr; Jun) at Paris' eastern forest, the Bois de Vincennes, combining a Think Tank 'ideas laboratory' raising awareness of ecological issues with artisan producers and indie, electro and hip-hop acts.

Take part in workshops, events and more through the Paris Good Fashion (parisgoodfashion.fr) initiative focused on improving sourcing, traceability, ecofriendly processes and circular economies as part of Paris' aim to become the world's most sustainable fashion capital by 2024.

Snap up bargain-priced unsold items at merchants such as bakeries via the app Too Good to Go (toogoodtogo.fr), which helps prevent food waste.

SUPPORT LOCAL

Choose fresh produce at *bio* (organic) markets, like Marché Raspail (Sunday), Marché Biologique des Batignolles (Saturday), Marché Biologique Brancusi (Saturday) and Marché Biologique Place du Père Chaillet (Wednesday and Saturday).

Buy sustainable clothing from Sézane (sezane.com), an affordable label that donates many of its proceeds to its own children's charity, Demain.

Browse exquisite handcrafted items, all made in French designers' studios, at Empreintes (empreintes-paris.com).

LEARN MORE

Discover Black Paris on a guided tour with Entrée to Black Paris (entreetoblackparis.com).

Take a walking or kick-scooter tour of Paris' multicultural northeastern neighbourhoods with Ça Se Visite (ca-se-visite.fr).

Learn about Islamic culture on Institut des Cultures d'Islam (institut-cultures-islam.org) tours.

Understand Paris' sustainability through tourist-office tours (en.parisinfo.com/guided-tours/142576/Sustainable-Visit).

LEAVE A SMALL FOOTPRINT

Cycle through the city with Paris' bike-share scheme Vélib', which has thousands of classic and electric bikes at docking stations citywide for low-impact travel.

Zoom around with Cityscoot (cityscoot.eu; per minute from €0.28), a similar scheme with the electric equivalent of 50cc mopeds, located via an app.

Look out for the highly anticipated 'flying water taxis' (electric hydrofoils) from SeaBubbles (seabubbles.fr).

CLIMATE CHANGE & TRAVEL

It's impossible to ignore the impact we have when travelling, and the importance of making changes where we can. Lonely Planet urges all travellers to engage with their travel carbon footprint. There are many carbon calculators online that allow travellers to estimate the carbon emissions generated by their journey; try resurgence.org/resources/carbon-calculator.html. Many airlines and booking sites offer travellers the option of offsetting the impact of greenhouse gas emissions by contributing to climate-friendly initiatives around the world. We continue to offset the carbon footprint of all Lonely Planet staff travel, while recognising this is a mitigation more than a solution.

RESOURCES

paris.fr/pages/les-marches-parisiens-2428

velib-metropole.fr

en.parisinfo.com/what-to-see-in-paris/sustainable-tourism-in-paris/eco-responsible-accommodation

littleafrica.fr

ESSENTIAL NUTS-AND-BOLTS

ACCESSIBLE TRAVEL

Access can be difficult in Paris for *visiteurs handicapés* (visitors with disabilities) but things are improving.

Buses are an alternative to the mostly inaccessible metro for those in a *fauteuil roulant* (wheelchair). Taxis G7 (g7.fr) has vehicles equipped for passengers with disabilities.

The 'Tourisme & Handicap' initiative identifies cultural attractions, hotels and restaurants that have facilities for those with physical, cognitive, visual and/or hearing disabilities; all display the label at their entrances.

The main tourist office has a service called ACCEO, which makes it possible for people who are deaf or hearing impaired to ask for information.

A French sign-language operator helps users to communicate via a webcam, microphone and speakers. Instant speech transcription is available, too. Visit en.parisinfo.com/accessibility.

Download the Accessible Paris guide (en.parisinfo.com/what-to-see-in-paris/visiting-paris-with-a-disability/accessible-paris-guide).

Online FACIL'iti (facil-iti.com) lets you customise parisinfo.com according to motor, sensory and/or cognitive needs.

Search a database of accessible venues on jaccede.com and its app.

FAST FACTS

Time Zone
Central European Time

Country Code
33

Electricity
Electricity
220V/50Hz AC

GOOD TO KNOW

Many nationalities will require ETIAS pre-travel authorisation from late 2022; see ec.europa.eu.

On escalators, stand on the left, walk on the right; on footpaths, walk on the right.

Parisians don't speak loudly – keep your voice at a similar volume.

The legal drinking age in France is 18; some areas in Paris restrict alcohol consumption in public places after certain hours.

France uses the metric system for weights and measurements.

GREETINGS

Greet anyone you interact with, like shopkeepers, with '*bonjour*' ('*bonsoir*' at night)/'*au revoir*'. The custom of *la bise* (cheek-kissing) has reduced due to the pandemic.

TOURIST INFORMATION

Paris' main tourist office (parisinfo.com) is at the Hôtel de Ville. It sells tickets for tours and several attractions, plus museum and transport passes.

TOILETS
Cafes don't appreciate non-customers using their facilities; try big hotels and major department stores.

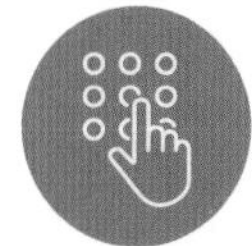

TELEPHONE
Calling abroad from Paris, dial France's international access code (00) before the country code.

SMOKING
Banned in indoor public spaces (including hotel rooms), but permitted on pavement terraces.

OPENING HOURS
Typically bars and cafes open 7am to 2am, museums 10am to 6pm (closed Monday or Tuesday), restaurants noon to 2pm and 7.30pm to 10.30pm (days vary), and shops 10am to 7pm Monday to Saturday; smaller shops may close for lunch and sometimes on Mondays.

FAMILY TRAVEL

The tourist office (parisinfo.com) lists museums and activities for kids.

Most restaurants welcome children; many offer a *menu enfant* (children's menu).

Under 18s (or a younger cut-off age) receive discounted or free entry to sights.

Rent strollers, car seats, high chairs, travel beds and more from companies such as Kidelio (kidelio.com).

Go to Paris Mômes (parismomes.fr) for Parisian kid culture (up to 12 years).

Hotels can often organise babysitters for guests.

WI-FI
Many cafes and bars in Paris have free wi-fi for customers. Free wi-fi is also available in hundreds of public places, including parks, libraries and municipal buildings; look for a purple 'Zone Wi-Fi' sign. To connect, select the 'PARIS_WI-FI_' network. Locations are mapped at paris.fr/wifi.

SAMANTHAINALAOHLSEN/SHUTTERSTOCK ©

LGBTIQ+ TRAVELLERS

The main nightlife hub is Le Marais, especially the areas around rue Ste-Croix de la Bretonnerie and rue des Archives, and eastwards to rue Vieille du Temple. Châtelet also has several popular bars and clubs.

Pride takes place around late June, headlined by the Marche des Fiertés parade.

Guided tours are operated by the Gay Locals (thegaylocals.com); its website is also a good resource for venues.

The Centre LGBT Paris-Île de France (centrelgbtparis.org) has information for LGBTIQ+ travellers.

LANGUAGE

Standard French is taught and spoken throughout France. This said, regional accents and dialects are an important part of identity in certain regions, but you'll have no trouble being understood anywhere if you stick to standard French, which we've used in this chapter.

The sounds used in spoken French can almost all be found in English. There are a couple of exceptions: nasal vowels (represented in our pronunciation guides by *o* or *u* followed by an almost inaudible nasal consonant sound *m, n* or *ng*), the 'funny' *u* (*ew* in our guides) and the deep-in-the-throat *r*. Bearing these few points in mind and reading our pronunciation guides below as if they were English, you'll be understood just fine.

BASICS

Hello.	*Bonjour.*	bon·zhoor
Goodbye.	*Au revoir.*	o·rer·vwa
Yes./No.	*Oui./Non.*	wee/non
Please.	*S'il vous plaît.*	seel voo play
Thank you.	*Merci.*	mair·see
Excuse me.	*Excusez-moi.*	ek·skew·zay·mwa
Sorry.	*Pardon.*	par·don

What's your name?
Comment vous appelez-vous? — ko·mon voo·za·play voo

My name is ...
Je m'appelle ... — zher ma·pel ...

Do you speak English?
Parlez-vous anglais? — par·lay·voo ong·glay

I don't understand.
Je ne comprends pas. — zher ner kom·pron pa

TIME & NUMBERS

What time is it?	*Quelle heure est-il?*	kel er ay til
It's (10) o'clock.	*Il est (dix) heures.*	il ay (deez) er
It's half past (10).	*Il est (dix) heures et demie.*	il ay (deez) er ay day·mee.

morning	*matin*	ma·tun
afternoon	*après-midi*	a·pray·mee·dee
evening	*soir*	swar
yesterday	*hier*	yair
today	*aujourd'hui*	o·zhoor·dwee
tomorrow	*demain*	der·mun

1	*un*	un	**6**	*six*	sees
2	*deux*	der	**7**	*sept*	set
3	*trois*	trwa	**8**	*huit*	weet
4	*quatre*	ka·trer	**9**	*neuf*	nerf
5	*cinq*	sungk	**10**	*dix*	dees

EMERGENCIES

Help!	*Au secours!*	o skoor
Leave me alone!	*Fichez-moi la paix!*	fee·shay·mwa la pay
Call the police!	*Appelez la police.*	a·play la po·lees
I'm lost.	*Je suis perdu/perdue.*	zher swee pair·dew (m/f)

Index

000 Map pages

J

L

M

N

O

P